P9-EKY-375

THE READERS' CHOICE

THE READERS' CHOICE

200 Book Club Favorites

Victoria Golden McMains

Quill
An Imprint of HarperCollins*Publishers*

HarperCollins books may be purchased for educational, business, or sales promotional use. For information please write: Special Markets Department, HarperCollins Publishers Inc., 10 East 53rd Street, New York, NY 10022.

FIRST PERENNIAL EDITION 2000

Designed by Jessica Shatan

Library of Congress Cataloging-in-Publication Data has been applied for.

ISBN 0-688-17435-3

00 01 02 03 04 ❖/RRD 10 9 8 7 6 5 4 3 2 1

For Michael, Adam, and Reed

ACKNOWLEDGMENTS

Thanks to my mother and father, Dorothy and Alfred Golden, who encouraged me to read, did plenty of it themselves, and always supported me in my writing. Any mother who takes her three-year-old child to the library to get a card can be assumed to be a lover of reading.

Without my book club, there would have been no book. My deepest appreciation to members past and present: Monica Anderson, Vicki Bailey, Hillary Costin, Tricia Coxhead, Patty Dahl, Roxanne Edelen, Kathryn Eisler LeMay, Margo Merck, Susan Mitchell, Bretta Rambo, Martha Scull, and Pamela Street. Our gatherings have been wonderfully enriching, and the resulting friendships a treasure.

Special thanks to certain avid readers who helped to find books: Jo Loarie and Susan Mitchell, the two most voracious, well-informed, and articulate literature lovers I've known; and Pamela Street, a dedicated reader of other print media as well as a lover of books—thanks for all of the publishing-related clippings and great ideas! My appreciation, too, to Wendy Milner-Calloway, Ruth Goldhammer, and Cheryl Hulsman for special help in referring books.

I'd like to acknowledge Pete Golis, editorial director of *The Press Democrat,* who made me incredibly happy by matching my enthusiasm with his own when I first suggested the idea of a monthly book review column named "Book Club Favorites."

I'd like to pay tribute to Marly Rusoff at William Morrow, who saw the value in a book like this and who has consistently worked to further the cause of literature in a time when fine writing has often been allowed to languish. It was a pleasure to work with her and the always-enthusiastic Toni Sciarra at Quill. The latter is proof that excellent, dedicated editors still do exist. My gratitude to my agent, Joe Regal at Russell & Volkening, another rare advocate of good literature in days of difficult publishing.

My appreciation to Levin & Company and Toyon Books, two remarkable independent bookstores that have managed to thrive in a town of nine thousand—and also to answer my continuing requests for help in searching down information about publishers, books, and authors.

And finally, my gratitude to Mike Murphy behind the counter at the Healdsburg post office, who blessed the envelope when I sent off my proposal to William Morrow. I hope this doesn't cause a run on the post office.

CONTENTS

THE READERS' CHOICE

Discovering Treasures: Good Books, New Friendships, Insights About Our Lives

Something wonderful is happening to books. People are reading them. The American public, once accused of planting itself in front of the television, has spearheaded a rapidly growing movement in the form of reading groups. Oprah has one. National Public Radio has one. Every small bookstore can refer you to one. The Denver area alone has three hundred.

Why are we doing this? Apart from the fact that it's enormously satisfying to escape into an alternate reality created by a talented author, we are probably seeking community. We commute to work, we come home and cook dinner, we do the laundry and the shopping. Who has the time or energy to hang out regularly with neighbors? Setting a date once a month to talk about provocative books with like-minded friends is one way to establish a new form of community. Picking a book to discuss takes the conversation to a higher plane. Instead of griping about tax season or engaging in gossip, we mull over larger human issues that authors set before us. We talk about the books and we talk about our lives within the context of a larger world, using the springboard that the author provides.

Even if a book club is not for you, but you're reading this, you probably enjoy lingering in bookstores. In the small town where I live, they're among the few places open in the evenings. You can see locals and tourists alike engaging in the dreamy business of browsing the shelves. The question is, then, given all the choices, what will you read?

The Readers' Choice is intended to give you a special treat. This list of two hundred favorite books has been culled from rave recommendations by more than seventy reading groups in California, Oregon, Colorado, and New York. Many of these books are little-known gems. All of them have been recommended by groups of people rather than a single reviewer. Although contemporary fiction predominates on the list, approximately one fourth are nonfiction, mostly personal adventure or biography. What you'll find here are highly satisfying narratives, often extremely well crafted and always sensitively drawn by writers who largely qualify for the designation "literary."

If you're a book club member, you'll immediately understand the need for such a list. The first question outsiders ask book clubbers is, "What have you read that's good?" The first question members of different book clubs ask each other is, "What have you read that's good?" Simply sampling a book's first page or first chapter may not tell you whether the whole thing is going to knock you out; many books pick up steam as they go along. A recommendation by a single bookstore employee is no insurance that the book will suit your taste. Book reviews are helpful, but again offer the opinion of only one person. Best-seller lists are interesting but are not nearly adequate guides to reading.

Why Best-seller Lists Are Not Enough

Reading clubs usually stay away from *The New York Times Book Review* best-seller list. Especially on the fiction side, books on this list tend to feature formula writing offering some combination of Murder, Mayhem, Millions, Shopping, and Sex

(MMMSS). In the recent past, the nonfiction side has showcased celebrity memoirs or memoirs by unknowns with an MMMSS story to tell, which are not always well written and usually not a source of literary or any other kind of inspiration.

Book clubs are hungry for another kind of writing, what the publishing world refers to as "the midlist book." These are well-crafted, thoughtful books, mostly novels, that cover a broad range of subjects and themes. Usually structured in a traditional way, with a clear beginning, middle, and end, they tend not to concentrate on sensational action or violence, but rather tell the stories of people facing some kind of personal challenge or conflict and growing in the process. Often, it is the manner of telling—the writer's style, voice, and vision—that makes the story so interesting, rather than the story events themselves. Maxine Chernoff's *American Heaven* and Ann Patchett's *The Magician's Assistant* are ideal examples. Both are great little novels of love and suspense that display literary finesse. Both grab you and hold you until the very last page, not so much because you're wondering whether the characters are going to die or be maimed or swept off their feet by passion, but instead whether they will come through their problems with hearts and minds intact. These books fall in between the extremes of literary avant garde, or experimental, writing and the formula, MMMSS writing of Danielle Steel or Michael Crichton.

Ironically, the New York publishing world has proclaimed the death of the midlist several times in the past decade or so, believing that these books didn't sell in large enough quantities to justify their existence. The catch is that publishers usually aren't willing to throw adequate promotion money at a non-MMMSS book, and marketing most often is the key to publishing success. There is a special irony in this, as books like *American Heaven* or *The Magician's Assistant* would probably sell like hotcakes if the reading public simply knew about them.

A small number of midlist books do appear on *The New York Times Book Review* best-seller list, but usually because they have some kind of angle that makes publishers feel they're more salable and worth the extra promotion: They are written by a proven, successful author like Margaret Atwood or Anne Tyler, or they touch upon popular topics such as dysfunctional families (Tobias Wolff, Rick Bragg) or multiculturalism (Amy Tan, Barbara Kingsolver). And there have been the wonderful exceptions by unknown writers: Sales soared for Charles Frazier's *Cold Mountain* when independent bookstores eagerly spread the word about his superbly crafted Civil War–era saga. In addition, and quite significantly, Oprah Winfrey's TV and on-line book club has catapulted a number of quietly published books of literary merit into the public spotlight; the resulting demand by her audience has caused a number of midlisters to be shipped to bookstores in quantities of one million or so.

Still, literary books on the best-seller lists lately have been the exception, not the rule. Fortunately, as the number of midlist books published by major houses has shrunk, their authors can still hope for publication by smaller presses around the country, such as Coffee House *(American Heaven),* University of New Mexico *(La Mollie and the King of Tears),* and Chronicle Books *(A Minus Tide).*

However, there's hope for a reversal in the so-called death of the midlist, as more and more of us join book clubs and purchase our monthly selections in the stores. As Winfrey discovered, nationwide there are hundreds of thousands of us who savor a sensitive, well-crafted novel and who appreciate some help in finding it. This is one more important reason why book clubs have become such a popular phenomenon in recent times. We are helping each other to find books worth reading.

How to Form a Book Club

Why Would You Want To?

If you're so busy with the rest of your life that searching for and reading good books is a treat you don't often allow yourself, belonging to a book club will give you a good reason to do exactly that. The search will become a lot easier, since all of the group's members will be sharing their book tips.

Just as important as reading, however, is the social aspect of reading groups mentioned earlier. Unless you have a standing date to meet at the gym or to plan a school fund-raiser, you probably only see your friends occasionally and talk on the phone sporadically. A monthly book club meeting is a great way to fill in that gap. You'll tend to respect the date and look forward to it eagerly.

When you do meet with friends in this context, you'll find that literature provides a compelling focus for conversation. Although you'll probably talk about other things as well, including your kids and the price of gasoline, the discussion is likely to be more gratifying than usual. Discussion of an author's themes, intentions, and characters provides a broader context for analyzing issues in your own world.

In my own group, some of our best discussions have been about topics as diverse as slavery, self-esteem, death and dying, interracial marriage, poverty, insanity, and Third World politics, with examples from our own family histories, personal experiences, and other readings.

Enjoy the satisfying sense of community that arises among the members of a book club. It is community in the most basic sense: people gathering to exchange ideas.

Who Would Join?

Ask a few friends. Ask them to ask their friends. Three or four people are enough to start.

If that doesn't pan out, go to your local bookstore, which may keep a list of people who want to join book clubs or may be able to give you the names of contacts for existing groups. Be bold. Connect with strangers. One of the pleasures of our group is that we've come to know people we otherwise wouldn't have chosen as friends on our own. The differences in politics, outlook, and personal style among us add spice to our conversations and make for interesting, surprising friendships.

If you're nervous about meeting with strangers, see if the bookstore is willing to allow you to gather there. Or pick a local café.

Once your group has been meeting for a while and has established a good dynamic, you'll probably become protective of that dynamic. At that point, you may choose to be more careful about membership selection, admitting people whom at least one of you knows well.

Are Book Club Members All Women?

For years it seemed that way, but men are now getting into the act. You'll find that a number of men recommended the books listed here. I haven't come across many all-men groups, but I have encountered clubs that are randomly coed or are composed of couples.

According to *The New York Times,* it is a widely held belief in the book business that far more women buy books than men, with as much as 70 to 80 percent of fiction purchased by women. It makes sense, then, that book club membership has been predominantly female. However, at least a few men have expressed regrets to me about the dearth of men's or coed book clubs and have said what a shame it is that men are missing out on the camaraderie and stimulating conversation these groups provide. It's encouraging to see that the tide is changing.

When Will You Meet?

My own group is composed of women with flexible work schedules; this means we can meet at lunch and stay through midafternoon. Most working people find evenings better. Allow at least two or three hours for your gatherings.

How Often?

Once a month is the typical arrangement. This gives everyone more than enough time to buy or share the book and read it. However, if you are new mothers and fathers reading parenting books together, you may want to meet once a week, especially if you're full-time caregivers desperate for adult conversation.

Will You Serve Food?

Our group meets over potluck lunch; we delight in conversing across a table full of good food. Our meetings are more social occasions than scholarly gatherings. Groups vary greatly in their approach, from no food to plenty, from structured discussions to easygoing conversation. Decide if you'd like to talk over a casual meal or would rather focus entirely on the book and maybe have light refreshment afterward.

At our meetings, the guests bring salads and other entrées and the hostess provides drinks and dessert. Each month a different member hosts the gathering at her home.

How Many Members?

If you're going to talk about books over dinner, you'll probably want to limit the size of your group to the number that can fit around your tables comfortably or sit around living rooms with dishes on their laps.

If there's no meal involved, the size of the group is up to you. My group has ten people; I've seen a group with thirty. However, the latter had a very organized approach to discussion.

How to Choose a Book

Of course, you can begin by using this guide. Beyond that, I suggest the following.

Through trial and error, most book clubs arrive at the decision that at least one person should have read the book before it is chosen. The club can then make its selection based on a personal recommendation. There's still no guarantee that most members will appreciate the book, but if at least one member has enjoyed it, the chances are improved greatly.

In my group, we take turns pitching our suggestions and then we decide. Somehow we never take a formal vote; one book seems naturally to win out over the others, on the basis of a particularly appealing recommendation.

Over time, you may find that some members consistently suggest certain types of books for the club. Establish at the outset what types of literature you'd like to try, so there are no hard feelings. Fiction? Nonfiction? Contemporary work only? Classics? Women writers? Spiritual writings? Genres such as mystery, thrillers, or science fiction? Everything?

Some groups are drawn together by a common goal, such as a desire to mull over books on child development or the wish to learn more about African American authors. You may find that your needs and desires change over time, leading you to prefer other readings. Periodically the group can reassess its goals.

There is also the question of hardcover versus paperback. If you're interested in reading newly published books, you can avoid some of the expense by having a book-buying partner. One month you purchase the chosen book, read it, and then lend it to your partner; the next month he or she does the same. In addition, many bookstores, particularly independently owned stores, will give discounts to clubs if the members order multiple copies of one book at the same time; inquire at your local bookshop.

While my club prefers to pick the next month's selection at the current meeting, some clubs like to schedule the entire year's choices in advance, with seasonal factors in mind. They may plan to read longer books during times of the year when people have vacations and may steer away from somber, more depressing tomes during the worst of dreary, winter weather.

There is an advantage, however, to waiting until the last minute to choose. If a member has just completed a book on his or her own and is really excited about it, everyone can quickly jump in and share it. If a new book has received excellent reviews and the club is eager to try it, one member can screen it, and if it passes muster, the rest of you can order copies as a group and quickly satisfy your curiosity as well.

Research the Author

When you meet to discuss a book, the conversation is enhanced if you have background on the writer. Upon selecting a title, you can ask the person who recommended it to gather a bit of author information.

Many public libraries carry a multivolume reference work called *Contemporary Authors* that is very helpful. More modern libraries have it on-line, with the entries regularly updated by the publisher. Articles in *The New York Times Book Review* or *Book* magazine are also helpful. Check the back of your book for a reader's guide and also see if the publisher provides a Web site that may give both author and book information.

What Exactly Will You Talk About?

Begin with the question "Did this book work for you?"

Why?

Did the author do a good job of drawing the characters? Was there a full description of each person, or did a picture gradually emerge from telling details: bits of speech, comments by other characters, an occasional clue to physical appearance? Did the characters seem real? Did you identify with them?

Did the writer create a setting that you could easily see? Did you feel as though you'd entered another world? Did you learn anything new by being there?

Was there a compelling problem or conflict at the outset that drew you in and made you want to know what would happen next? If not, what made you keep reading?

What did you think of the author's use of language? Was it spare or thick with description? Was it humorous? Poetic? How did this affect your reading of the book? Are there any passages of special beauty or effectiveness that you want to point out to the group?

How did you feel about the voice in which the story was told? Did one of the main characters narrate? If there was a narrator, did he or she have a special perspective that made you care about the events described?

What was the point of the story? Did it inspire you?

Was this a book that stayed with you for days or weeks afterward? Why?

Have you read anything else by this author? How did it compare?

Disagreement Is Good!

Don't fall silent if someone or everyone else says, "I couldn't stand the main character" or "I didn't like the book."

Disagreement is good. It can lead to interesting discussion. Don't let it stop you cold. Disagreement gives you something meaty to talk about.

To keep conversation going, you may have to overcome a bit of shyness or lack of confidence in your own opinion, if you did happen to like the book. Do it. It's worth it.

You don't have to tell anyone they're wrong. Simply ask, "Why didn't you like the protagonist?" or "What bothered you about the book?" Ask the critics to compare the book to others in a similar vein that did work for them. Ask how they might have changed the author's writing to improve it. Then, after a while, you can let drop that you absolutely loved the protagonist or the whole book. And say why.

What Happens If Someone Doesn't Read the Book?
In our group, nothing. You could go for months without reading the books, and it would be okay. (However, if many of us did this for long, we'd want to examine why.) The most important thing for us is seeing each other. Sometimes a member finds, upon looking at the selection, that she is absolutely not interested. Also, while some of us read four or five books in a month, others find it hard to get one under their belt.

So we attend meetings whether we've completed the selection or not. Often it's easy to participate in the discussion anyway, because the conversation expands from the author's work to broader issues. To protect the conversation against cries of "Don't give away the ending!" we have an agreement that we will not hesitate to discuss any aspect of the book at its designated reading.

Some groups make it a rule that each selection must be read and that members can miss reading only one or two selections before they are disqualified from club membership. Decide early on how you want to handle it.

Keep Track of Your Book List
It took our group a while to realize that it's helpful to have a record of what we've read, especially when relatives or friends ask us to share our favorites. You might designate one of your group as record-keeper.

In our county at least one club—consisting mainly of schoolteachers—has a formal rating system by which they score each book after group discussion. Members vote using a scale of 1 to 10, and the results are recorded on their official club list.

If you do keep a record of your group's favorites, please e-mail them to me at vgmcmains@aol.com or send them to Book Club Favorites, Sunday Forum, *The Press Democrat,* P.O. Box 569, Santa Rosa, California 95402. I screen recommendations, and if I choose to read one of your favorites, I'll write a review if I'm also enthusiastic. By sending me the favorite picks of your reading club or of your circle of family and friends, you may be helping to compile volume two of *The Readers' Choice: 200 Book Club Favorites.*

Our Club

We have no name; we simply think of ourselves as Book Club. The ten of us live north of San Francisco, with one in the hills of Marin, a few in Santa Rosa, a city of 128,000, and the rest just north, in the wine country of Sonoma County and on the Mendocino coast. We have been full-time moms, an emergency room doctor, a nurse, a hotel architect, a therapist, winery and vineyard owners, writers, activists, and a hospice administrator. Most of us are newcomers to the region, having joined the thousands who moved here in the past couple of decades from places like Los Angeles, San Francisco, and New York to live among the vine-covered hills and valleys and along the Russian River.

Our book club began in 1989 when several mothers who usually stopped to chat in the parking lot of their children's school decided they'd like to meet in another setting. Since then, we've had a few members come and go as schedules changed or people moved away. Although we've relished attending our book club since the earliest days, we've found it's become even better with time, in spite of periods when only a few people could show up or when personal crises made our lives more important to discuss than the books.

We have fairly eclectic tastes, ranging from E. M. Forster to Annie Dillard, Isabel Allende to Anne Lamott. Rarely do we all like the same book. In fact, one or two of us almost consistently disagree, but that's okay and is part of the fun. On those rare occasions when everyone present loves the book, it's a special pleasure.

A few of us are second-generation book club members, continuing a practice that our mothers enjoyed. Although the movement has recently exploded into a huge phenomenon, reading groups in the United States actually date back to the early nineteenth century. Although we didn't have any grand aspirations or sense of history when we decided to get together and talk about the books, we're proud to be part of that tradition.

Enjoy the Journey

The following two hundred books are great responses to that frequently asked question "What have you read that's good?" Each is a favorite of a group of readers, either members of a formal book club or a chain of friends and relatives who shared the book and loved it. I read each book as well before describing it here.

Each listing in the next pages is indicated as paperback or hardcover, its status when *The Readers' Choice* went to print. For those who stick strictly to paperback, keep in mind that, by the time you read this, a number of books listed as hardcover may have been issued in less expensive paperback editions.

Following each book review are several questions that may serve as food for thought, either for you as an individual reader or for use by your book club.

All of these books were in print and available through bookstores when *The Readers' Choice* was written. However, if a few of the little-known gems praised here have sadly gone out of print by the time you read this, please ask your bookstore for help. Many can place special orders with book-finding services.

For all those who asked if they could have a collection of my monthly "Book Club Favorites" columns in *The Press Democrat,* here it is. Enjoy!

The Readers' Choice: 200 Book Club Favorites

Fire on the Mountain, by Edward Abbey, University of New Mexico Press (paperback)

Fire on the Mountain is a story of both strength and simplicity, an inspiring tale about a New Mexico rancher trying to hold back the authority of the U.S. government as it lays claim to his land. Told from the point of view of a twelve-year-old grandson who has come to visit for the summer, Abbey's novel traces the actions of John Vogelin as he refuses to allow the neighboring White Sands Missile Range to annex his property.

Abbey's love of the desert and mountains comes through poignantly in his descriptions of cottonwood trees and riverbeds, grama grass and sand dunes. The tender-and-tough relationship between grandfather and grandson lends force to the story, emerging in the give-and-take of very effective dialogue.

The story's power is enhanced by the knowledge that Abbey's fiction was inspired by real events. John Prather, a New Mexico cattleman, waged a similar battle against the federal government when it tried to make his ranch part of White Sands.

Abbey, who died in 1989, has come to be known as a father of the modern environmental movement. Although he didn't like to be labeled an environmentalist, Abbey once called himself an "agrarian anarchist." "If a label is required," he commented, "say that I am one who loved the unfenced country."

Abbey worked for fifteen years as a park ranger and fire lookout for the National Park Service in the Southwest and also taught writing at the University of Arizona. In the early 1950s he was a Fulbright Fellow, and in 1975 he became a Guggenheim Fellow. He authored twenty books, nine of them novels. *The Monkey Wrench Gang* may be his most notorious fiction work: It is an account of an environmental group's attempt to blow up a dam in Arizona.

Abbey expresses deep love and respect for both the land and its older inhabitants. However, he is also clear about the compelling reasons why land might be co-opted for other uses. Does Abbey present any answers to the dilemma posed in the book, of nature versus people and their technology?

The Romance Reader, by Pearl Abraham, Riverhead Books (paperback)

In the novel *The Romance Reader,* a young girl trapped within the confines of Hasidic Jewish culture tells what it is like to be surrounded by mainstream American life and yet be required to follow the narrowly defined rules of an ultra-Orthodox sect dating from the Jewish ghettos of eighteenth-century Poland.

Author Pearl Abraham weaves her own firsthand knowledge of Hasidism into the story of Rachel, a rebellious New York teenager of the 1960s who would like to wear sheer stockings, swim in a bathing suit, and read contemporary novels. Rachel's simple desires are shocking to her rabbi father, her dutiful mother, and their conservative community, who believe that women's heads should be shaved at marriage, that the female body should be hidden, and that the only books worth reading are religious in nature.

Abraham grew up in a Hasidic community and now teaches writing at New York University. She portrays the parameters of Hasidic life in a lively, moving way by detailing what Rachel cannot have rather than by writing a lengthy exposition on Hasidism. Rachel's daring forays to the public library to obtain books of classic American literature or her clandestine pursuit of lifeguard certification endear her to the reader. By our standards, her yearnings are innocent; by her family's standards, they are perfidious.

Abraham is also the author of *Giving Up America,* a novel that traces the disintegration of a marriage and continues her examination of Orthodox Jewish religion and culture.

Like so many others whose families are new to this country, Rachel prefers to leave behind centuries of strict tradition to dive into the American melting pot. In doing so, she is forced to choose between offending her parents and freely embracing a new way of life. Does it seem to you that Abraham's novel presents a criticism of Hasidic life or simply a study of it?

Rachel's rebellion has been compared to Huck Finn's brave journey in Mark Twain's HUCKLEBERRY FINN *and Holden Caulfield's struggles in J. D. Salinger's* THE CATCHER IN THE RYE. *How similar do you think her story is to these classics?*

Skirts, by Mimi Albert, Baskerville Publishers (hardcover)

You may have to ask your favorite bookstore to order this book from Baskerville, but it is well worth the effort. Albert has written a mesmerizing story of three young women on their own in New York City's Greenwich Village in the early 1960s, seeking independence and excitement among the Beat Generation rather than following the home-and-motherhood route expected of most girls then.

Albert writes powerfully of the seducer and seduced as she introduces Zalman, the tall, handsome son of a rabbi, who suggests "turning on" to all of life, including drugs. He is both an alluring figure and an ominous one as he leads the particularly innocent Helene deeper and deeper into his exotic world.

Throughout the novel, Albert's language is eloquent, direct, and vividly descriptive. Interspersed through her intense, dramatic narrative are wonderfully playful bits of writing that are often hilarious.

It's surprising that twenty years elapsed between publication of Albert's first book, *The Second Story Man,* which was praised in a *New York Times* book review as "perfectly written," and the appearance of *Skirts,* which was a nominee for the Bay Area Book Reviewers Association Award for fiction in 1994. In the interim, Albert lived and studied in India, published short fiction, and lived and taught in northern California's wine country. Today she teaches creative writing at the University of California Extension at Berkeley and is a California Arts Council artist in residence at the National Institute of Arts and Disabilities. As of this writing, she is finishing a new novel, *Through Black Seas.*

Helene, Ruth, and Victoria have a common cultural heritage but seem to share little in terms of personality and goals. Do you believe in their friendship? What connects them?

Ruth is a particularly rough-edged character. What is it that makes you care about her?

How odd or unusual do the views that were held toward women in the early sixties seem in today's milieu?

Tuesdays with Morrie: An Old Man, a Young Man, and Life's Greatest Lesson, by Mitch Albom, Doubleday (hardcover)

How can a book about death be upbeat? If the man dying is Morrie Schwartz, it's quite possible. Sportswriter Mitch Albom has written a fitting tribute to his one-of-a-kind college professor, letting Morrie's words provide a great deal of inspiration about life as well as death.

Although they were close friends during Albom's days as a student at Brandeis University, Albom let his relationship with his favorite professor lapse after he left school to pursue a career as a musician and then as a journalist. Late one night, twenty years later, while switching TV channels, he heard a familiar voice. It was Morrie, being interviewed about his impending death by Ted Koppel, the host of ABC-TV's *Nightline.*

The story that Albom tells about this plucky little man who once commanded rooms full of sociology students with his wit and his insight and who also loved to dance the night away is compelling in and of itself. It is made even more interesting with the addition of Albom's story, which is typical of so many of his baby-boom generation: Driven by a need to achieve and perform, he finds professional success to be strangely empty. Sitting alongside his ailing former mentor, tape-recording their sessions together, Albom attempts to preserve for himself and others the wisdom that Morrie has to offer.

Albom, who writes for the *Detroit Free Press,* has been voted America's number one sports columnist ten times by the Associated Press Sports Editors. He is the author of the best-selling *Bo* and *Fab Five* and has published four collections of his columns.

Morrie has a lot of things to say about how life should be lived and how death is best approached. Do his pronouncements ever seem to go over the top in terms of confidence or arrogance? What is it that makes us want to embrace the delivered wisdom of this supremely confident man?

Reservation Blues, by Sherman Alexie, Warner Books (paperback)

If you've seen the movie *Smoke Signals,* you already know about the fresh, funny style of Native American writer Sherman Alexie. The characters and setting for that film, based largely on Alexie's first book, *The Lone Ranger and Tonto Fistfight in Heaven,* appear again in *Reservation Blues* with the same irresistible humor and distinctive point of view.

Winner of the American Book Award in 1995, *Reservation Blues* tells what happens when blues legend Robert Johnson magically finds his way to the crossroads at the Spokane Indian Reservation in Washington. His guitar is passed into the hands of Victor, a troubled young man who becomes no less troublesome but extremely talented as the member of a new rock group, Coyote Springs. Alexie's novel follows Victor, Junior, and the very likable Thomas Builds-the-Fire as they attempt to pull themselves out of the poverty of reservation life and contend with the specter of rock-and-roll stardom.

A member of the Cour d'Alene tribe, Alexie grew up on the Spokane Indian reservation. His fiction also includes *Indian Killer,* a novel about a Native American serial killer who seeks revenge for his people's genocide by murdering whites. Although the critically acclaimed book sounds extremely depressing, it shows the same sardonic humor and imaginative characterization that lighten Alexie's portrayal of the sordid features of reservation life in his previous novels. Alexie is also the author of books of poetry, including *Old Shirts & New Skins, First Indian on the Moon,* and *The Summer of Black Widows.*

What do you think of the portrayal of women in RESERVATION BLUES? *Is Alexie simply being amusing in naming them Betty and Veronica, Checkers and Chess, or is he demeaning them?*

Alexie uses a fair amount of fantasy in his story, including the miraculous appearance of Robert Johnson. Still, his portrayal of Native Americans has a gritty, authentic quality. Does this novel portray important truths about the lives of American Indians, or is it more a playful romp?

Paula, by Isabel Allende, translated from the Spanish by Margaret Sayers Peden, HarperPerennial (paperback)

If you are one of those people who didn't appreciate the sumptuous, thickly descriptive writing of Isabel Allende's wildly successful novels *Eva Luna* and *The House of the Spirits,* try this book. *Paula* is the straightforward telling of the author's very colorful family history interwoven with an account of her young daughter's death from a rare disease. The writing is vivid but economical; Allende has a lot of anecdotes to tell, and she gets quickly to the point.

Death is a key element in the story and yet doesn't cast a pall over it. As Allende distracts herself by writing this long letter to Paula, who rests for months in a coma, she distracts us as well.

How did one person come to have so many unusual relatives? Part of the fascination of this nonfiction work is the account of the 1973 overthrow of Chile's President Salvador Allende, the author's uncle. Just as memorable is the depiction of the author's stepfather, better known as "Tío Ramón, the direct descendant of Jesus Christ," self-described as the ugliest man of his generation. In addition, hovering in the drapes of her bedroom is the ghost of Isabel Allende's grandmother Memé, known for her spiritual powers.

Having lived in Peru, Chile, Lebanon, Spain, and Venezuela, Allende now resides in northern California. She is also the author of *Aphrodite: A Memoir of the Senses,* which combines research on aphrodisiacs with Allende's personal memories and favorite, earthy recipes, and *Daughter of Fortune,* the fictional story of a young Chilean who follows the father of her child to California during the 1849 goldrush.

It would be easy for Allende, at this vulnerable point in her life, to idealize her relationship with her daughter. Are there signs that she's guilty of this?

Dialogue can be critical in moving along a story and in building character. What do you think of Allende's voice in this memoir and its importance in creating her own character?

In the Time of the Butterflies, by Julia Alvarez, Plume (paperback)

Although fiction, *In the Time of the Butterflies* is based on the true story of the Mirabel sisters who defied Trujillo, the malevolent dictator in their native Dominican Republic, and then died in 1960 at the hands of his thugs.

The four sisters, as drawn by Alvarez, are captivating. You'll want to get to know them better and to understand exactly what caused their deaths. Furthermore, the villains in this story are so thoroughly evil that, if you don't know the story of Trujillo, you'll want to savor the story of how he was toppled.

Your fascination will be heightened precisely because *In the Time of the Butterflies* was inspired by actual events. It's hard not to wonder how such a normal family could have been prompted to take heroic actions that would make them legends in their own time.

Unlike much modern Hispanic writing, Alvarez's story is not drenched in lavish prose, although the author does a beautiful job of re-creating time and place. Alvarez relies on the expressive, colorful voices of her characters to create memorable portraits and scenes.

Poet and novelist Alvarez is also the author of the best-selling *How the Garcia Girls Lost Their Accents* and its sequel, *Yo!* Her collected essays centering on family and literature are available in *Something to Declare. In the Time of the Butterflies* was a nominee for the 1995 National Book Critics Circle Award.

Does it disturb you that Alvarez has taken the liberty of combining fact with fiction? How does this technique affect your belief in the validity of the entire story, including the political events?

Were you confused by the leaps between past and present and the alternating perspective of the four sisters?

IN THE TIME OF THE BUTTERFLIES *is an unusual retelling of history, in that it centers on female rather than male bravery. Did the heroines seem fully drawn, or did they seem only to be icons of womanly courage?*

Bless Me, Ultima, by Rudolfo Anaya, Warner Books (paperback)

A favorite selection of many book clubs, *Bless Me, Ultima,* was the winner in the 1970s of the Premio Quinto Sol, the national Chicano literary award, and Rudolfo Anaya was hailed as the nation's foremost Latino author for both this book and his novel *Albuquerque,* which won the PEN Center West Award for fiction.

Set in New Mexico, in the borderland between a small village and the huge *llano,* or plain, *Bless Me, Ultima* is an Hispanic boy's coming-of-age story. Young Antonio is torn between his father's side of the family, the cowboys who ride and work on the *llano,* and his mother's side, the farmers whose lives are connected to the village and who are related to the region's first Catholic priest. The six-year-old is asked to begin preparing for adult life and, in so doing, to choose sides.

Anaya draws a number of conflicts here, between Hispanic and American culture, between Catholicism and paganism, between what parents expect of their children and what those children in the end must choose to do. He points out an interesting conflict built in to the people of the Southwest: the inherited tension that resulted from blending the blood of the Spanish conquistadores, a wild and often violent group of adventurers, with the blood of relatively peace-loving, sedentary native farmers.

Antonio's life is forever altered when his aunt Ultima, a *curandera,* or healer, comes to live with his family. Ultima teaches Antonio how to gather and use herbs and, more important, how to gather the strength and self-knowledge that will lead to satisfying adulthood.

Anaya was thought to be in the vanguard of changing perceptions about Hispanic identity when this book was first written. Do his characterizations seem dated now? How do his characters' senses of identity compare with those of Hispanic people in more recent books like T. Coraghessan Boyle's THE TORTILLA CURTAIN *and Luis Rodriquez's* ALWAYS RUNNING*?*

Hidden Latitudes, by Alison Anderson, Washington Square Press (paperback)

Imagine Amelia Earhart stranded on a tropical island near the site of her plane crash. Imagine a young couple forty years later, their sailboat blown off course to that very same island. Alison Anderson has done just that and done it superbly.

Will seventy-year-old Amelia reveal herself? Over the course of her imprisonment on this verdant but desolate island, she has faced enough danger and disappointment to keep her from rushing out to meet her guests. Robin and Lucy, terrified at the failure of their engine in these remote waters, distracted by the chasm in their marriage, only gradually see signs that they are not alone.

There are other threads that create suspense: Can this marriage be saved? More to the point, can these lives be saved?

Anderson writes simply and convincingly, alternating between Amelia's voice and a third-person narrative of Robin and Lucy. As Amelia unfolds for us the story of her four decades in the Pacific, we watch the young couple struggle to save themselves. Amelia's time on the island has included moments of transcendent beauty as well as danger, so that her fascinating memories provide relief for the characters' harsh dilemmas.

Don't confuse this book with *I Was Amelia Earhart,* another novel that was published at approximately the same time. The other book received a lot of attention and made *The New York Times Book Review* best-seller list; this one was published to quiet praise and was nominated for a Bay Area Book Reviewers Association Award for fiction, but received only limited promotion.

An accomplished sailor, teacher, and translator, Alison Anderson has written a superb first novel.

Did you have any difficulty accepting the premise that Amelia Earhart might have survived on this little island?

If the book works for you, it provides a kind of vacation from your own existence. What is it about Anderson's writing that helps you to transcend time and place so thoroughly, to be transported to her fictional island?

Midnight Champagne, by A. Manette Ansay, William Morrow (hardcover)

Heralded by *The Utne Reader* in 1998 as one of the top ten new faces of fiction, A. Manette Ansay comes to full power in her fifth novel, *Midnight Champagne.* Her plucky use of language and her ability to present multiple interesting characters in provocative situations unite with a tightly woven plot to produce a story that is both engaging and suspenseful.

The entire novel unfolds within the confines of a wedding ceremony and dinner reception—and a host of intriguing scenarios tied to the day's affair. Set in a snow-laden wedding chapel and lodge on the shore of Lake Michigan, the marriage celebration pulls together numerous couples in various stages of love and aversion. The young couple exchanging rings have known each other for only three months. A husband-and-wife team who check into the lodge have known each other far too long and far too violently. In between are all kinds of variations on the romance theme, expressed with both humor and pathos.

What creates the suspense? Ansay displays the frailties of each key player and at the same time makes most of her major characters so likable that we worry about the potential threats they pose to themselves or to others.

Continuing a tradition begun in a previous novel, *River Angel,* Ansay dabbles in the use of ghosts, but with relative restraint. By the time these visitors make their appearance, they are but one more possibility for drama in a lodge full of the unexpected.

Ansay is also the author of *Sister* and *Vinegar Hill;* the latter was an Oprah Winfrey book club selection.

There's a growing sense of awful danger related to one of the characters. What do you think of the very vague, gradual way Ansay reveals this person and his actions?

At the outset it seems sad that April is being married in an old, ill-fitting wedding gown that does not become her. Does this seem important by the end of the book? Why?

The Robber Bride, by Margaret Atwood, Anchor Books (paperback)

Margaret Atwood is a very funny woman. You might not guess this from reading *The Handmaid's Tale* or *Cat's Eye,* two of her darker novels, but her humor is evident in *The Robber Bride,* woven into the accelerating drama. (If you are lucky enough to have an opportunity to hear Atwood speak, do it. She's a natural wit and enjoys playing to an audience.)

In *The Robber Bride,* Atwood creates a hypnotically attractive female named Zenia who wreaks romantic havoc wherever she goes. The three other main characters in the book are women drawn together by their common wounds at Zenia's hands and their attempts to fend off this nightmare femme fatale.

Comforted at first by the knowledge that Zenia is dead, the three women meet occasionally to enjoy lunch. On one of these outings, Zenia breezes into the restaurant—alive and well enough to endanger their marriage and relationships and to throw their lives into chaos once more.

Atwood is a catty observer of human frailty; her tale points out the ways in which we grant power to others and the obstacles we face in making moral choices.

The most recent works of this Canadian novelist, short story writer, poet, and literary critic have garnered the most attention, but you might also want to try an excellent older book, *Bodily Harm,* which at first glance seems like a simple mystery but in fact is a novel of much broader range, including a number of issues of interest to women. Other fiction by Atwood you'll probably want to check out: the novel *Alias Grace* and a collection of short stories called *Wilderness Tips.*

Serious, hefty women villains are few and far between in modern literature. In writing this novel, Atwood asked herself, "Where have all the Lady Macbeths gone?" For all of us who grew up with male characters dominating the books we read, is there a kind of pleasure in encountering an extremely powerful female villain as well as finding middle-aged women protagonists to admire?

THE ROBBER BRIDE *could be described as a social comedy. Is it more than good entertainment? Did the characters and their relationships seem real to you, and did Atwood cause you to reflect on certain contemporary dilemmas and conflicts?*

The Flamingo Rising, by Larry Baker, Ballantine Books (paperback)

Even though the author wants you to think otherwise, there is no big crisis or dilemma to move this story forward—but that's okay. The setting is so unusual and the characters so completely one-of-a-kind, that you'll want to keep reading simply to see what becomes of them. A feud between the owners of a funeral home and the world's largest drive-in movie in Jacksonville, Florida, as well as the promise of a large fire and other life-altering events add to the spice, but mainly Larry Baker has created an extended family that you'll want to become part of.

Narrator Abe and his sister Louise were adopted as small babies in Korea by Hubert Lee, an American soldier on his way home from the war. The children grow up with two loving but unorthodox parents in a residence built inside the tower of the drive-in, a monstrous beachside structure large enough to show movies to shrimp boats pulling their catch to shore at the end of a day. Hubert insists that anyone employed by him must live with him, and so characters as diverse as a petite railroad man named Pete, a goofy but graceful pilot named Judge Lester, a blonde beauty named Polly, and a rabid dog named Frank all interact unpredictably and often with great humor.

Some suspense does arise when Abe falls in love with the daughter of his father's archenemy, the owner of the neighboring funeral home. Abe and Grace's love story provides a kind of calm center from the crazy events swirling through the novel.

THE FLAMINGO RISING *is Baker's first novel. While many have praised it as wildly exuberant and inventive, the book may show some signs of inexperience. Do you see anything about the writing mechanics or construction of plot that might need fine-tuning?*

There is a tragic surprise at the end of Baker's novel. Did it come as a complete shock, or were there clues that prepared you for this particular event?

The huge Flamingo drive-in can be seen as an unorthodox symbol of American culture. What do you think Baker is saying about American ambition, American taste, and American illusions?

Slaves in the Family, Edward Ball, Ballantine Books (paperback)

A descendant of one of the oldest slave-holding families in the South, Edward Ball explores his family's history as slave owners and traders and seeks to reveal the secret history—secret, at least, on the white side of the family—of all those people of color who were also the descendants of his white ancestors.

As the son of a minister with a modest income, Ball knew none of the trappings of wealth that had been second nature to generations of Balls living on plantations near Charleston, South Carolina. However, as an adult he realized that he and other members of his extended family lived with a certain sense of privilege arising from their connection to a plantation dynasty. This odd sense of superiority and an intense curiosity about his family's past led him to leave his journalism career in New York and settle in Charleston, which he used as a home base to conduct extensive research through both written records and personal interviews.

When the Civil War ended, at least 842 slaves were emancipated from Ball family tracts. The author estimates that today there are 75,000 to 100,000 living descendants of freed Ball slaves residing throughout the United States. His accounts of his contacts with quite a few of these people and of the stories they have to tell are fascinating, as are the historical details he uses as connective tissue in this compelling book.

One of the sad facts that emerges from Ball's history is that Charleston was the major entry point for captive Africans arriving in North America. Accustomed as we are to reading about Ellis Island as the nostalgic entryway to the United States for waves of European immigrants, it's shocking to realize that thousands of other Americans-to-be first experienced their country in the form of a harsh coastal prison from which they would be sold to the highest bidders.

Winner of both the National Book Award and the Southern Book Award for nonfiction, *Slaves in the Family* can bog down a bit with all of the fine detail that Ball provides. An abridged, audiotape version of the book produced by Simon & Schuster and read by the author is a stirring alternative for those not willing to sit still for quite so extensive a history.

At times it seems that the United States will always, in one way or another, suffer the aftereffects of having enslaved a portion of its population. Does Ball's book say anything that encourages you to believe that blacks and whites can overcome the deep wounds caused by slavery?

After reading this book, what do you think of the accuracy and usefulness of questionnaires that ask us to define ourselves according to race?

Cloudsplitter, by Russell Banks, HarperPerennial (paperback)

If you remember him from history class, John Brown and his attack on Harpers Ferry may seem only an odd footnote to the beginning of the Civil War. Read this book, and that will change. In *Cloudsplitter,* Russell Banks has done a stunning job of creating a full-blooded portrait of this man obsessed with ending slavery and of the son who struggled to grow up in his shadow. *Cloudsplitter* is crafted as a novel, but it feels like the truth, and the power of Banks's writing is bound to shake you.

Forty years after the events at Harpers Ferry, Owen Brown decides to tell his story as the only surviving son of the infamous American political terrorist many considered a madman. What unfolds is both a spellbinding tale of father-son conflict and of the political and social landscape that preceded the war between the states.

Brown may have been obsessed and he may have been rigid in his beliefs, but as Banks portrays him, he was a morally upright man who believed that none should rest as long as human beings were enslaved. Be that as it may, what was it like to be the son of a man willing to sacrifice his life and his family in the name of freedom for others? Banks details Owen's difficulty in trying to please his father and at the same time to grow up in some kind of normal way. The task was Herculean. As Owen states at the outset, he may as well have died at Harpers Ferry, for after the death of his father, nothing would ever seem quite right again.

Banks is the author of numerous novels, among them *The Sweet Hereafter, Rule of the Bone, Affliction,* and *Continental Drift.*

As the overbearing, enormous figure of John Brown emerges full-blown in the capable hands of Russell Banks, the character of his son Owen slowly wilts. What are some of the most telling ways that Banks reveals the decline of Owen Brown?

Banks did extensive historical research in preparing to write his novel. Do you think his fictional re-creation of the John Brown story enhances our knowledge of U.S. history or muddies the waters of historical fact?

Regeneration, by Pat Barker, Plume (paperback)

You may never have heard of British author Pat Barker, but you'll wonder why when you've read *Regeneration.* Her very humane, winning novel based in a "loony bin" in Britain during World War I tells the stories of soldiers being treated for shell shock and of a therapist who suffers the stress of helping these men prepare to return to face the depravity of war.

One of the patients Dr. William Rivers must treat is Siegfried Sassoon, a decorated military hero who has decided that the war is a senseless slaughter and that he will no longer serve as an officer. The only thing that his superiors can think to do is to label him as mentally unsound and send him in for reprogramming, or "regeneration." How Rivers and Sassoon resolve this problem is a major thread of Barker's story.

Barker has done an astounding job of bringing to life a distant time and a nation tangled in a terrible war. We care about her characters, we feel their passions and their traumas, and we hope fervently that they will recover their ability to lead decent lives. A particularly striking feature of *Regeneration* is that it reads like a traditional novel, catching you up in the intimate dramas of numerous characters, and yet, when you are done, a note from the author informs you that her characters were real. A neurologist and social anthropologist named W. H. R. Rivers did treat an officer/poet/war protester named Sassoon and a poet named Wilfred Owen, and many of the events inside and out of the mental hospital actually did happen.

Regeneration is the first book in a trilogy that also includes *The Eye in the Door* and *The Ghost Road,* which won England's prestigious Booker Prize in 1995. Barker is also the author of the critically acclaimed novel, *Another World.*

Although REGENERATION *could be classified as an historical novel, it is much more. How does Barker use emotions and questions of personal conscience to take her book to a higher plane?*

How does Barker manage to convey scenes of terror and disgust and at the same time create a story dominated by feelings of warmth and wonder?

The Whereabouts of Eneas McNulty, by Sebastian Barry, Viking (hardcover)

Ireland seems to be turning out one extremely talented author after another, as witnessed by the writing in Niall Williams's *Four Letters of Love* and Jeannette Haien's *The All of It.* Here is another beautifully crafted novel, this one so lyrical in its prose that it calls to be read aloud.

In his small village of Sligo, Eneas McNulty is an innocent among angry partisans. When he chooses to solve the problem of hard times and slim employment prospects by taking a job with the Royal Irish Constabulary, the British-led police force, he alters his life irrevocably.

Although this is a tale of wandering and loss of home, the character of Eneas is so endearing that you want to travel with him and hope for a happy ending. Novelist Sebastian Barry makes it worthwhile to endure Eneas's travails by introducing an unusual cast of supporting characters as well as sojourns at exotic locations, telling it all in prose of memorable beauty. *Eneas McNulty* is reminiscent of *The English Patient* in the way its language sweeps over you in a lovely, seductive rhythm.

Barry is the author of three books of poems and three books of fiction. He has also written for the theater and is best known for the award-winning *The Steward of Christendom.*

Barry's novel has been said to possess elements of James Joyce and Dylan Thomas, particularly in the tone and power of its language. Can the same be said of Barry's characterizations? Would you say that Eneas is a familiar Irish stereotype, or is he a distinctive and new literary creation?

The author takes us to diverse countries, including England, Scotland, the United States, and Nigeria. In doing so, he raises further questions about nationalism, colonialism, and political violence. What do you think he's trying to tell the reader about these issues?

By the end of Eneas's life, we feel that we've been on a long, often hard journey. Do you have any sense of satisfaction for the main character? What do you think he has achieved?

Maiden Voyage, by Cynthia Bass, Bantam Books (paperback)

Coming-of-age stories are a popular modern form and so are tales about the *Titanic,* but Cynthia Bass's book is unique in that it is the only coming-of-age story that involves the sinking of the *Titanic.* Bass has very effectively re-created the first and only voyage of the ship that was to be the wonder of its time, making its destruction a pivotal event in the life of twelve-year-old Sumner Jordan.

It might have been enough to research and describe the *Titanic,* a boat so well engineered that it was supposed to be incapable of sinking, then lead us through its cavernous kitchens and gleaming corridors, seeing them through a child's eyes and having us tremble once the iceberg hits. Bass has done much more. She has created a cast of intriguing characters, each with his or her own picayune habits and colorful agendas, so that we very much want to trace their fates before, during, and after the great disaster of 1912.

Sumner is a precocious child, an aspiring poet and the son of a leading American feminist, who lives in the tumultuous early years of the century, when world war was imminent and women were fighting for the right to vote. He leaves his Boston family to visit his estranged father in London, and as a special treat arranged by his mother, he returns home solo on the largest, most lavish man-made object on the face of the planet. When the ship hits the iceberg, Sumner grapples with the edict "women and children first" and the moral dilemma it poses.

Bass is also the author of *Sherman's March,* another historical novel. A former student of history at the University of California at Berkeley, her work shows the results of both meticulous research and vivid imagination.

What do you think of Bass's choice of illuminating a women's rights theme as experienced and interpreted by a young boy?

All details about the TITANIC *presented in* MAIDEN VOYAGE *are given with great accuracy; do you feel that the author should have spent even more time on the ship and its sinking or that she made the right choice in balancing Sumner's story with the disaster?*

The Diving Bell and the Butterfly, by Jean-Dominique Bauby, translated from the French by Jeremy Leggatt, Vintage Books (paperback)

It's hard to conceive just how this book was written. Petite in size, it is huge in accomplishment. In 1995 Bauby was editor-in-chief of *Elle* magazine in Paris when he was struck down by a massive stroke. Unable to move anything but his left eyelid, he found a way to dictate this book and not be silenced. His brief memoir became a number one best-seller in England and France.

A man of forty-three, the father of two young children, and the possessor of both superior wit and imagination, Bauby draws you quickly into his new, locked-in world. He feels, he says, as though a huge diving bell is sitting on his chest, and yet he is able to soar at times like a butterfly, thanks to the character of the human mind. Reading this elegant work, you are privileged to soar with him.

Until Bauby dictated this book a blink at a time, no one had ever before personally described the experience of being locked in an unresponsive body. Bauby recalls bits of his past, reflects on his predicament, even conjures up delectable meals to cook and to eat, and allows us to accompany him through the world as he now experiences it. Reading his descriptions of food, you'll envy his ability to evoke gourmet treats so thoroughly. Traveling with him to the beach, you'll wonder if, on your own, you would appreciate every sight and sound so completely. Learning about his gutsy attempts to let his friends know that he had not become a vegetable—by sending them a sort of newsletter—you'll only admire his fortitude.

This is not a sickbed memoir but rather a successful attempt to overcome infirmity: a memorable offering of a man blessed with sensitivity and the ability to communicate.

You might find that you are drawn into this book by fascination with the morbid details of Bauby's medical crisis. Given his situation, it would be easy to feel only one emotion toward Bauby: pity. What keeps this memoir from being maudlin?

Bauby expresses his sensations, memories, and fantasies with great specificity. Does this slow down his narrative or strengthen it?

Warriors Don't Cry: A Searing Memoir of the Battle to Integrate Little Rock's Central High, by Melba Pattillo Beals, Washington Square Press (paperback)

Until you read this riveting book, you're not likely to truly understand the hardships of fighting for southern integration in the 1950s and 1960s. Melba Beals was one of nine bright, talented African American students chosen to integrate Little Rock's Central High School in 1957. It has taken forty years for the pain of that experience to recede enough for her to write a thorough account.

Among the tales of terror and hatred, however, come many inspiring stories of family love and a few of interracial friendship. While the rest of the nation probably assumed that the black teenagers making history by attending Central High were well protected by federal troops and then state troopers, the truth is that Melba, her friends, and their families were physically and verbally assaulted every day of the school year. The heroics of the nine students and their families were echoed in the acts of certain friends and even strangers.

As you read about the tortures the nine black students endured, you'll be amazed that mere children were so determined and so strong. Encouraged by others to believe that their efforts would have a profound influence on the civil rights movement in America, they did in fact become warriors.

Beals's writing is plainspoken and to the point. Her voice takes on the youthful innocence of the teenager she once was, as many of her recollections are taken from a journal she kept while attending Central High.

Beals worked as a reporter for NBC and today is a communications consultant in San Francisco. She has written a sequel to her childhood memoir: *White Is a State of Mind.*

Beals's book puts you right in Little Rock with her. What are the elements of her writing that make her memories come to life so effectively?

Can you think of any equivalent acts of courage on behalf of human rights or any other social issues that have occurred in the United States in recent times?

The Boys of My Youth, by Jo Ann Beard, Back Bay Books (paperback)

Jo Ann Beard's memoir has been described by some critics as a very moving description of an ordinary life—as if ordinary life might not be filled with extraordinary drama at times. Beard disproves this "unusual description of the ordinary" in two ways: First, one of her stories concerns a type of event that most of us will never experience—a shooting at the University of Iowa, in which six of her associates were gunned down by a disgruntled student. Second, Beard's descriptions of the more typical days of her life are loaded with drama and humor and pathos that point out just how memorable conventional life can be.

The Boys of My Youth is a loose collection of vignettes spanning Beard's childhood in the 1960s and her adulthood. She emerges as a spunky, pale little girl who can make life hell for her parents when her doll Hal is removed from her grasp . . . a preteen who can toughen up to deal with the aftermath of her father's drunk driving . . . and a dog-loving woman who won't take divorce lightly. Through it all, she is able to look wryly at her own antics as well as those of her family and friends.

By the way, the title story is not really about the boys of Beard's youth, in spite of the picture of the bed on the cover. It is more about the lack of boys in Beard's youth and the importance of having a lifelong good friend, and the book is all the more amusing and heartwarming because of it.

Beard seems to have an uncanny ability to remember the smallest particulars of her childhood—and to communicate them with a perfect mix of wry humor and childlike simplicity. Her book was first written as fiction and then reclassified by the publisher as nonfiction, probably to take advantage of the craze for memoir. What do you think of this blurring line between fiction and nonfiction, as more and more writers draw pictures of their past with detail that may involve more guesswork than actual memory?

Comedy and grief alternate in these stories in an arresting way. What do you think of how Beard entwines the suspenseful story of the murders of her friends and employers with offbeat interludes in which she pretends that her collie is a Maserati?

A Minus Tide, by Robin Beeman, Chronicle Books (hardcover)

This tiny book is small in the way a diamond is. Beeman's novella sparkles with expert storytelling and characterization. Like a minus tide, an extremely low tide that reveals things not usually seen, her intimate story lays bare five interconnected lives.

Two couples living in a small town along the northern California coast are reeling in the aftermath of the death of a visitor. Sally, an odd, bewitching woman who has gone over the cliff in her car, is tied to the other four as a sibling, lover, or friend. Each chapter belongs to one of these four telling the story of their interwoven lives from his or her perspective.

The language is precisely crafted; Beeman is sparing with adjectives but draws vibrant,, intense, often amusing pictures. For example: ''Mattie's show was a wild success. The gallery, a chi-chi place with clientele from the city, was packed. Champagne, oozing cheeses, little fresh fruit tarts, lots of tanned skin, bleached teeth, and good posture. Mattie's watercolors are a delight, even when they're puzzling.''

Beeman's characters are distinctive and real precisely because she has revealed their odd little flaws. With these believable souls, she weaves mystery, romance, and drama.

Beeman has also written an excellent collection of short tales, *A Parallel Life and Other Stories,* ranging in style from quirky humor to deadly serious, covering territory from rural Louisiana to the coast of California. Her short story ''Work It, Girlfriend'' appeared in a collection by northern California writers called *Cartwheels on the Faultline.*

If the chapters were not labeled "Mattie," "Evan," "Joel," and "Anna," would you be able to distinguish each narrator's voice? Can you point out the bits of dialogue or the way of viewing the world that mark each different character?

By the end of the story, what is your impression of Sally? Is it possible to have a definitive view of her after hearing the various characters speak of her?

Moghul Buffet, by Cheryl Benard, Farrar, Straus and Giroux (hardcover)

What an unexpected delight. First-time novelist Cheryl Benard plops us down in Pakistan with an awkward American businessman, involves him in a murder mystery, tosses in women hidden under chadors and a few militant Middle Eastern feminists, and along the way is wryly funny.

Moghul Buffet displays an impressive familiarity with Pakistan; although Benard is not Pakistani, she is a world traveler and splits her time between the United States and Austria. Director of a Viennese research institute, she is the author of numerous successful nonfiction books written in German, primarily on women's issues.

Her sad-sack-but-likable businessman, Micky Malone, lives in Bethesda, Maryland, and does not relish the idea of traveling to far-off places, especially in the Third World. Nevertheless, when his partner becomes acutely ill, he must take his place on a junket to Pakistan to complete a deal selling their company's prefabricated buildings. His misgivings escalate when a staffer from the American consulate warns him about Peshawar, the border town where he is staying: "—recent car bombings, don't linger if you hear an explosion because there is almost always a second one to follow, avoid bus terminals and the bazaar—"

Meanwhile Benard wraps us up in other stories about local people: the police investigator and his modern wife; a young girl trapped in slavery in a wealthy man's home; and an expatriate American woman who is working on behalf of the poor. Although each of them helps to raise serious, timely issues, including mention of the Taliban, Islamic militant rebels, at the nearby refugee camp, the plucky narrative keeps the story entertaining at the same time.

A particularly satisfying aspect of this book is the way Micky's character emerges more fully as time goes by and then is transformed by the events that befall him. Did you believe this transformation? Were there hints that this might happen?

Were you startled by the existence of modern feminists in Pakistan? What else did you learn about that country in the course of reading this book?

Who did carry out the murders? What were the clues?

***Plain and Simple: A Woman's Journey to the Amish,* by Sue Bender, HarperSanFrancisco (paperback)**

Sue Bender is a Berkeley artist and therapist, mother of two sons, holder of two graduate degrees from Harvard and Berkeley, who one day stepped outside her frantic, stressful life to go live with the Amish.

This was not an easy thing to do. The Amish are a private people; they do not particularly welcome outsiders. Nevertheless, Bender managed to live with two families for a number of months in farm communities in Iowa and Ohio. The visit transformed her, and in its simple telling, her book explains why

Bender had lived a life of lists, of things to do from morning to night. Like many of us, she was always hurrying to the next item, so that it could be checked off to make way for the next.

The Amish, she found, savor each task in their day. They find joy in every job, whether preparing dinner or clearing a field. There is no hurry to get chores out of the way, but rather a quiet appreciation of the pleasures inherent in a piece of work. After living in their company, Bender was able to return home and establish a new pattern for her own life, as well as to write a soothing, lovely book encouraging the rest of us to do the same.

Since writing *Plain and Simple,* she has authored a follow-up book entitled *Everyday Sacred: A Woman's Journey Home,* in which she gives examples from her daily life explaining how she has learned to live with "just enough" and at the same time to experience each day fully.

Has reading this book made any difference in the way you organize or experience your own life?

Can you imagine making a journey like the one Bender did? Does the ability to leave your regular routine behind and leap into a new, radically different reality rely solely on personal desperation?

Bitter Grounds, by Sandra Benitez, Hyperion (paperback)

Winner of the American Book Award in 1998, *Bitter Grounds* does two apparently opposing things well: It presents a cozy generational saga of two families of women, and it details the recent political history of strife-torn El Salvador. Author Sandra Benitez wraps you warmly in the stories of a poor family and a rich family tied to El Salvador's coffee plantations, but not so warmly that you don't feel the terrors imposed by government forces or guerrilla soldiers.

Following pairs of mothers and daughters caught up in both romantic passion and political fervor, Benitez manages to draw a vivid history that is free of sappy emotion or political polemic. Tantalizing specifics drawn from her own childhood in Salvador range from a recipe for sweet and salt tamales to the languorous feeling of lounging in a warm, fragrance-filled courtyard.

Benitez grew up in El Salvador in the 1940s and 1950s, often serving as a scribe for the illiterate women working in her home and becoming privy to their heartbreak at having to leave villages and families behind to find employment in the capital. In the 1970s, she learned firsthand the repercussions of oppression when friends and family became targets of the growing revolution. Now a resident of the United States, she has written a powerful book of fiction based in part on her life experience.

It's interesting to note that Benitez's first novel was written when she was fifty-two. It's another book club favorite: *A Place Where the Sea Remembers,* which won the first Barnes and Noble Discover Great New Writers Award in 1993.

Benitez makes clear the issues that confront both the rich and poor in El Salvador. By the end of the book, have you decided who the villains are? What message do you think the author is trying to convey about the civil war in this tiny country?

The popular radio soap opera LOS DOS *provides comic counterpoint to the anguish experienced at one time or another by each of the book's heroines. Do you ever feel that Benitez has slipped over the line into the same sort of melodrama in her own story?*

Max Perkins: Editor of Genius, by A. Scott Berg, Riverhead Books (paperback)

Winner of the 1978 National Book Award for nonfiction, this biography has timeless appeal for what it reveals about famous American authors, publishing behind the scenes, and the work of a man who was probably America's greatest editor. Ernest Hemingway, F. Scott Fitzgerald, and Thomas Wolfe were among the many in Max Perkins's debt.

In these days of celebrity memoirs and publishing aimed for mass consumption, the idea of an editor who would spend countless hours with his authors helping to craft literary fiction is an exotic one. Word has it that the economics of book publishing have made this sort of editing assistance extremely rare nowadays; if a manuscript needs fine-tuning, it is more likely that the author's agent will make some suggestions—or that the author will hire a freelance editor—because the publishing house is not likely to do so.

The irony here is that when this excellent retelling of Max Perkins's colorful life and times was first published, his example was seen as the ultimate of what a good editor could be. Now his story symbolizes a glorious time past, one for which many modern authors hold great nostalgia.

Berg's book is loaded with interesting anecdotes, including a description of how Perkins gave Marjorie Kinnan Rawlings the idea for *The Yearling* and how he virtually distilled and helped to write Wolfe's *Look Homeward, Angel.*

Berg is also the author of *Goldwyn: A Biography* and *Lindbergh*; the latter won the Pulitzer Prize in 1999.

Would you say that this is more a biography of Perkins or a collection of stories about the authors he helped? Would you have preferred to know more about Perkins?

Do you think it's appropriate to call Perkins the editor of Thomas Wolfe's LOOK HOMEWARD, ANGEL, *or the collaborator? What do you think of his literary relationship with Wolfe? Do you see any reason why Perkins should not have worked with Wolfe in this way?*

Talk Before Sleep, by Elizabeth Berg, Delta Books (paperback)

This is a novel about women's friendships; it's about laughter and intimacy and the things women will do for one another. The fact that one of the two main characters is dying does not set the tone for Berg's story, but instead puts these friendships in extremely sharp focus and makes us prize them even more.

The friends of the dying woman are an unlikely group: a fast-track businesswoman, a militant gay woman, and a former nurse who is a conventional wife and mom. Each could be a flat stereotype, and each is most definitely not. These women astound and annoy one another, and together they find ways to have pleasure in the worst of situations. The men also seem real; they are both irritating and sympathetic. Friendship is to be honored, Berg lets us know, but it is part of a larger picture that includes other important elements, like husbands, lovers, and children.

Berg has a wonderful way with words. Whether she is describing white bed sheets flapping on the clothesline as if they wanted to escape or a wife walking away from a romantic restaurant dinner that is not really that at all, her choice of images and dialogue is perfect.

Berg is also the author of *Range of Motion, Durable Goods, Joy School,* and *The Pull of the Moon.*

In the brief prologue, Berg tells us that this novel was inspired by the death of a good friend, and that, in writing TALK BEFORE SLEEP, *she both wanted to help herself get over this loss and also make a plea for more research into the causes and prevention of breast cancer. Were you aware of these ulterior motives once you were into the tale? Did the writing ever seem pedantic or overly sentimental?*

Were you put off by Ruth's feeling that she should return to her husband? Could you understand why she would think of doing such a thing, and did this make her seem real—or surprisingly weak?

What do you think of Berg's decision to have Ruth already accepting her approaching death at the outset of the novel? Did it lessen the drama any? Why do you think the author chose to set things up this way?

I'm on My Way but Your Foot Is on My Head: A Black Woman's Story of Getting Over Life's Hurdles, by Bertice Berry, Fireside (paperback)

How can a black girl succeed when her mother is alcoholic, a bright and shining older sister falls prey to drugs, and teachers tell her she has no future? Read Berry's book and see.

You may not know comedienne and former talk show hostess Bertice Berry, but you are likely to fall in love with her while reading her memoir. Originally published under the title *Bertice: The World According to Me,* Berry's memoir is an upbeat, inspiring account of how one young black girl born to poverty in Wilmington, Delaware, made her way to become a college professor and then a professional entertainer.

This is not serious writing. It is fluffy with quick philosophy and advice. It jumps from anecdote to anecdote on subjects as diverse as racism, diet and exercise, and spirituality. However, this is winning writing because a vibrant, intelligent character emerges from the pages, one who makes us applaud.

It's hard not to like a professor who so thoroughly enjoys making her students laugh that she eventually goes on the road as a comedienne. Berry offers interesting advice on teaching, especially the insanity of grading on a curve. Although administrators chastised her for her approach, Berry believed that education was not a contest, and that if she was able to help all of her students arrive at the correct answers, she had the right to give them all A's.

Berry is also the author of two comedy collections: *Sckraight from the Ghetto: You Know You're Ghetto If . . .* and *You Still Ghetto: You Know You're Still Ghetto If . . .*

Berry was born the sixth of seven children in a poor black family and faced a childhood marked by difficulty. What do you think were the factors that made it possible for her to withstand numerous serious challenges and emerge a success?

Do you think the style of the book is appropriate in that it expresses Berry's comic mode, or do you think it would have benefited from a more cohesive, chronological narrative?

Brazzaville Beach, by William Boyd, Daniel M. Barber (paperback)

Scientist Hope Clearwater lazes on a beach at the edge of Africa pondering recent brutal events she witnessed while studying chimpanzees, and very quickly we are pulled into a compelling story touching on questions of human destiny and fate.

Boyd spins two tales here: the unfolding drama of the primates' secret existence and the story of Hope's failed marriage to a troubled mathematician. In an unnamed African nation, Hope had worked in a nature preserve under the direction of a famed primatologist, dedicating herself to studying a band of chimps and learning the most intimate details of their lives. In the course of doing so, she uncovered certain grotesque facts about the animals that disrupted accepted theory about primate behavior—and threatened her own career.

The author is expert at creating suspense and also at bringing to life a believable, interesting female character possessing strength and intellect. The chimps seem just as authentic, thanks to assistance provided to Boyd by noted primate researcher Jane Goodall.

Boyd is also the author of the novels *The Blue Afternoon; Armadillo; An Ice Cream War,* which won the Booker Prize; and *A Good Man in Africa,* which won England's prestigious Whitbread and Somerset Maugham Awards. Born in Ghana, Boyd was educated at the universities of Nice, Glasgow, and Oxford. Today the novelist and screenwriter lives in London.

In BRAZZAVILLE BEACH, *Boyd offers specialized knowledge of chimpanzees and of developing nations as well as expertly drawing his female narrator. Can you think of any other English or American contemporary novelists who exhibit this ease at depicting foreign countries and exotic subject matter?*

What do you think of Boyd's choice to begin his novel at the end of the story, after all of the events have transpired? Do you mind traveling to the past in flashbacks? Do you think the story would have been stronger if the author had simply begun at the beginning?

The Tortilla Curtain, by T. Coraghessan Boyle, Penguin Books (paperback)

In this masterpiece, Boyle creates two worlds, that of illegal immigrants barely subsisting in a southern California canyon and that of white Americans living the good life nearby in a gated community.

It would have been easy for Boyle to mock Delaney and Kyra Mossbacher's affluent San Fernando Valley lifestyle, but he doesn't. Instead of playing the couple's attitudes and behavior for broad humor, he renders them as people you can understand. At the same time, following the desperate travails of Candido and America Rincon, Boyle could have lapsed into melodrama; he does not. As you read about the ennui of the first couple and the pain of the second, you hope that the two worlds will intersect, with some sort of redemption for each.

An interesting thread through this novel is Delaney's study of environment, particularly his ironic notes on immigrant flora and fauna. As the people in his tale struggle with questions of Mexican immigration, Boyle serves up through Delaney a fascinating collection of facts about the numerous life-forms that have made their way to the United States and that we now take for granted as members of our ecosystem.

Boyle is the author of a diverse array of novels, including *The Road to Wellville, Riven Rock, East Is East,* and *World's End,* for which he won the PEN/Faulkner Award. *The Tortilla Curtain* was the winner of the Prix Medicis Étranger.

Delaney and Kyra are living the ultimate American dream—or are they? There is a vague unease to their way of life. Meanwhile, Candido and America struggle to gain a foothold on the American dream and suffer greatly for their efforts. What do you think Boyle is trying to say about the ideals America represents? What do you think he would say the true American dream should be?

What do you think of Boyle's characterization of Delaney's and Kyra's so-called liberal neighbors? Is it believable that liberals would behave like this? Do these characters seem one-dimensional, or do they seem like real people?

The Mists of Avalon, by Marion Zimmer Bradley, A Del Rey Book/Ballantine (paperback)

Here's a nice, big book to get lost in, one that's so satisfying you'll wish for a sequel.

Marion Zimmer Bradley has taken the liberty of re-creating the Arthurian legend so that women are the main actors. They are the heroes and the villains, the creators of life and the keepers of knowledge, as well as the powers behind the throne.

Arthur's sister Morgaine aims to grab Britain back from the Christians and reestablish the worship of the Mother Goddess. Queen Gwenhwyfar has to choose between her duty to Arthur and the new God and her passion for Lancelot. Arthur is not particularly a hero in this tale.

Bradley has accomplished this absorbing novel not just by weaving her story expertly, but by constructing a mythical time and place so that we believe every detail of the landscape is real. She thoroughly studied the geography of Somerset, England, the purported site of Camelot and Guinevere's kingdom; texts on comparative religions including the Druids and Celtic faiths; and immersed herself in the many books touching on King Arthur.

Bradley followed *The Mists of Avalon* with two prequels, *The Forest House,* which you may not find as compelling as the original book, and *Lady of Avalon,* which is best read after *The Mists of Avalon,* even though it precedes it in time. She is also the author of *The Catch Trap* and *The Firebrand* and has written numerous science fiction, fantasy, and gothic romance stories with an upbeat feminist slant, which she refers to as her "potboilers."

Viviane is the priestess of the magical Isle of Avalon, which becomes more difficult to reach as people turn away from its goddess-oriented religion. Viviane aims to find a king who will be loyal to Avalon as well as to Christianity. In the world that she has created, do you think Bradley really believes that it's possible for a nature-based religion to coexist with Christian belief?

Theory of War, by Joan Brady, Fawcett Columbine (paperback)

Here's a little-known fact: White children were sold as slaves in the years just following the Civil War. This was not an uncommon practice among the destitute families of former soldiers; they would "bind over" a child to a stranger until adulthood for a flat fee of $15 to $25. Author Joan Brady's grandfather became a slave in this fashion at the age of four, and she has based her jolting, absorbing novel on this awful piece of family history.

With this story, Brady became in 1993 the first woman to win Britain's Whitbread Book Award, both for Book of the Year and Novel of the Year. Although she was born in San Francisco and educated at Columbia University, Brady now makes her home in England.

Sometimes it's difficult to stay with a novel that dwells so heavily upon tragic events, but *Theory of War* gets beyond this problem in a number of ways. The modern-day narrator is a cantankerous granddaughter whose salty, sometimes witty comments pique your curiosity and provide relief of sorts. Although Jonathan Carrick is permanently scarred by the events of his childhood, not everything that befalls him in the course of this novel is dreadful. Furthermore, Brady's references to military philosopher Karl von Clausewitz in referring to Jonathan's dealings with archenemy Senator George Stoke give you hope that Jonathan will somehow be the victor in the end.

A former ballerina, Brady is also the author of an autobiography, *The Unmaking of a Dancer,* and a novel, *The Imposter.*

Brady is interested in how one's identity forms. Jonathan Carrick's childhood as a slave seems to poison not only him but also the generations that follow. Do you think that Brady is saying this poison is inescapable?

THEORY OF WAR *is rough around the edges in both voice and structure. Do you think Brady purposely designed her novel in this raw, jarring way to add to the reader's shock at the events she describes?*

***All Over but the Shoutin'*, by Rick Bragg, Vintage Books (paperback)**

If there was ever a wonderful tribute to a mother, this is it. Rick Bragg's account of his life as a poor southern white boy who managed to overcome almost every variety of difficulty that poverty can bring is, at the heart, a story of one woman's willingness to sacrifice her own life for that of her children.

Today Bragg is a national correspondent for *The New York Times* based in Atlanta, Georgia, and the holder of a Pulitzer Prize in journalism. His stark stories covering the urban disabused seem to have grown out of a sensitivity instilled by his own harsh childhood in rural Alabama.

Bragg's family was repeatedly abandoned by his father, a man tortured by alcoholism and haunted by his war experience. Bragg's mother picked cotton and cleaned houses so that her children wouldn't go hungry, but the years of drudgery and self-denial took a tremendous physical toll on her. When Bragg was awarded the Pulitzer Prize, his mother's initial reaction, after extreme pride in her son, was that she couldn't come to New York for the ceremony because she wasn't fit to be seen in distinguished company.

As you read Bragg's book, you will probably find yourself repeatedly returning to the photo of the woman on the cover: his mother, as a strong, gorgeous young woman untainted by the years that lay ahead.

Although Bragg expresses anger and sadness regarding his family life, the book is uplifting because there's also humor and substantial admiration for various members of his family. In describing his career and what it was like to be a back-country boy making his way among journalism's Ivy League elite, Bragg also provides plenty of interesting anecdotes about his reporter's life.

Bragg writes, "Of all the lessons my mother tried to teach me, the most important was that every life deserves a certain amount of dignity, no matter how poor or damaged the shell that carries it." Has he honored this credo in his writing?

Some say that the reason memoir has become more popular than the novel in recent times is that authors have had the audacity to bare all in telling their personal stories, making memoir more truthful than the novel. Is that what makes Bragg's book so moving?

Hotel du Lac, by Anita Brookner, Vintage Books (paperback)

British author Anita Brookner writes quiet novels that seethe with emotion and pose difficult questions. Is it realistic to expect romantic love? What are the gaps between art and reality? What can women be in the world?

As in *Hotel du Lac,* which won the Booker Prize in 1984, Brookner's main characters tend to be sensitive, solitary women who achieve some sort of insight. Doesn't sound like a lot of action, you say? You're right. But when the novel is done, a lot will have happened.

In *Hotel du Lac,* thirty-nine-year-old Edith Hope is a romance novelist who jilts her fiancé on their wedding day. Family and friends fear that she is headed for a nervous breakdown and send her off to Switzerland for a stay in a lakeside resort. She spends her days observing the other guests, writing letters to her married lover, and working on her latest novel. Although in conversation with her friends she pokes fun at romantic love, in her dreams and in her books she longs for it.

The author of more than fifteen novels, Brookner has a remarkable ability to turn out lucid, accomplished work in virtually one draft. An international authority on eighteenth- and nineteenth-century French artists, she taught for a number of years at Cambridge and at the Courtauld Institute of Arts in London, producing her fiction during summers off from teaching. Eventually she left academia to devote herself entirely to novel writing. Among her critically acclaimed books are *Altered States, Brief Lives, Falling Slowly, Family and Friends,* and *Incidents in the Rue Laugier.*

Brookner has been praised repeatedly for her wit, intelligence, and honesty as a writer, but her response is that she is merely writing love stories. Do you think that's true? Does her novel reveal much about human behavior, motives, and the little oddities of character that people in real life won't discuss but a good novelist can explain?

What do you think Brookner is trying to say about true love? Can two people ever create a truly gratifying, peaceful existence together? Do you think she's saying that the key to happiness is renouncing the idea of love?

The Kin of Ata Are Waiting for You, by Dorothy Bryant, Random House (paperback)

If you've never read any of Dorothy Bryant's books, this is a great one with which to start. The Berkeley author has turned out an array of novels that are not only uniformly absorbing and well written but also startlingly different from one another in their choice of settings and characters: *Ella Price's Journal, Miss Giardino,* and *The Garden of Eros* are other favorites.

The Kin of Ata is the only Bryant book written in the fantasy genre. It is the tale of a dissolute man who seems to have killed not only his girlfriend but himself. He comes to, however, in an unfamiliar world where all signs of violence and ugliness are absent. How he will get along in this strange, appealing land and what sort of effect it will have on his personal character are the questions that pull us through the story.

Originally published in 1976, *The Kin of Ata* is just as fresh and provocative today as it was more than twenty years ago. Once you've read the book and lived in Bryant's fantasy world, you want to hang on in that realm, revisiting it in your mind for a long time following. Bryant has something of a following, with one fan in northern California sporting a license plate that reads "Ata Kin."

The wide divergence in styles among her books led to difficulties for Bryant in dealing with New York publishers, who asked for more fantasies like *Kin of Ata* or more contemporary fiction in the mold of *Ella Price's Journal.* Bryant's dissatisfaction with the conglomerate machinery of publishing and her desire to see her books remain in print once they were published led her to form her own company, Ata Books in Berkeley. Her publications are available through local bookstores.

Bryant's novel has been described as "a beautiful, symbolic journey of the soul." In selecting a main character who is morally repugnant, has Bryant made it more difficult or easier for us to take to heart her spiritual journey?

Two worlds are linked here: the everyday world we consider real and a dreamlike world that Bryant leads us to believe is the true reality. How does she manage to make this jump between worlds without seeming too fantastical?

Flight of Passage, by Rinker Buck, Hyperion (paperback)

When Rinker and Kernahan Buck, ages fifteen and seventeen, flew coast to coast in 1966 in a Piper Cub airplane without a radio, it didn't occur to them that they might be breaking records or that their feat might attract the attention of the entire nation. Or that thirty years later, their story might make great reading.

They made their flight because the idea was irresistible. At least to Kern, it was. Raised at the knee of a barnstorming pilot who loved to relate stories of his conquests, mild-mannered Kern caught his father's flying fever. He asked his younger brother Rinker to come along because he needed a navigator. Neither boy suspected how thoroughly their adventure would alter their own relationship or their dealings with their strong-willed father.

Read this book for three reasons: high adventure, a fascinating biography of daredevil pilot Tom Buck, and the satisfying transformation of brothers from adversaries to friends. Once the boys leave New Jersey in their tiny plane, you'll find it hard to stop turning pages. When they make it to the Rockies, you'll wonder how Rinker survived to write the book.

In between telling how he and his brother bought the Piper for $300, restored it during the winter, then set off on their six-day quest, Rinker reveals the details of his father's colorful life. A magazine editor, political activist, and spokesman for Alcoholics Anonymous, the senior Buck was haunted by his days of glory as a pilot and by the crash that cost him a leg.

The expert, evocative writing in *Flight of Passage* reflects the career of the younger Buck, now an accomplished journalist. This is his first book.

Buck's memoir is a page-turner. What are the elements of his writing that make you want to gobble up this book?

Can you imagine two young boys taking a daring journey like this today? Would insurance and questions of liability get in the way? How about changes in the law?

Blue Jelly: Love Lost and the Lessons of Canning, by Debby Bull, Hyperion (paperback)

This has got to be the oddest, funniest bit of memoir to come down the pike during these past few years of memoir mania. Former *Rolling Stone* writer Debby Bull, after breaking up with her boyfriend, is shaken out of her state of self-pity when she hears the song title "I'm So Miserable Without You It's Almost Like I've Got You Back." She will cure her broken heart, she decides, by making jam.

In between recipes for crab apple jelly and blueberry butter, Bull takes you meandering around the countryside, visiting out-of-the-way places like the World Museum of the Potato and meeting characters like the lady who invented the Loving Relationships Workshop. Every once in a while you are treated to a quote from a celebrity she once covered for *Rolling Stone* or *Interview* magazines, such as Freddy Fender or Roy Rogers. After sampling some New Age philosophies and pondering words from the stars, she is hit by a number of bits of wisdom that she gladly shares with us.

No, this is not full-scale memoir; it's so brief it's barely a book. Bull gives only a small piece of her life story, but this little morsel is tasty. Although the recipes look good, don't worry if you're not interested. Read this book simply because the writing is uproarious and the glimpse of Bull intriguing. Whether you're into jam making or not, her book is a good way to chase the blues away.

BLUE JELLY *is wry and offbeat, although honest emotion comes through in the very adept writing. Given the unusual nature of Bull's book, was the ending too predictable?*

Bull notes that Sylvia Plath stuck her head in the oven as a way of dealing with disappointment, "but warming canning jars is a much healthier use of gas." Do any other authors come to mind in connection with this book? How would you compare Nora Ephron's attitude in HEARTBURN *with Bull's perspective here?*

Kindred, by Octavia Butler, Beacon Press (paperback)

Although you'll find this book on the science fiction shelf, it has little to do with science and everything to do with American history. In fact, it's a great follow-up to Charles Frazier's *Cold Mountain,* Sherley Anne Williams's *Dessa Rose,* or Edward Ball's *Slaves in the Family,* if you're hungry for stories about the antebellum South. In Butler's fantasy tale, a young African American woman named Dana is yanked from the relative comfort of modern-day southern California into the harsh reality of slave culture in 1819 Maryland.

It's not important exactly how this time travel is achieved; Butler makes the wise choice of not trying to explain it. Dana is as puzzled by the leap as we are; what becomes immediately crucial is how she will cope with life on a southern plantation, where the body and soul of a black person are threatened at every turn.

It's best just to dive into the book and ignore the introduction at the outset. While Robert Crossley's preface is well-meaning and does establish Butler's historical authenticity, it is unnecessary. The suspense of Dana's situation and the generous detail with which the author describes plantation life are enough to convince you that the story is well worth reading.

Perhaps the only shortcoming in *Kindred* is the occasionally wooden dialogue. However, the easy flow of Dana's thoughts and the careful weaving of the story more than compensate for an occasionally stilted exchange.

Butler is the author of numerous science fiction novels, that, unlike *Kindred,* are set in the future. She was the winner of that genre's Nebula Award and twice the winner of the Hugo Award.

By taking a modern woman and placing her in slavery times, does Butler give us a special ability to empathize with the plight of the slave? If you've read DESSA ROSE, *do you find that the point of view of a visitor has more impact than that of a slave?*

Does Butler adequately answer the question "How could anyone allow themselves to be made a slave?"

A Good Scent from a Strange Mountain, by Robert Olen Butler, Penguin Books (paperback)

Winner of the Pulitzer Prize in 1993, *Good Scent from a Strange Mountain* depicts with great sensitivity the varied, colorful lives of Vietnamese immigrants residing in Louisiana.

There are a number of remarkable things about these short stories. They are told in many different voices—those of a suburban wife with a taste for game shows, a middle-aged husband touched by his wife's sorrow, a young mother speaking to her unborn child, a lonely businessman who owns one of John Lennon's shoes—and each one feels entirely authentic. The dialogue and narration have the distinctive rhythm of Vietnamese speaking English. The writing is startling in its effectiveness and its delicacy. In Butler's hands, the characters come unforgettably alive.

Butler first came to know the Vietnamese while serving with army intelligence in Vietnam in 1971 and working as interpreter for the U.S. adviser to the mayor of Saigon. His free hours were spent on the streets of Saigon, talking to and falling in love with the city's inhabitants. After returning to the United States and writing six novels, Butler was offered a teaching job at McNeese University in Louisiana. It was then, flying over bayou country and recognizing its resemblance to the Mekong Delta, that *Good Scent* was born.

Three of Butler's earlier books were set in Vietnam: *The Alleys of Eden, On Distant Ground,* and *The Deuce.* Don't be caught unawares, however, by the more recently published *They Whisper,* which is a novel devoted purely to sexuality. He is also the author of the critically acclaimed short story collection, *Tabloid Dreams,* and the novel, *The Deep Green Sea.*

Butler creates enormous empathy for his characters, so that you are caught unawares by the depth of sympathy you feel and are even embarrassed that you hadn't previously imagined the complexity and passion of these lives. How does he achieve this kind of empathy?

The Djinn in the Nightingale's Eye: Five Fairy Stories, by A. S. Byatt, Vintage International (paperback)

A. S. Byatt is best known among book clubs for her Booker Prize–winning novel, *Possession.* Here is another favorite, a more recent book that is somewhat unorthodox in its approach. It appears Byatt decided to have a different kind of literary pleasure by setting herself the challenge of writing stories in the Victorian fairy-tale mold but with an eye to twentieth-century concerns and even twentieth-century settings.

She presents five stories of varying length, with the title tale the longest, almost a novella. In each of these, Byatt spins out words and ideas with such apparent ease and grace that repeatedly her literary mastery will take your breath away. Whether it is sexual obsession, personal revelation, or sly political commentary she's offering, she entertains us even as she gets us to think. Dragons, humble people on a quest, and three-wish scenarios are seen from a fresh, unexpected point of view, but with the vibrant, lush language of a traditional British storyteller.

The title tale is a special treat, because it's easy to imagine Byatt, a rather chunky, older woman, as the heroine of this erotic story. The matronly Dr. Gillian Perholt travels the world as a "narratologist," both telling and analyzing stories at international conferences. Women's lives in fiction, she points out, "are the stories of stopped energies . . . and all come to that moment of strangling, willed oblivion." Dr. Perholt's own energies are unstopped when she meets up with a genie. The results are enticing.

Byatt's recent books include *Elementals: Stories of Fire and Ice, Babel Tower, Angels and Insects,* and *The Matisse Stories.*

At least two major themes can be seen in "Dragons' Breath," one involving boredom and the other a human tendency to avoid facing crisis until it has trampled us. Can you find particularly affecting passages that describe a shift away from boredom and toward emotional intensity? Can you think of recent historical parallels to the story of the villagers?

What do you think is Byatt's message in her title story?

Andorra, by Peter Cameron, Plume (paperback)

You'll find it easy to settle into the sunny, dreamy mountain paradise of Andorra along with Alexander Fox, as he escapes personal tragedy in Peter Cameron's haunting novel. However, almost from the outset, there is tension as well as glorious vacation weather. As Alexander meets a collection of friendly locals in this town in the Pyrenees, between France and Spain, his new home on the one hand seems too pleasant to be true and on the other, a little too mysterious to seem safe.

Should Cameron's novel be classified a mystery? Possibly, but it is also a literary piece of work, with the author distinguishing himself by his skillful use of wit and characterization rather than through scenes of action or overt danger. In fact, *Andorra* could also be called a comedy of manners, as well as a meditation on truth and on the possibility of leaving tragedy behind. As Alexander falls into an awkward love affair and is tempted by another, there are so many tantalizing and complex undercurrents, you'll enjoy wondering, "What is *really* going on here?"

Dead bodies do turn up in Andorra, and, given the mysterious nature of the place and its residents, we are tantalized throughout by questions of who are the good guys and who are not.

Cameron is also the author of the novels *Leap Year* and *The Weekend* as well as the short story collection *The Half You Don't Know.*

Part of the mystery in Cameron's novel arises from the way Alexander Fox keeps secrets from the reader as well as from the other inhabitants of the town of La Plata. Did you find this frustrating, or were you willing to go along with Cameron as he waited to unveil Fox's story?

ANDORRA *could be described as minimalist fiction, in that Cameron is so sparing in providing descriptive detail. Did this bother you? Was the description he did provide adequate in evoking character, action, and place?*

There are clues from the outset of the novel that Andorra is not a real place. What are these clues, and what do you think this country is supposed to symbolize?

Emperor of the Air, by Ethan Canin, HarperPerennial (paperback)

Although a star of the literary world, Ethan Canin seems to be relatively unknown to the public at large—which is a shame, because his writing is clear and direct and packs a wallop. Whether examining the life of a failed baseball player whose wife drags him on real estate searches or that of a teenage boy who hides in the trunk of his father's car while his dad is on a date, Canin grabs us with unexpected bits of human drama and makes us care.

This collection of stories, which was Canin's first book, is notable in its ability to bring to life characters of different sexes and different ages. It is also an example of exquisite narrative and dialogue that rings true. Ironically, although Canin is most admired by the literary world, his writing is very much down to earth and accessible, aimed directly at the heart as well as the intellect.

In tales such as "We Are Nighttime Travelers," in which a retired couple rediscover their love for each other, and "Star Food," in which a young boy studying the heavens realizes he can't expose a thief stealing from his parents' grocery store, Canin finds loveliness and surprise in the everyday lives of people.

Particularly remarkable is the fact that Canin wrote these tales while a medical student in Boston. It would be unusual for any writer to create stories this good, but to have done it while facing the rigors of medical school makes Canin seem all the more gifted.

During his medical residency in California, Canin wrote a collection of stories published as *The Palace Thief.* More recently he was the author of the novels *Blue River* and *For Kings and Planets.*

Canin's stories can be reread over time with repeated delight. Some have called them classics. What are the aspects of his writing that make Canin's fiction seem timeless?

EMPEROR OF THE AIR *has been praised for its originality. How does Canin manage to write about regular people leading ordinary lives and still seem fresh in his approach?*

Jack Maggs, by Peter Carey, Vintage International (paperback)

A number one best-seller in England and Australia, *Jack Maggs* has all the ingredients for mass appeal: a strong, mysterious character driven by obsession, a vivid historical backdrop, romance, humor, and hints of sordid deeds. Carey's novel also boasts elements of good literature: dazzling characterization, strong narrative, and believable dialogue that moves the action along.

Jack Maggs is a tribute to Charles Dickens's *Great Expectations,* with Maggs the mystery man returning to London rather than Australian convict Abel Magwitch. We immediately want to know what his mission is. Why is this obviously wealthy man willing to take a position as a servant in a London household? Will he reveal his secrets—and thereby endanger his life—while under hypnosis by an enterprising English author?

Although set in Dickens's day and based on a Dickens novel, Carey's style is much different than that of the classic author. The latter was paid by the word, and he took his time to describe people and places. Carey is very much to the point; he avoids the stuffy, formal Victorian language seen in Dickens's work. Still, his tale exudes the flavor of England in the 1800s via brief, telling descriptions of the minutia of everyday life, such as the standards for selecting a footman or the ingredients for brass polish.

Carey's novel *Oscar and Lucinda* won Britain's prestigious Booker Prize. The author of numerous novels and a collection of stories, the Australian-born writer now resides in New York.

JACK MAGGS *is as much a criticism of Dickens's era as it is a tribute to Dickens. What are some of the disturbing social conditions and behavior that Carey spotlights?*

The figure of Tobias Oates provides an opportunity for Carey to poke fun at the conduct of writers both modern and Victorian. Did Oates seem more a caricature than a flesh-and-blood person?

Sleeping in Flame, by Jonathan Carroll, Vintage Books (paperback)

If you like offbeat fiction, *Sleeping in Flame* is likely to win your heart. Jonathan Carroll's novel is a surprising tossed salad of humor, romance, and otherworldly events carried out by people who at first seem unusual only in the sense that they are glamorous. The ending to this story is so out of the ordinary that it would be a betrayal to give any sort of hint of it.

The only real problem with *Sleeping in Flame* is that you might be jolted uncomfortably if you don't understand the tale is going to turn weird.

Carroll begins his story calmly enough with a former American actor turned screenwriter who lives in Vienna, relishes its café society, and enjoys a close, working relationship with a director friend. However, when Walker Easterling meets Maris York, a beautiful model trying to escape an angry lover, his life begins to turn topsy-turvy.

Carroll's writing is playful; he is not afraid to imagine wildly or to assume that you will follow him down a bizarre and sometimes frightening path. What makes you willing to follow is the utter accessibility of his main character, the sweetness of the love between him and Maris York, and the fact that Carroll can joke around while offering stark drama. Author Pat Conroy has said, "Jonathan Carroll is a cult waiting to be born." It's easy to imagine that this might be true.

Carroll is also the author of *Kissing the Beehive, The Land of Laughs,* and *Voice of Our Shadow,* to name a few of his novels. Unfortunately, his older books are out of print. *Kissing the Beehive* and *Sleeping in Flame* are still available in bookstores.

Carroll pulls us in with an easy, conversational style and almost lulls us with good feelings about his main characters. Then the rug is pulled out from under us, and a story of a much different flavor takes over. How did you feel about having this done to you?

Carroll enjoys a broad audience in Europe. Do you think he is offering something different from most American contemporary fiction? What are the elements of his style that distinguish it from other modern novels you've read?

My Antonia, by Willa Cather, Houghton Mifflin (paperback)

How many people, when asked to identify America's finest writers, would name Willa Cather? Somehow she has been overlooked in the lists that include F. Scott Fitzgerald, Ernest Hemingway, and Mark Twain, and yet she ranks among them for the simple excellence of her prose and the way she has captured life in the American heartland.

My Antonia is a coming-of-age tale and love story set on the prairie, a common locale for Cather's work. Born in Virginia in 1873, Cather moved with her family to Red Cloud, Nebraska, when she was ten. Her formative years spent living on the prairie among immigrant farmers gave rise to the robust, indelible characters who would later populate her books.

Antonia Shimerda is one of those immigrants, a young Bohemian girl with only a few words of English who arrives with her family in Black Hawk, Nebraska, at the same time as Jim Burden, the narrator, a recently orphaned boy of ten. The novel chronicles the bitter challenges Antonia's poverty-stricken family must face in their new land, and the growing admiration and affection Jim feels for the strong-willed, lovely Antonia.

The author of twelve novels, four collections of short stories, two volumes of essays, and one collection of poems, Cather won the Pulitzer Prize in 1923 for her book *One of Ours*. Other favorites among her work are *O Pioneers!* and *Death Comes for the Archbishop*. *My Antonia* was her personal favorite.

The great American prairie, Cather reminds us, was settled by immigrants from many different countries. In her hands, the newcomer Antonia becomes one of the great American heroines. What are the qualities that Cather extols via this character?

If Antonia is a hero, how does Jim compare? Is his character as completely formed? Does their relationship stand at the fore in this book, or do the portraits of individual characters?

Wild Swans, by Jung Chang, Anchor Books (paperback)

From the very first sentence, this true account of one family's life in modern China rivets you with drama, and over the course of 508 pages it rarely lets up. "At the age of fifteen my grandmother became the concubine of a warlord general . . ." writes Jung Chang, now a resident of London, and then she proceeds to lead you through the often traumatic events that befell her grandmother, parents, and brothers and sisters as the Communist revolution pummeled them and millions of other Chinese citizens.

If you've ever romanticized Chairman Mao, read this book. If you think you know the extent of his violent revolution, read this book anyway. The historical details of the Communists' rise to power, when added to the intimate details of Chang's family struggle, add up to an ultimate education about modern China.

Although the Communists came to power by destroying the corrupt and terrifying Kuomintang, at first bringing relief from hunger and brutality, very shortly Mao created a holocaust that claimed some forty million Chinese lives via famine, military torture, and civil chaos of unbelievable proportions.

Yes, this is a long book and not always easy to read because of its heavy emotional toll. You're likely to stay with it, however, for several reasons. There's the sheer fascination of China revealed from the point of view of an insider. There are many heroes along the way, whose continuing bravery in the face of terrible danger will make you want to hear their stories to the very end. And, of course, you'll want to know how the young woman who was granddaughter to a concubine, daughter of a Communist official, and herself a member of the Red Guard, found her way to the Western world.

We tend to talk about "The Holocaust" as if there has been only one in modern history. Is there anything we can learn from this book that will help us in the future to recognize and stop massive crimes against humanity?

Chang's history begins with feudal society in twentieth-century China. Given the degree of social and technological change that China has experienced in the past one hundred years, can you imagine leaps like this having taken place without violence?

Hunger, by Lan Samantha Chang, W. W. Norton & Company (hardcover)

Lan Samantha Chang has the gift of concise, elegant prose that hits with great force. Her short fiction re-creates the high impact that can result from relations between people. In each of her stories, her characters are desperately hungry for love, recognition, fame, or the old country. We watch them heroically or inanely struggle toward these aims, but no matter how bittersweet the battle, Chang conveys a feeling of strength and endurance. Surprisingly, much of the force of her stories builds in silent actions and unspoken thoughts.

The novella-length title story of *Hunger* concerns two immigrants from China who meet and fall in love in New York. When the husband's promising career as a violinist takes an unexpected turn, his family's future shifts dramatically. With great finesse Chang plays out the complex emotions of daughters, wife, and husband as dreams of talent and success ensnare them.

In all six stories, Chang examines questions of love and destiny with the talent of a gifted artist. A graduate of Yale and the University of Iowa, she held the Wallace Stegner and Truman Capote Fellowships at Stanford University. *Hunger* is her first book.

Chang has an ability to show how small rifts can open between people and deepen to broad chasms. Can you think of crucial moments in these stories when relationships were irrevocably altered?

Although the father in "Hunger" becomes impossibly demanding and grim, Chang doesn't allow him to become a one-dimensional villain. How does she avoid that pitfall?

The narrative in HUNGER *is spare, with each word carefully chosen. The dialogue, as well, is thoughtfully orchestrated, revealing only what is needed and conveying the flavor of the old world. The wife in "Hunger" says, "Some Chinese make their fortunes in America . . . Tian and I were not among them. Perhaps we lacked the forgetfulness that is essential to moving on." Can you find other examples of narrative or dialogue that seem to echo the rhythms of the characters' mother tongue?*

American Heaven, by Maxine Chernoff, Coffee House Press (hardcover)

Here's another author you'll wonder why you missed until now. *American Heaven* is a tour de force in which the characters speak through voices so powerful and true that you'll have difficulty believing this is fiction. The high stakes in their lives and the unexpected ties among Chernoff's people will also seize your attention.

A professor of creative writing at San Francisco State University, Chernoff is also the author of *Plain Grief,* the award-winning *Bop,* and *Signs of Devotion.*

In *American Heaven,* Chernoff has created four diverse people and thrown them together in the same Chicago apartment building: Irena, a recent Polish immigrant, formerly a mathematician, who has become a caretaker for an aging jazz musician; Harrison Waters, the African American jazz musician whose days of glory are past; Jack Kaufman, an ailing Jewish gangster; and Elizabeth, Jack's young caregiver.

The suspense arises from the disparate characters' interactions with one another, the menace of Jack's criminal livelihood, the secrets lurking in Elizabeth's past, and the precariousness of Irena's struggle to build a new life.

At first you'll think it's Irena you want to know in this story, for her quiet voice carries tremendous force as she registers the differences between people, thought, and day-to-day existence in America and Poland. Soon, however, other voices take on significance, in strikingly different styles of expression. Which voice in this book was the most important to you?

Chernoff seems to be studying the way we tend to jump to conclusions about people based on career, nationality, manners, and other factors apart from personality. Each of her characters is revealed in stages, so that our first impressions seem incomplete or false. In this story of exile, love, and friendship, what major theme do you think she's trying to express?

Goodbye Without Leaving, by Laurie Colwin, HarperPerennial (paperback)

When she died in 1992, Laurie Colwin left behind melancholy fans who loved her wacky humor and her telling observations of modern life. In books like *A Big Storm Knocked It Over* and *Happy All the Time,* she proved herself unusual: She was a writer who could grip readers with milder issues like love, happiness, and self-fulfillment rather than violence and graphic sex.

Goodbye Without Leaving is the best of the lot. Colwin tells the story of Geraldine Coleshares, who gives up graduate studies in English at the University of Chicago to become the only white backup singer for a rhythm and blues act. Her rock and roll days with Vernon and Ruby Shakely and the Shakettes make everything that comes after—marriage, a more regular job, parenthood—seem dull by comparison. And herein lies the problem: how to lead a normal life and at the same time experience thrills and pleasures.

Geraldine's voice is a wonderful blend of dreamy fun and witty self-contempt. How could there be any comparison, she asks us, between struggling over a doctoral thesis entitled "Jane Austen and the War of the Sexes" and spending your days on a bus with shock absorbers so fabulous that you could easily gloss your nails with Poison Grape or sparkling Merry Berry? "On stage," she says, "I felt a way I had never felt before. I was an eagle, an angel. My body was made of some pure liquid substance and would do whatever I asked it to. . . . The big questions fell away. There were no questions—only answers. The kind of ecstasy people found in religion, I found in being a Shakette."

Geraldine is searching for happiness away from the mainstream of white, middle-class America. As she resists her family's efforts to pull her back to the conventional, do you think she makes the right choices? Does she win true happiness in the end?

Colwin's humor puts her in the company of writers like Susan Isaacs and Nora Ephron. While seasoned with wit and amusement, their works pose serious questions as well. Do you think the humor diminishes the impact of their themes?

Body & Soul, by Frank Conroy, Delta (paperback)

Body & Soul is a good, old-fashioned story: There's a hero we can root for; he overcomes extreme adversity to achieve a dream; there are hard knocks along the way; and while we are worrying over the main character we become residents of a different time and place.

Nowadays too many authors have cheapened this big, heroic story form by using a formula: Give easy, quick characterizations, then add shopping, sex, and/or violence, and mix with rags-to-riches. Conroy has not done this.

Director of the Writers' Workshop at the University of Iowa, Conroy has crafted his novel with acute, straightforward language. Carefully he introduces us to six-year-old Claude, trapped in an apartment by day while his mother drives cabs on the streets of New York. As the boy learns to play an old piano tucked away in his basement apartment and shows a startling musical talent, other people come into his life, and they, too, are developed as full, flesh-and-blood characters with interesting stories of their own.

You may not understand every detail of Conroy's information about music theory, but the fact that he has included it, detailing Claude's development as a prodigy, gives the story another strong dimension. So, too, does Conroy's description of the changing New York scene from the 1930s through the 1960s.

Conroy has also written an engaging memoir, *Stop-Time.*

Perhaps the only disappointing thing about BODY & SOUL *is that Conroy doesn't take as much time and care in developing characters in the latter third of his story. The ending seems rushed, and a few situations involve coincidences perhaps too big to swallow. Did this diminish your pleasure in the book, or did the author build enough momentum that you found the ending satisfying?*

It could be said that BODY & SOUL *is a story about the transforming power of music. However, successful novels are usually driven by a major conflict or dilemma that the main character must overcome. In the case of this story, what would you say is the major struggle?*

The Power of One, by Bryce Courtenay, Ballantine Books (paperback)

Don't avoid this novel just because it was made into a terrible movie. The book is spellbinding, an epic tale set in modern South Africa. When our group finished reading it, everyone wanted to know, "Who *is* this author?"

It turns out that the author is an Australian advertising man and newspaper columnist whose books are quite popular in that country. The next book of his to appear on our shores was the nonfiction *April Fool's Day: A Modern Love Story.*

The Power of One follows a young, frail victim as he aims for the improbable goal of welterweight champion of the world. You'll root for him all the way and be held to the edge of your seat wondering what strange magic or odd character will come his way next.

This is probably the only novel you'll ever read where the young hero sets off to school lugging his "chook," or pet chicken, with him. The protagonist, Peekay, is born in the years just before World War II, an English-speaking child among English-hating Afrikaners. He is nursed by a black woman—one more thing to identify him with the "wrong" people: the native Africans newly experiencing official apartheid. An abandoned child mistreated by his own, he is fortunate to gain the strong and loving guardianship of Doc, one of the more spectacular, noble, and unusual characters you're likely to encounter in your reading adventures.

THE POWER OF ONE *develops the influence of home and community as a major force in Peekay's life. In accomplishing this, Courtenay attacks apartheid. Does the book seem like a vehicle for expressing anti-apartheid sentiment or does it integrate this theme as a natural part of the story?*

A page-turner like THE POWER OF ONE *could be dismissed as mass-appeal fiction simply because it's so readable. What are the aspects of Courtenay's writing that qualify his work as good literature?*

Necessary Madness, by Jenn Crowell, Warner Books (paperback)

It's enough that this book is beautifully written, an understated story of love and loss surrounding an American woman in her thirties living in London with her young son. However, the fact that it was authored by a seventeen-year-old American who had never been married or a mother or been to England makes it absolutely remarkable.

Many writers spend decades trying to achieve Crowell's steady, elegant use of language, in which every word counts and nothing is extra. If a novelist can also create a fully believable protagonist who suffers weakness and yet is likable, that is a sure sign of literary talent. Crowell has done this and more. She has completely drawn a woman old enough to be her mother, then created a complex relationship between that woman and her aging mother. Furthermore, her London setting and references to British culture feel comfortable and authentic.

The story is simple. After eight years of marriage, Gloria Burgess loses her husband to leukemia. Living in an adopted country, struggling to be a decent parent, alienated from her own family back home, she must fight overwhelming grief. Although tempted to succumb to madness, she begins to find her way beyond it. Delving into the past, she recollects her parents' failed relationship, trying to learn something from their mistaken notions of love. Flashbacks to her love affair with her artist husband provide a positive, upbeat counterpoint to the story of her struggle in the present.

When *Necessary Madness* was published in 1997, Jenn Crowell was a sophomore at Goucher College in Maryland.

An intriguing friendship develops between Gloria and Jascha Kremsky, an artist friend of her dead husband. What do you think of the way Crowell handles this relationship and piques our curiosity with the various possibilities that might ensue?

Although critics gave Crowell rave reviews, there were a few grumbles about occasional lapses into melodrama. Do you think she ever went too far in her emotional descriptions of Gloria's and Bill's life together or his death from leukemia?

The Diary of Mattie Spenser, by Sandra Dallas, Griffin Trade Paperback (paperback)

A diary hidden in an old suitcase brings to life the dreams and travails of a young woman on the Colorado frontier in the years just following the Civil War, in Denver author Sandra Dallas's novel. Although *The Diary of Mattie Spenser* begins as a quiet, simple account of Mattie's unexpected marriage to a handsome local boy and their journey by covered wagon away from the boundaries of polite civilization, the tale quickly becomes not at all quiet and not at all simple. Frontier brutality, complicated relationships, the tensions of disparate people thrown together in a small community, and the pains of domestic life in a rough setting add up to an extremely compelling story.

At the heart of the novel are three stories: pioneers facing the rigors of western settlement, the drama between two people whose marriage faces severe tests, and the question of whether the ideals and attitudes of an innocent young woman can survive intact in a rough, isolated setting.

Dallas has done her homework in re-creating the historical setting. Her ability to reveal character in small gestures and poignant reflection adds to the authenticity. So does her rendition of Mattie's voice, which has a certain sweetness that soon becomes tempered by the traumas of frontier life. By the time you're done reading this fictional diary, the realism and emotions will make you believe it's true.

Dallas is also the author of *The Persian Pickle Club* and *Buster Midnight's Cafe.*

As the story progresses, Mattie's attitudes shift on matters of "loose women," Indians, and black people. What other indicators are there of her personal growth?

By the end of the novel, would you say that Mattie had become a strong, independent woman? Or, is it possible that she lost herself bit by bit, through the building of a sod house, the birth and death of children, and miserable behavior by her husband? Were the compromises she made signs of weakness or fortitude?

Shark Dialogues, by Kiana Davenport, Plume (paperback)

You may have assumed that James Michener wrote the definitive book on Hawaii, but Kiana Davenport has written a new story of the islands that is fresh, magical, and passionate. Taking a fiercely female perspective, she focuses her tale on Pono, a native "kahuna" or seer, and her four granddaughters of mixed ancestry, tracing their family lines from early island days to the present.

Davenport is not afraid to alternate between lucid historical fact and stream-of-consciousness writing, giving us the larger picture and then taking us inside her characters' heads as they deal with life-and-death conflict. She also has no qualms about setting Hawaiian mystical beliefs alongside modern mainland practicality.

If you don't want to read another story about white people conquering, spreading disease, and undermining someone else's culture, don't read this book. If you relish drama, romance, and a slightly different take on history, go for it: *Shark Dialogues* is one of those books you'll read hour after hour, immersed in adventure, lulled by humid breezes, floating offshore with Pono in the warm currents.

Born and raised in the islands, Kiana Davenport is of Hawaiian and Anglo-American descent. A former Fiction Fellow at Radcliffe's Bunting Institute, she is a resident of Boston and Hawaii. A more recent novel of hers is *Song of the Exile.*

Throughout SHARK DIALOGUES *there burns a rage at the continuing pollution and commercial devastation of the Hawaiian islands by outsiders. Does Davenport offer any clues as to a realistic solution at this point in island history?*

In the story of seven generations of one Hawaiian family, we witness the modern history of the island. Pono, the grandmother and powerful dream-teller, is at the center of this tale, and although she is a heroine she is also shown as fearful. Did you falter at times in your feelings about her? Was it confusing to find that her daughters could not relate to her? Did this make her a richer character or did it make it hard to accept her?

Davenport's novel becomes fairly erotic at times. Did you find she went too far in this regard? Did this and the sometimes feverish romantic flavor diminish the book in any way for you?

36 Views of Mount Fuji: On Finding Myself in Japan, by Cathy N. Davidson, Plume (paperback)

Here's an engrossing account of the difficulties of truly coming to know a foreign culture. Having lived and worked in Japan as college professors and having established strong friendships there off and on for ten years, both Davidson and her husband were tempted to make Japan their new home at the end of the 1980s. However, as she reveals in her portraits of the people and the place, the difficulty of their goal was overwhelming.

Given all the Japan-bashing that has gone on over the past decade or so, Davidson's approach to that country is refreshing. She is able to see the blemishes but also to appreciate the finer things that culture has to offer.

To feel completely comfortable in an adopted country, one must thoroughly understand the language and the customs. Davidson came to believe that, in spite of her best efforts, she could spend a lifetime in Japan and still guess at proper behavior or correct expression. Paradoxically, she has painted what seems like a comprehensive portrait of the country in a series of vignettes that are both entertaining and insightful.

Are Japanese women as submissive as we assume? In a few very surprising ways, no. Have the Japanese come to dominate us in commerce, or has the West cowed them into submission? Davidson gives us an unusual view of the Japanese, with both affection and criticism, sharing the reasons why she fell in love with this Asian country.

She is also the author of the book *Closing: The Life and Death of an American Factory.*

Every time Davidson thinks she has a take on Japanese culture, she uncovers a new layer of meaning or unexpected nuance to contradict her previous view. Do you think the same would be true for a Japanese person trying to become acquainted with American culture?

In building a Japanese-style home for themselves in the United States, did the Davidsons create an environment that is probably more Japanese than what they found in modern Japan?

Pilgrim at Tinker Creek, by Annie Dillard, HarperPerennial (paperback)

Winner of the Pulitzer Prize in 1975, this nonfiction account of Annie Dillard's experiences living at the edge of Tinker Creek in a valley of Virginia's Blue Ridge is a beautiful ode to nature and a meditation on our ability to perceive and appreciate the natural world. It's also pretty funny at times, and at other times can be awfully violent.

Plan to read this book in short bursts so that you can both enjoy the colorful anecdotes and digest Dillard's intense musings. Her stories about the outrageous sexual habits of the praying mantis and the disgusting demise of a small green frog will leave you both amused and shocked—and probably looking for more. The material that comes in between, however, which questions human beings' ability to stay truly within the moment, to achieve ultimate awareness of the surrounding world, requires some thought.

What is particularly charming about Dillard is that she can be both romantic and irreverent. She rhapsodizes at length on her dazzling vision of light sparkling through the leaves of a sycamore tree, or she tells us, "Fish gotta swim and birds gotta fly; insects, it seems, gotta do one horrible thing after another."

Dillard is also the author of *An American Childhood,* a memoir of her youth in Pittsburgh, another book club favorite.

Eudora Welty said that PILGRIM AT TINKER CREEK *"is a form of meditation, written with headlong urgency, about seeing." Did reading this book influence your own ability and willingness to see the world around you?*

This is more than nature writing. Dillard observes her surroundings, then offers her observations as a springboard to ideas about consciousness and metaphysics. What are some of the spiritual ideas that you took away from this book?

There is no major action or narrative thrust to carry you through this book. What kept you going?

Arranged Marriage, by Chitra Banerjee Divakaruni, Anchor Books (paperback)

Winner of the American Book Award and the 1995 Bay Area Book Reviewers Association Award for fiction, Chitra Divakaruni's superb collection of short stories illuminates her countrywomen's lives in India and America. Indian-born Divakaruni now teaches creative writing at the University of Houston; she offers an excellent perspective of life between and within two cultures.

Whether describing the plight of a woman trapped in an abusive marriage in India or the quick adjustments required of a new, immigrant bride in California, she effectively reveals the contents of private lives, spilling out dreams and disappointments in a way that makes them seem universal.

In the same way that writers like Amy Tan and Maxine Hong Kingston have captured the voices of other cultures, Divakaruni beautifully re-creates the sounds and rhythms of Indian people. Her descriptions can be rich with imagery: ". . . when the sun hung above the lake as red as the marriage bindi on Mother's forehead, Grandpa-uncle caught a great rui fish that sent up sprays of rainbow water as it leaped and thrashed at the end of his line." Or, her dialogue and narrative can be crazy and abrupt with the style of a new world: An American aunt says, "This weekend he is taking us to the mall. So many big big shops there, you'll like it. He says he will buy pizza for dinner. Do you know pizza? Is it coming to India yet?"

The author of four volumes of poetry, Divakaruni is also the author of two novels, *The Mistress of Spices* and *Sister of My Heart.*

In "Doors" Divakaruni portrays the contrasting attitudes toward privacy in Eastern and Western cultures. What do you see as the major difference? Is the author offering a criticism?

Do you think Divakaruni is saying that love does not exist in traditional Indian marriages?

The idea of change is dealt with repeatedly in these stories. For the girls and women who face transition, is change seen as a terror or as a source of great promise?

The Mourners' Bench, by Susan Dodd, Quill (paperback)

Riveting suspense can arise merely from the excitement generated when two very different characters are thrown into intimate contact. This chemistry happens in *The Mourners Bench,* a novel that will turn your head with the disparity between the two main characters' voices. In fact, it is likely to surprise you that one author can so effectively create two such different voices: one of a southern woman raised in modest circumstances, the other of a New England academic born to privilege.

As the story opens, William (Wim) has come to find Leandra at her isolated cabin in rural North Carolina, where she makes a modest living mending dolls. They haven't seen each other for years. Now William is dying.

Slowly Susan Dodd unfolds the events that first shoved together this unlikely twosome and then tore them apart, alternating between awkwardness in the present and trauma in the past. What holds you is the delicious proposition that the two might finally love each other with some happiness and comfort. Although this is a small story, it has the power of a Faulkner tale, to whom Dodd pays homage.

Dodd is also the author of *Mamaw, Hellbent Men and Their Cities, Old Wives' Tales,* and *No Earthly Notion.* Her latest book is *O Careless Love,* a collection of stories that explore the often inconvenient and unlikely aspects of love, including a memorable tale about an endodontist who repairs a patient's freshly broken heart while performing a root canal.

Dodd tells a romantic, earthy story without becoming effusive about passion or sex. Does her lack of graphic detail diminish the drama or add to the power of a tale told about two shy people?

There are fairly complex emotions at work here as Leandra and Wim approach and retreat from each other in a suspenseful kind of dance. Did the author make it clear why they had such difficulty making true contact with each other?

Did you understand how Leandra and Wim could each love Leandra's sister and at the same time dread her behavior?

A Yellow Raft in Blue Water, by Michael Dorris, Warner Books (paperback)

The late Michael Dorris and his wife, novelist Louise Erdrich, are known for their numerous critically acclaimed books featuring Native Americans as their heroines and heroes. In his moving debut novel, *A Yellow Raft in Blue Water,* Dorris told the story of an Indian mother, daughter, and granddaughter torn by disturbing secrets yet bound by family love, varying the perspective so that we see each woman's point of view.

Just as we think we've begun to grasp the essence of what has happened, Dorris pulls us back to take another look. The *Rashomon* effect is particularly potent if you choose to listen to this book on tape; in fact, you may find that the novel begins slowly and that the recorded version, narrated beautifully by Colleen Dewhurst, may pull you in more quickly, as the distinctive voice of Rayona, the teenager, punches out her account of a visit to her eccentric mom in the hospital.

The highly praised *Cloud Chamber* was Dorris's sequel to *Yellow Raft.* Rayona also shows up as an eleven-year-old in one of Dorris's children's books, *The Window.*

Dorris and Erdrich credited each other as collaborators in every one of their works, although they were most often listed as individual authors. However, they shared the writing credit equally for *The Crown of Columbus,* a suspense novel about a Native American anthropologist who discovers Christopher Columbus's lost diary and then follows a trail for buried treasure to the Bahamas.

Dorris was a member of the Modoc tribe but also was of French and Irish descent; many of his and Erdrich's characters reflect the multiple ancestry that is true of so many Americans. In addition to being a storyteller, he was also an anthropologist, historian, and social critic. His book about fetal alcohol syndrome and his adopted son, *The Broken Cord,* won the National Book Critics Circle Award in 1990.

Dorris's death was an apparent suicide spurred by accusations that he had been an abusive parent and a child molester. How do these accusations affect your reaction to his work? In judging an artist's work, is it appropriate to consider the details of his or her private life, or should the writing stand on its own?

"I never grew up, but I got old. I'm a woman who's lived for fifty-seven years and worn resentment like a medicine charm for forty." Dorris was not afraid to show his characters' frailties. How did this affect your ability to care about them?

The Solace of Open Spaces, by Gretel Ehrlich, Penguin Books (paperback)

Gretel Ehrlich was a documentary filmmaker when she came to Wyoming in 1976, but the people and the place so thoroughly captivated her that she left behind her movie career to herd, calve, and brand sheep—and to write about the American West. Her filmmaker's sensitivity shows up in an exacting eye for revealing objects, words, or gestures that capture the essence of a place and its people.

In *The Solace of Open Spaces,* Ehrlich introduces us to an array of endearing frontier characters she met as a ranch hand learning to work with sheep. Her observations are funny and telling as she erases our stereotypes of cowboys and ranch hands, replacing them with quirky, unique cameos of both women and men. At the same time, she submerges us in the dramatic weather patterns of Wyoming, where, "When it's fifty below, the mercury bottoms out and jiggles there as if laughing at those of us still above ground." It also gets pretty windy, as you'll see.

When she first arrived in Wyoming, Ehrlich was grieving over the death of a close man friend. As she tackles the tough ranch work and falls in love with the landscape, you feel that she is slowly healing, though she avoids directly addressing this question. However, the book will provide a kind of solace for you as well, if you let it.

"The truest art I would strive for in any work," she says, "would be to give the page the same qualities as earth: weather would land on it harshly, light would elucidate the most difficult truths; wind would sweep away obtuse padding." Repeatedly, Ehrlich has accomplished this feat.

Ehrlich is also the author of *A Match to the Heart,* an account of her near-lethal experience when she was struck by lightning, and *Questions of Heaven: The Chinese Journeys of an American Buddhist.*

As a social observer, historian, and naturalist, Ehrlich has made a valuable contribution to our record of the American West. As you look back on this book, what in particular do you remember as new and surprising information about the people and landscape of Wyoming?

Heartburn, by Nora Ephron, Vintage Books (paperback)

A court case resulted from the publication of this book, which tells you just how funny and cutting it is. Ephron's novel is based on the breakup of her marriage to Carl Bernstein, of Watergate reporting fame. Ex-husband Bernstein got the judge to say that Ephron could never write material based on him or their children again.

If you saw the movie of *Heartburn,* forget it. There was no resemblance to the novel, even though Ephron wrote the screenplay. All of the fun was left out of the movie version. This can happen when a story that depends upon a witty narrator is translated to the screen but the narration doesn't survive.

Heartburn is the tale of a woman seven months pregnant who learns that her marriage is over; her husband has fallen in love with another woman. "The most unfair thing about this whole business," she says, "is that I can't even date." The heroine, Rachel Samstat, is a cookbook writer, and so there are plenty of recipes interspersed with the melancholy, anger, and amusing commentary. For many readers, the scenario described by Rachel, in which a husband asks, "Where's the butter?" became a classic means of explaining the devious behavior of the modern adult male.

Heartburn was first published in 1983 and seemed to mark a turning point in Ephron's writing career. Formerly an essayist/humorist, she subsequently gained entry into the film world as a writer, director, and producer. She wrote and directed *Sleepless in Seattle* and *This Is My Life* and wrote and produced *My Blue Heaven.* Her writing credits also include *Silkwood* and *When Harry Met Sally.*

An essential part of the humor in this book is Rachel's ability to poke fun at herself as well as at her husband, Mark, and his lover, Thelma. Why is this so important in a book like this? What were your favorite moments when Rachel looks ridiculous?

Rachel points out that marriage seems to be closely connected with the accumulation of material possessions. The way she puts it is funny, but it's also social commentary. What other bits of social commentary stand out for you in HEARTBURN?

***The Spirit Catches You and You Fall Down: A Hmong Child, Her American Doctors, and the Collision of Two Cultures,* by Anne Fadiman, The Noonday Press (paperback)**

Incredible is an overused word, but it does describe the perseverance of the Hmong people through centuries of travail in China, Laos, and now the United States. Anne Fadiman's gift for narrative and her sympathy for the heroic Hmong combine to create a deeply moving chronicle of the struggle that occurred when the culture of these steadfast people met the equally strong culture of the American medical community in a small teaching hospital in central California in the 1980s.

Lia Lee was a baby girl suffering from severe epileptic seizures when her parents brought her to the hospital in Merced. Although highly trained and compassionate, the doctors there were not prepared to communicate adequately with Lia's Hmong parents, whose worldview and understanding of illness were so different from theirs, they might have come from another planet, let alone another continent.

Although Fadiman studied the ensuing crisis with the same thoroughness that a good anthropologist might have, she presents her findings in a highly readable fashion. She alternates between Lia's suspenseful story and a fascinating history of the Hmong, including their contribution to our country's secret war in Laos as employees of the CIA and their sad fate as American welfare recipients. Fadiman also presents suggestions for avoiding the sort of cross-cultural medical disaster that befell Lia's family.

The Spirit Catches You and You Fall Down was the winner of the National Book Critics Circle Award for nonfiction in 1997. Fadiman is editor of *The American Scholar* and is also the author of *Ex Libris: Confessions of a Common Reader,* another book club favorite, a highly enjoyable collection of essays on her and her family's love affair with books.

Hmong refugees in French Guiana were given their own land to farm and quickly became self-sufficient, supplying more than 70 percent of that South American country's fresh vegetables. Do you accept the American government's claim that they couldn't do the same for Hmong refugees in our country?

No matter what the spiritual beliefs of the parents, American doctors put the welfare of a child first, providing the treatment they believe is best. Does this make it impossible to take into account cultural differences between doctor and patient?

***Daughter of Persia: A Woman's Journey from Her Father's Harem Through the Islamic Revolution*, by Sattareh Farman Farmaian with Dona Munker, Anchor Books (paperback)**

Two stories will mesmerize you in *Daughter of Persia.* The first is that of a young girl born into a harem who became an educated woman and founded the first school of social work in Iran. The second is the tale of twentieth-century Persia/Iran and how that country came to be ripe for takeover by Ayatollah Khomeini.

Farman Farmaian offers a special perspective in presenting this personal and national history: Her life has almost spanned the century, she attended school both in Iran and in the United States, and she has known world leaders as well as having worked with the poorest of the poor. Furthermore, she was fortunate to be born to a man who saw the value of education for both his daughters and his sons; the wise shazdeh saw that Iran's future would be tumultuous and that his progeny were more likely to survive if he made certain they were strong, intellectually flexible, and educated.

Both the author's autobiography and Iran's history contain many surprises if you've depended only on popular media for your knowledge of Iran. For example, the Shah who preceded Khomeini was not purely corrupt and tyrannical; he brought many of the benefits of modern life to a Third World country. Also, Farman Farmaian's mother was pleased to be one of many wives, as the other women provided her with badly needed companionship.

In 1979 Farman Farmaian escaped Iran and eventually made her way to Los Angeles, where she continues her career in social work.

In the news and in our personal conversations about world politics, we tend to talk about individual countries as if their entire citizenry were of one mind-set. Did this book help to dispel this notion and to make you more sensitive to the plight of people living in countries we consider our enemies?

What lessons did you take away from Farman Farmaian's description of the rule of the Shah and his replacement by Ayatollah Khomeini?

Birdsong, by Sebastian Faulks, Vintage Books (paperback)

In constructing a novel that might simply have been a war story and a romance, Faulks has gone much further: He has created complex characters and explored the deepest reaches of their minds.

Faulks leaps from a broken love affair between a young Frenchwoman and an Englishman living in France, to the trenches of World War I, to modern-day England, all the while threading story strands back and forth, binding together decades with themes of love, honor, and commitment.

Birdsong is an interesting combination of romanticism and grit. The descriptions of the lice living on the soldiers and in their clothing are as vivid as the passionate scenes between two lovers or the wistful longing of a tunnel-digger for his sweet, innocent son back home.

This is a dense novel, loaded with characters, thick with feelings and philosophy, set in a landscape that is lushly idyllic or rife with peril. If you know nothing about the use of tunnels to foil the enemy during World War I, you'll know plenty by the time you finish this book. Faulks has added significantly to the work of novelists Pat Barker and Sebastien Japrisot in building our awareness of the nightmare some called The Great War.

Faulks was voted Author of the Year for *Birdsong* in 1995 by the British Book Awards. The London resident is also the author of *A Fool's Alphabet* and *Charlotte Gray.*

Faulks switches gears several times in the course of his novel, taking us from a highly erotic love affair into the degradations of the trenches and then into modern-day England where a young woman tries to trace her ancestry and uncover the stories of the men we've just seen. Do you feel thrown about by these leaps, or did they seem like necessary relief from the intensity of the writing just past?

In today's fiction, authors less frequently use the omniscient narrator to tell their stories. Would you have preferred to witness these events from the point of view of one or more of the characters?

Learning to Bow: An American Teacher in a Japanese School (also titled _Learning to Bow: Inside the Heart of Japan_), by Bruce S. Feiler, Ticknor & Fields (paperback)

When he enters a ritual bath naked with his new teaching colleagues and discovers that he's the only one without a towel strategically placed, Bruce Feiler begins a sometimes hilarious and often provocative acquaintance with Japanese culture. Fresh out of Yale, Feiler has been hired to teach English to junior high students in Sano, Japan, but often he is the one doing the learning.

As Feiler comes to speak Japanese more fluently and develops friendships, the society that seemed entirely alien begins to make sense. His description of education, parenting, and home life gave the first glimpse of grass-roots Japanese culture provided by a westerner who had taught in Japanese schools.

Learning to Bow describes an educational system claimed by some to be the best in the world—one that is almost entirely different from our own. Although it would be difficult to adopt the complete Japanese system in our own culture so devoted to individual rights, it might be instructive to take notes. What happens when students and teachers regularly mop the classroom floor and wash the windows at the end of the school day? What happens when students are sent out into the neighborhood to clean up trash? Maybe pride of ownership and community concern.

Feiler is also the author of *Dreaming Out Loud: Garth Brooks, Wynona Judd, Wade Hayes, and the Changing Face of Nashville,* which offers an inside look at country music, and *Under the Big Top: A Season with the Circus.*

Feiler shows obvious delight in this opportunity to observe the Japanese people and their community up close. In addition to his enthusiasm, what were the elements of his approach that made it possible for him to gain entry to this society?

While Feiler found much to admire about the Japanese way of life, what were some of the more disturbing social difficulties he described? Did you see any similarity to our own culture in these areas?

The Book Shop, by Penelope Fitzgerald, Mariner Books (paperback)

If you insist on happy endings, this novel is not for you. However, keep in mind that you'll be missing out on the work of a talented author who knows how to draw character, inject dry humor, and paint scenes from ordinary life with the skill of a master. Reading Penelope Fitzgerald's compact little book is like eating a tasty olive; the pleasure comes from its sharp, quick flavor and the feeling that perhaps you'd like more.

One of England's most celebrated contemporary authors, Fitzgerald won the prestigious Booker Prize in 1979 for *Offshore*. Alfred Corn wrote in *The New York Times Book Review*, "The career of the English novelist Penelope Fitzgerald offers the best argument I know for a publishing debut made late in life. Her first novel appeared in 1977, when she was 60."

In *The Book Shop*, Fitzgerald tells the story of a widow living in a small town who decides she will do something meaningful with her life by opening a bookshop. Florence Green's simple plan evokes surprisingly negative responses from certain key people in town, and most of Fitzgerald's novel describes how her main character quietly faces the opposition to pursue her dream. In the course of achieving her goal, Florence bumps into an assortment of people, each intriguing.

Fitzgerald is also the author of *The Blue Flower*, which won the 1997 National Book Critics Circle Award, *Innocence*, *The Beginning of Spring*, *The Gate of Angels*, and *Human Voices*.

THE BOOK SHOP *could be called a tragicomedy of manners, targeting mainly the provincial English countryside of the 1950s. Do you think Fitzgerald's pointed attack on the small-mindedness of certain people is an interesting period piece or that its theme offers universal truths that extend to other times and settings?*

Was there a reason for the poltergeist, or was Fitzgerald simply having fun with ghosts?

Florence divides people into "exterminators and exterminatees." Do you think the author sees the world purely in this way?

River: One Man's Journey Down the Colorado, Source to Sea, by Colin Fletcher, Vintage Books (paperback)

Reading *River* is like taking a soothing, prolonged vacation. Colin Fletcher's book about his seventeen-hundred-mile rafting trip down the Colorado River is a meditation on the joys of escaping civilization, with a fair amount of adventure thrown in.

Well known to environmentalists and to avid backpackers, Fletcher has written a number of books about his experiences outdoors, including his walk from Mexico to Oregon in the 1950s *(The Thousand Mile Summer)* and his two-month hike through the Grand Canyon in the 1960s *(The Man Who Walked Through Time).*

In *River* he details his six-month journey in 1989 from the source of the Colorado in Wyoming to its conclusion at the Gulf of California. This was not a particularly easy feat for a sixty-seven-year-old who had recently undergone heart surgery and was having trouble recovering from the flu. In fact, the idea of Fletcher traveling anywhere seems downright crazy at first and lends suspense to his tale.

Encounters with a variety of wildlife, as well as with friendly and unfriendly Americans, and the passing panorama of eye-popping rock formations pepper his descriptions of the river. Given his lack of experience in white-water rafting, Fletcher's travels over numerous challenging rapids also lend excitement.

If you enjoy *River* and are sorry when the journey is over, you'll definitely want to check out a book called *Raven's Exile* by author/naturalist Ellen Meloy. Meloy has written an absorbing chronicle of a season along the river in Desolation Canyon with her husband, Mark, a river ranger in Utah's red-rock canyon country.

Among Fletcher's observations come reactions to the sounds of the river and its surroundings: rushing water, machinery, birdcalls. Can you think of other nature writers who use this much auditory description to conjure up environment?

Fletcher makes his journey a symbolic one, as he speaks of testing himself in old age and ponders the passage of time, loves lost, and mortality. Do his musings seem dated, or do they stand the test of time since he first wrote these words in 1989?

The Sportswriter, by Richard Ford, Vintage Books (paperback)

This is not a book that you'd call a pleasure to read. The events won't grab you, sweep you up, and carry you forward in a great rush. Yet *The Sportswriter* is a powerful novel, one that brought Ford great acclaim in the literary world and is worth reading for one very significant reason: It reveals in an eloquent way the psyche of a modern American male.

For any woman who has ever complained that she doesn't understand how men think, here's extensive revelation.

Frank Bascombe, the sportswriter of the title, is a man in his late thirties whose young son has died, whose marriage has crumbled, and whose promising career as a novelist has fizzled to nothing. Why would you want to stay with him in this dreary situation? Because he has a rich inner life that makes him endearing.

And this is where the tension in the story lies. We know Frank is sensitive, we share his pleasure in small, dreamy moments, and yet we come to see clearly that he is unable and unwilling to express this side of himself to anyone near and dear. In fact, he fears the dreaminess that overcomes him at times. What's more, he resorts to dishonesty with others and with himself rather than reveal his tender inner core.

A surprisingly sympathetic character in the book is Vicki, the girlfriend who seems to be a total error on Frank's part. She plays along with his insincere chatter and grates on your nerves because of her lack of finesse, yet, in the end, she is the one with an important lesson to teach.

Ford's sequel to this book, *Independence Day,* was the winner of the Pulitzer Prize in 1996.

There's a lot in this book to ponder: Frank's choice of a girlfriend, the contrast between his inner life and outer life, his relationship with his roommate, his insistence that he was wise to give up fiction writing. What do you think of the lack of commentary or clear point of view on these issues by the author?

Sleeping in Velvet, by Thaisa Frank, Black Sparrow Press (paperback)

You could call this a collection of short stories, but it's more a series of moods and slices of life exquisitely captured. Frank's stories tend not to have a beginning, middle, and end but rather an unfolding, and at the end of each, you may sigh with contentment and recognition, or at least will feel that you've been someplace real.

On the other hand, *Sleeping in Velvet* also contains some offbeat little tales like "Captain Crunch" and "The Short and Unhappy Life of HAL the Computer"—odd, tongue-in-cheek, little fantasy pieces that are very cleverly written.

The idea of hiding, as expressed so beautifully in "The White Coat," could be said to inhabit most of these stories. In Frank's tale, the white coat is an ermine garment once used to camouflage refugees who were fleeing the Nazis in a snowy northern clime. Frank's protagonist asks for an opportunity to try on the magical coat and briefly disappears. This fantastical element inhabits a number of Frank's tales and seems tied to the slippery quality of her narrative, which wavers between prose and poetry.

An Oakland resident, Frank teaches at the University of San Francisco and also has a private practice as a psychotherapist. She is coauthor of *Finding Your Writer's Voice* and the author of two other books of fiction: *Desire* and *A Brief History of Camouflage. Sleeping in Velvet* was a nominee for the 1997 Bay Area Book Reviewers Association Award for fiction.

As you read these stories, you may be tempted to look for signs of the therapist who wrote them. Were there clues that the author is accustomed to thinking psychoanalytically? Would this make her any different than most sensitive fiction writers?

In "The Story of Miss Edna," Frank tells of an odd experience that occurs when a school bids farewell to a retiring kindergarten teacher. What do you think of the way emotions become strangely turned around? How does the ending of this very short story relate to the emotional boomerang that precedes it?

Cold Mountain, by Charles Frazier, Vintage Books (paperback)

If you follow *The New York Times Book Review* best-seller list, you don't need an introduction to this book. However, if you are one of those people who steer away from the popular fiction list in pursuit of more serious writing, you'll be very pleasantly surprised by Frazier's finely told story about a Civil War soldier named Inman who decides to leave his hospital bed and walk home even though the conflict is still raging. The prospect of seeing his love Ada and their remote North Carolina mountain community carries the war-scarred soldier over rough miles and through harrowing encounters with strangers.

Frazier alternates his chapters between Inman's journey and Ada's life back home, providing in the young woman's upbeat tale some very welcome relief from the soldier's travails. Although we first meet Ada when she is close to starvation, as a formerly affluent intellectual who has no idea how to survive on her own in the countryside, her life takes a promising turn when a loner named Ruby offers to work Ada's farm with her.

Frazier's novel is filled with details of nature, agrarian life, and the social milieu of the 1860s. His information about the Civil War and that era is said to be quite accurate. His prose has the rhythm and elegance of writing of that period, lending the novel further authenticity.

Cold Mountain was the winner of the National Book Award for fiction in 1997.

Frazier describes Ada's family history and recent past in detail but neglects to fill in Inman's life before the war. Why do you think the author did this? Do you consider his omission a flaw in this remarkable novel? Could Frazier's decision relate to the fact that Inman was based on one of his relatives?

Both Inman and Ada experience serious inner turmoil as the novel progresses. How would you describe each one's personal, interior odyssey?

COLD MOUNTAIN *takes its time to build momentum. After the slow start, can you see rising and falling motion in each chapter about Inman? Would you say there is a moral or lesson to be gained from each segment of his journey?*

The Mirror, by Lynn Freed, Ballantine Books (paperback)

There are so many wonderful things about this novel by northern California author Lynn Freed. Told in the voice of a young Englishwoman who has immigrated to South Africa just after World War I, the spunky and sometimes cranky words of Agnes La Grange will hook your interest and not let go until you have learned just what kind of life she ultimately makes for herself.

As with most successful fiction, Freed's story feels so genuine that you want to believe it's entirely true. In addition to her expertise at creating characters and settings, Freed tempts you to believe in Agnes's world by providing black-and-white photos of the locale in which her story unfolds.

The biggest reason for nestling this book in your lap is that the challenges the main character faces are so compelling. Agnes's deepest desires are to experience adventure, to achieve something worthwhile, and to know passion but not be dominated by a man. Given the time in which she lives, this is a particularly tall order, and it is a pleasure to watch her struggle and not succumb to Edwardian mores.

In Agnes's narrative, a truly distinctive character emerges, with her often caustic observations revealing as much about herself as they do about the other people in her life. Agnes's personal flaws make her seem like someone we'd know; the reader roots for her to overcome her own shortcomings as well as the obstacles thrown up by others in her quest to escape a mediocre life.

Freed was born and grew up in Durban, South Africa, and has written two other novels set in that country: *Home Ground* and *The Bungalow*. She is also the author of *Heart Change*.

Agnes is ruthlessly honest and not entirely likable. How far can an author go in giving her heroine infuriating qualities before we no longer care about her?

Agnes is determined never to lose herself to compromise. There are moments when she feels strongly the power of being alive. By the end of the novel, has she been entirely true to her goals? Would you say her life has been a success?

The Long Rain, by Peter Gadol, St. Martin's (paperback)

Here's an unusual twist on a murder mystery: We know the killer, we know he killed by accident, and we wonder how he will extricate himself from the nightmare of having become a hit-and-run driver. In Peter Gadol's gripping *The Long Rain,* attorney Jason Dark not only hides his involvement in the death of a teenage boy on a lonely mountain highway but also ends up defending the transient mistakenly accused of killing the youth.

The author of three other relatively diverse novels, Gadol is not a mystery/suspense writer per se, but rather the author of quality contemporary fiction. In *The Long Rain* he focuses his talents on creating a vivid wine country tableau in California's Central Valley, painting a portrait of a young family, and slowly revealing a main character who can evoke both our sympathy and our disgust.

Gadol does an excellent job of miring Jason in the complications and miseries created by lies piled upon lies. By the end of *The Long Rain,* if you are willing to put up with Jason's initial mistakes, you will find yourself eagerly turning pages to find out how and whether he will set things right.

Interspersed with Jason's dire dilemma are satisfying descriptions of his work rebuilding his father's winery. From pruning the vines to squeezing the grapes, Gadol provides an earthy, engaging view of vineyard life and wine making that gives his novel further depth.

Gadol is also the author of *Closer to the Sun, The Mystery Roast,* and *Coyote.*

There are strange parallels between protagonist Jason Dark and low-life Troy Frantz, the man accused of the hit-and-run. Both are separated from their wives and teenage sons, both have committed crimes. Do you think Gadol intended Frantz to be Dark's alter ego?

THE LONG RAIN *is a story of moral failure and the search for redemption. Did you understand how Jason Dark could have made the mistakes that he did? What was it about him that made you sympathize with him and wish for an outcome that would restore his dignity?*

Dreaming in Cuban, by Cristina Garcia, Ballantine Books (paperback)

Cristina Garcia's novel about three generations of Cuban women is irresistible from the very first page: A little old lady equipped with binoculars sits on her front porch guarding the coast of Cuba. From grandmother Celia, Garcia introduces us to two more generations of a lusty Latino family living in Cuba and the United States, weaving a story around revolution, immigration, lost love, and the conflicts that arise among women with differing politics and spiritual visions.

The widowed matriarch Celia supports Castro's revolution, believing that her people must work together on behalf of the common good. Her older daughter, Lourdes, has abandoned the island to open the Yankee Doodle Bakery in Brooklyn, with the hope of establishing franchises across the nation. Lourdes's daughter Pilar has trouble communicating with her mother and nurses a slowly waning spiritual bond with her grandmother back in Cuba. Meanwhile, Celia's youngest child, Felicia, continues to live in Cuba, but suffers insanity and seeks relief from a healer following the African-based Santeria religion.

Garcia tells her tale with a kind of magical realism. The characters are believable, the events could be true, yet so much that is mystical happens in these women's minds and hearts that the writing takes on a surreal quality. The book is about the death of dreams and the birth of new ones, about loss and regeneration.

Garcia's latest novel is *The Aguero Sisters.*

DREAMING IN CUBAN *captures that island's poetry and mysticism. While Lourdes fights to escape the visionary tradition of her family, Felicia immerses herself in it. What do you make of the repeated appearance of Lourdes's dead father? Is Garcia saying that Lourdes is wrong in rejecting the dreamworld?*

Charms for the Easy Life, by Kaye Gibbons, Avon Books (paperback)

This is not your typical novel about three generations of women. It's funny, it's offbeat, and Grandma is a midwife/healer who can take care of herself, thank you.

Gibbons, who has a gift for language as well as storytelling, has written a number of memorable books *(Ellen Foster, A Virtuous Woman, A Cure for Dreams, Sights Unseen, On the Occasion of My Last Afternoon)*, each with its own distinctive flavor. This one has a certain pioneer spirit, in which the main character, Charlie Kate, makes her way without a man in the turn-of-the century South by using intellect, guts, compassion, and an impressive knowledge of folk medicine. The conflict comes in part from an equally smart daughter who has made finding the right man her goal in life. By the time we reach World War II, the book's narrator, Charlie's granddaughter, touches us with questions about her own future and who she should be, given the examples of the two strong, sparring women who are her family.

Another important issue for Charlie is the development of modern medicine. Much of her success rests on her abilities as a healer, in a time when the midwife was often the most important medical person in a community. We watch as doctors take over the landscape, some of them with unscrupulous ways, looking down their noses at the centuries of practical folk medicine that Charlie and others like her have had to offer.

Gibbons knows how to have a good time. Her characters are endearing, she makes us laugh, and she leads us down a satisfying path, where strong women will win in the end and love is an interesting possibility.

CHARMS FOR THE EASY LIFE *was inspired by oral histories gleaned by the WPA, a Depression-era government agency that created jobs for scholars and artists as well as for construction workers. In spite of its basis in reality, Charlie's story sometimes seems incredible because of her extreme independence and lack of concern about social mores. Were you willing to believe in this brand of southern feminism? Would you say the book had a fairy-tale quality?*

Gibbons portrays three strong women, two of them sometimes at war with each other. Did you take sides in this conflict, or were you able to sympathize with each?

If you read ELLEN FOSTER, *which was a groundbreaking book on child abuse, were you able to accept the change of tone in* CHARMS FOR THE EASY LIFE?

Victory over Japan, by Ellen Gilchrist, Little, Brown and Company (paperback)

Ellen Gilchrist is among the best of American short story writers. Her bewitching tales share a crucial element with the work of many other southern writers: The characters are crazy and unpredictable in a way that makes them lovable and also makes us want to find out what will happen next.

Winner of the 1984 National Book Award for fiction, *Victory over Japan* was the second of her many books and a great example of her ability to create dangerous, funny women.

Miss Rhoda wanders through many of Gilchrist's stories. She is the kind of unruly teenager who can make a father pray to God for assistance and the kind of adult woman who can announce, "I'm stuffed. . . . How can I eat all this? I won't be able to move, much less make love to you. I am going to make love to you. You know that, don't you?" She breezes her way in and out of this collection, through a broad canvas of experiences.

The frothy, rollicking style of Gilchrist's storytelling makes you wish for longer, more sustained work. However, be cautious when selecting from among her novels: *The Annunciation* and *Sarah Conley* don't seem to hold a candle to her short stories, but *The Anna Papers* and *Anabasis* were well received.

Other Gilchrist short story collections include the award-winning *In the Land of Dreamy Dreams, Drunk with Love, The Courts of Love,* and *Flights of Angels.*

There's an amiable, light quality to Gilchrist's writing that might make it seem less than serious literature. Does her combination of comedy and poignancy diminish the significance of her work or make it memorable?

Rhoda Katherine Manning has been described as the quintessential Steel Magnolia. Do you think she's a representative character of the American South, or is she more the image of what we enjoy imagining a southern woman to be? Would you describe her as caricature, a cartoon figure, or a flesh-and-blood, believable person?

Part of the fun of Gilchrist's writing is watching the men respond to her tricky females. Often her women have issues with men over which the ladies seek revenge. Do you think she is fair in her characterization of men?

Creek Walk and Other Stories, by Molly Giles, Scribner (paperback)

Most readers have not heard of Molly Giles, but by now her name should rightfully have taken a place among American literary heavyweights. A mentor to authors such as Amy Tan and Melba Beals, a master writer in her own right, and a nominee for the Pulitzer Prize, Giles has now produced her second collection of short fiction, *Creek Walk and Other Stories.*

If there is any way you can attend a reading by Giles, do so. Her writing is excellent, but her reading of it makes it marvelous.

Giles writes of women struggling with a variety of challenges, from facing down the Trailside Killer to tangling with the oddities of fame. "The Blessed Among Us" is a tantalizing story inspired by her friendship with novelist Amy Tan, although the main character, Iona, is an Hispanic American rather than a Chinese American. Giles's humor and pathos in describing the reaction of Iona's writers' group to Iona's sudden fame pack a wonderful wallop. "Talking to Strangers," cast in an entirely different mold than "The Blessed," told in the voice of a murdered young woman, will give you the willies but will impress you with its virtuosity in an entirely different way. Of the fourteen stories included here, most are memorable for their characters and their drama.

In addition to the Pulitzer nomination, *Rough Translations,* Giles's first collection, won the Flannery O'Connor Award for short fiction, the Boston Globe Award, and the Bay Area Book Reviewers Association Award for fiction. She is an associate professor of English at San Francisco State University.

Women emerge on the pages of Giles's work fully formed. Do her male characters come to life in the same way? Is the development of both male and female figures essential to the effectiveness of a story?

The stories in CREEK WALK *range from studies of the mundane, like "War," to harrowing investigations of violence, like "Talking to Strangers," to portraits of the surreal, as in "The Writers' Model." Do the more exotic tales reduce the impact of her stories of everyday life, or do the latter provide welcome relief?*

Kaaterskill Falls, by Allegra Goodman, Delta (paperback)

Although this is an impressive piece of work for a first novel, it should be pointed out that Allegra Goodman is also the author of two short story collections: *Total Immersion* and *The Family Markowitz*, which was a best-seller. This probably explains how Goodman could so skillfully take a quiet tale and lend it such strength.

Kaaterskill Falls is set in a tiny town in upstate New York where a small sect of Orthodox Jews comes to spend their summers. Not all are devout followers of Rav Elijah Kirshner, and so we follow several of them as they contend with modern desires, ghosts from the past, and questions of real estate development. Elizabeth Shulman is a restless mother of five married to a devout and kind man, wishing for something more than domestic chores to occupy her hours. Import company owner Andras Melish and his sisters are the only members of their family to have survived the Holocaust, and while his sisters thrive in the present, Andras lives in a state of sad isolation. His young daughter, Renee, befriends a girl outside of their close-knit community, and all kinds of new possibilities open to her.

Is this earthshaking, rivet-you-to-the-chair drama? No. But Goodman's captivating characters will win your attention and hold it. *Kaaterskill Falls* will also give you the satisfaction of traveling to another time and place, as the author envelops you in the sounds, tastes, and textures of Kaaterskill Falls and New York City's Washington Heights.

Daphne Merkin wrote in THE NEW YORK TIMES, *"There are times when one wishes for some passion—some unholy mess or some desperate humor—to erupt from the pages, but the darker impulses are not what interest Goodman. . . . Her truest talent is for imposing a shape on the little, everyday disturbances that distract most of her writing peers; she has an almost 19th-century ability to create a sense of linkage, of one existence impinging on the next." Others have complained, "no story, no emotion, nothing." Were Goodman's characterizations, her creation of community, and the subtle explosions of feeling enough to hold you?*

Goodman appears to have painted an accurate, succinct portrait of an American Hasidic life. Did her coverage seem kind or critical?

***No Ordinary Time: Franklin and Eleanor Roosevelt: The Home Front in World War II*, by Doris Kearns Goodwin, Touchstone Books (paperback)**

Any history book that begins with the bedroom arrangements in the White House is bound to capture your attention. What's more, Doris Kearns Goodwin's account of the Roosevelts and the United States from 1940 through 1945 continues to be interesting all the way through, 759 pages in all. This is probably why it won a Pulitzer Prize in 1995.

Goodwin's engaging—and relatively discreet—narration is filled with absorbing information about the first family, their associates, and a world at war. Throughout, there's the story of a marriage that no longer involved intimacy but had strong bonds of respect and partnership—and that resulted in huge accomplishments on behalf of the American people.

Goodwin has summarized a tremendous amount of research, along the way uncovering innumerable anecdotal incidents underlying important events. Full portraits of the Roosevelts emerge, personal failings included, as well as glimpses of foreign leaders.

Learn how Hitler had the British Army cornered on the beach at Dunkirk and could have destroyed them, but instead decided to take a three-day break. Read about the pathetic state of the U.S. military, which boasted men on horseback to fight German tanks, as we approached the war. Most of all, read about an American president who tended to act with confidence and courage on behalf of larger issues.

Goodwin is also the author of *The Fitzgeralds and the Kennedys, Lyndon Johnson and the American Dream,* and *Wait Till Next Year,* her memoir.

You don't have to like FDR to admire the grace with which he handled a multitude of challenges, all the while keeping in mind an overriding, intelligent plan. Although savvy about politics, he seemed to act primarily on behalf of a greater good, without blowing back and forth in the political winds. How does he compare to recent presidents in this regard? What are the factors that make it so hard for recent national leaders to act without regard to popularity?

How did Goodwin make her history book read more like a novel than a textbook? Try to separate out the different story lines moving through this volume. Take a look at her narrative skills and her ability to select what is important.

Personal History, by Katharine Graham, Vintage Books (paperback)

If you are curious about this inspiring memoir but are not willing to dig into a 642-page book, you have two other choices. You can listen to Graham's very human, engaging autobiography on a three-hour audiotape or take a particularly long car trip and listen to the unabridged version (thirty-three hours).

Any of these are worthwhile options. While the abridged tape leaves out much of Graham's Pulitzer Prize–winning *Personal History,* it does enable you to hear the author recount the short version herself—at times a very emotional experience—and to grasp easily why the life of the former publisher of *The Washington Post* has been a source of much interest.

If you already know that under Graham's leadership the *Post* published the Pentagon Papers and broke the Watergate scandal, in both cases challenging the authority of the U.S. government, it's important to understand that Katharine Graham never envisioned herself as a leader. Born to great wealth, she abandoned a brief career as a journalist to become a wife, mother, and socialite. When her husband died and she assumed leadership of a publishing empire, her competent stewardship was an unexpected, exhilarating achievement.

In describing her husband's decline into manic-depression and his infidelity, Graham never once says a harsh word about his lover or lapses into self-pity at the pain his illness inflicted on her. However, she is not shy about disclosing engrossing, behind-the-scenes details regarding the executive branch of government and business in the offices and press rooms of the *Post.*

Like NO ORDINARY TIME, *Graham's* PERSONAL HISTORY *reads like a novel while revealing important pieces of American history. Do her choices ever seem self-serving, or is she willing to show weaknesses that make a character seem authentic?*

Did the book ever seem too long? If so, what would you have cut?

Thinking in Pictures and Other Reports from My Life with Autism, by Temple Grandin, Vintage Books (paperback)

Thinking in Pictures is a remarkable, personal account of autism, given that one of the main symptoms of autism is an inability to communicate easily—or at all. Temple Grandin was the autistic woman described in Oliver Sacks's book *An Anthropologist on Mars,* and here she very capably takes up where Sacks left off.

You may think of autistic persons as wordless children rocking back and forth, screaming and inaccessible. Grandin shows us a much broader range of behavior that can be labeled autistic. She theorizes that degrees of autism may stretch along a continuum that includes Albert Einstein and Bill Gates as well as many of the people closest to us. She also tells how a shrieking, nonverbal child may grow to be a functioning adult and how the use of certain medications has made her own life easier.

The most important difference between her and other people, Grandin believes, is that she thinks in pictures. She seems to have no conversations in her mind, no means of discourse with herself, only a series of visual images that are highly complex.

Autistics often experience horrific sensory overload, with sounds both soft and loud reaching them at the same high-decibel level and the slightest touch causing excruciating pain. In response to her own conflicting need to be held and her fear of touch, Grandin invented a "squeeze machine" that allows her, and now other autistics, to control the strength and duration of a hug.

Grandin teaches animal science at Colorado State University and has designed one third of all the livestock handling facilities in the United States.

What do you think of Grandin's theory about blocked emotional development in autistics? Does this give clues to causes of emotional disturbance in other children?

Does Grandin's explanation of what it's like to think in pictures destroy the idea that language is necessary for thought?

Unravelling, by Elizabeth Graver, Harvest Books (paperback)

Although the haunting novel *Unravelling* is set in the 1800s, its young heroine possesses the spirit of a rebellious, modern young woman. A farm girl raised according to the strict mores of the times, Aimee Slater is nonetheless headstrong and impassioned, always wanting more than her family farm can offer, and Elizabeth Graver, in her first novel, aptly shows what might have happened to such a young woman in nineteenth-century New England. Graver's use of language is utterly graceful, and her story is simple but carefully drawn.

Against her parents' wishes, Aimee leaves their New Hampshire farm to work in the mills of Lowell, Massachusetts. We meet her years later, a woman in her thirties residing alone in the woods, visited only by a mute child and an outcast one-legged man, and we wonder how she arrived at this lonely juncture. Graver's story takes us backward to her separation from her rural life, her amazement at the ways of the city and factory, and the crises that befall her in Lowell. Then, gratefully, we move forward as the older Aimee finds a way to live outside of social confines.

This may be a debut novel, but it was not Graver's first attempt at writing. In 1991 she became the youngest person to receive the prestigious Drue Heinz Literature Prize for her short story collection, *Have You Seen Me?* She has also been the recipient of a Fulbright grant and a Guggenheim Fellowship. Her latest novel is *The Honey Thief,* another book club favorite.

Graver spins out Aimee's relationship with her mother in an intense, tangled way, placing their conflict at the book's core. Were you satisfied with the way the author handled their difficulties? Did the ending of the book seem appropriate?

Graver pins her story on historical fact. Does the air of authenticity keep Aimee's travails from lapsing into melodrama? If you did find her story melodramatic, was this a problem? How does UNRAVELLING *compare to* THE SCARLET LETTER?

The Caveman's Valentine, by George Dawes Green, Warner Books (paperback)

If you like detective-by-accident stories, this one's a doozy. A homeless man living in one of New York's parks finds a body dumped just outside his cave and decides to seek justice. In order to do so, he must overcome severe paranoid fantasies, clean himself up, and focus all of his newly organized wit on gaining entrance to the society he once fled.

Awarded the 1995 Edgar Award for a first mystery novel, Green's book is both funny and raunchy. (Toward the end of the book, sadomasochistic sex is an element of the story, so be warned.) Romulus Ledbetter is one of the more interesting heroes to come along the American fiction trail, as he struggles to silence his crazed babblings and to overcome his fear of Cornelius Gould Stuyvesant, an all-powerful, imaginary nemesis—and to make his way into a "normal" world that includes some fairly deranged characters of its own.

Green has concocted a truly sympathetic homeless person and will probably influence the way you view street people from now on. A Juilliard-trained musician, Ledbetter is also a former family man with a daughter about whom he cares deeply. His one-man war on evil, against the power broker he believes is responsible for all social problems, may be hard to follow at first, but hang on. Ledbetter is supposed to be hard to understand when first you encounter him.

Green's second novel was the best-selling *The Juror.*

The author manages to move his murder mystery right along without sacrificing characterization. Ledbetter is a vagrant, an intellect, and a psychotic. How does Green get us to empathize with him?

Ledbetter is severely paranoid. Is it believable that he could pull himself back together the way he did in order to reenter society? Does an author have a responsibility to cling entirely to what is possible or most probable?

Green has built his novel on a variety of issues that give it depth. In addition to the question of homicide and mental illness, what questions does the author ask us to consider?

Errands, by Judith Guest, Ballantine Books (hardcover)

Judith Guest amazed the literary world in 1976 when her first novel, *Ordinary People,* became the first unsolicited manuscript in twenty-six years to be accepted by the prestigious Viking Press. Her successful book went on to become an Academy Award–winning film. Later came *Second Heaven,* and now *Errands* continues her tradition of expert writing about the complexity of family life.

Errands tells of a young Midwestern family that must face the death of its father. Annie and her three children are so thoroughly disabled by the loss of husband and father Keith to cancer that at times you'll wonder why you should go on with them, watching their lives crumble. However, if you're willing to hang on through the pain of their travails, you'll be glad you did. Bit by bit, Guest allows normalcy to return to their lives, whether in the form of brothers reestablishing verbal contact or an aunt needing solace from them instead of the reverse.

Guest is a master at capturing the feeling and texture of family dialogue, especially of siblings bickering. Her cynical, traumatized teenagers seem very real, and when their self-protective reserve finally begins to melt, they never once seem sappy. The narrative is succinct and direct, with the shifting perspective from character to character leading you to feel like an intimate member of the family.

In getting us to identify with her people, Guest highlights certain moments, crystallizing a character's thoughts, bringing to the fore certain feelings or ideas that the rest of us have experienced but have not necessarily been able to articulate. What moments were particularly memorable in this way for you in her story?

Guest shows a special ability to bring to life the children in her book. A NEW YORK TIMES *review noted that the adults seem flat by comparison. Meanwhile,* BOOKLIST *said that Keith was so fully developed and interesting that the reader could hardly bear to lose him. What's your opinion about Guest's rendition of adults in this story?*

At first Annie may seem rather rigid and cold. However, it becomes clear that she is acting out the different roles of mother, sister, daughter, and employee to keep her family afloat. Is it believable that she would avoid her grief in this way?

Snow Falling on Cedars, David Guterson, Vintage Books (paperback)

Although Guterson's evocative, beautifully written novel is often billed as the story of a Japanese American on trial for murder in the Pacific Northwest or of Japanese American lives irrevocably altered by internment during World War II, *Snow Falling on Cedars* is also an affecting love story and an ode to an island.

This quiet book gradually gathers force as you read it: a slowly unfolding trial, snow piling on a thickly wooded island, secret memories of teenage love, brilliant summer days in strawberry fields and among the tide pools, a dispute over land, innocent lives twisted by blind hatred, a mysterious death on a fishing boat.

Ishmael Chambers is the one-man staff of the local paper on the island of San Piedro, north of Puget Sound in Washington. A veteran maimed during World War II, he must overcome personal demons to strive for accuracy and justice in the resolution of the court case. Meanwhile, Guterson shows us how the war has left a terrible mark on other residents of this small island.

Winner of the PEN/Faulkner Award in 1995, the novel illuminates the lives of a handful of the island's residents, each of them very different, few of them really knowing each other, and yet all of them closely intertwined. Several love stories are told as the characters come to life, with the various tales of passion an essential counterpoint to the parallel story of hatred.

Guterson is also the author of a collection of short stories, *The Country Ahead of Us, the Country Behind,* and another novel, *East of the Mountains.*

The forbidden romance portrayed in SNOW FALLING ON CEDARS *becomes more and more affecting as the novel unfolds. Is this merely because it is forbidden? What elements make this love story particularly moving?*

The Japanese American people living on San Piedro suffer terribly as a result of war hysteria. A deep sense of helplessness emerges as Guterson draws each of his characters and their past. What history lessons do you take away from Guterson's story? What do you think he's trying to tell us about an individual's ability to determine his or her own fate?

The All of It, by Jeannette Haien, HarperPerennial (paperback)

The death of a well-liked man in a small Irish town creates a terrible dilemma for the local priest. We first meet Father Declan de Loughry while he is fly-fishing in miserable weather, trying to ignore the rain and midges to struggle with a moral dilemma posed by the widow of his dead parishioner.

The dying man has uttered a deathbed confession that dissolves all assumptions the good Father has ever made about the couple. Enda and Kevin Dennehy lived a lie for fifty years by pretending to be husband and wife, and as Enda then tells Father Declan "the all of it," her tale shakes the priest to his core.

Just what *is* moral behavior? Jeannette Haien asks us. This very short book is not as quick a read as it looks. You'll want to take your time and think about it. First published in 1986, Haien's slim piece of fiction was a sleeper success that apparently grew in popularity as the result of word of mouth.

Haien's novel is presented in two voices, Enda's and Father Declan's. There is a delicious contrast between the two: The priest is reserved and pedagogical in tone, while speech flows from Enda in a spirited, warm rush. The story is also flavored by Haien's adept portrayal of Irish country life.

A concert pianist and teacher who lives in Manhattan and spends her summers in Connemara, Ireland, Haien is also the author of the novel *Matters of Chance.*

Can you find examples of a change in style of speech and in outlook on the part of Father Declan as Enda proceeds to tell her story?

On the one hand, Enda's revelations involve sin and scandal that Father Declan cannot ignore. On the other, there are mitigating circumstances and true love. Haien's ending leaves room for interpretation. What do you think the priest's final decision is?

Creative writing teachers often warn students that the use of flashback can slow down a story and diminish its impact. What do you think of Haien's choice to begin the story with Father Declan fishing for salmon, thinking back on what has transpired?

The Short History of a Prince, by Jane Hamilton, Anchor Books (paperback)

If you have found Jane Hamilton's writing extremely elegant but were too depressed by the excruciating downward spirals of her first two novels, here's a lovely surprise. Although centered on a family's loss of a young son, *The Short History of a Prince* has an altogether different sort of tone than *A Map of the World* and *The Book of Ruth.* Told in the funny, ironic voice of Walter, the surviving son, Hamilton's latest novel moves quickly past the basic facts of the disaster and gets down to the business of studying and following Walter's life.

And it's an interesting life that Walter has. He tells us about it from the perspective of a man in his late thirties, looking back on teenage years spent pursuing a career in ballet. Although he is gay, no big issue is made of this fact; in a refreshing, matter-of-fact way, Hamilton allows Walter's sexuality to be an important element of his persona but not the source of constant discussion or trauma.

It's clear from the outset that Walter will not be a professional dancer. At most, he is mediocre at the thing he loves best. The reader is pulled along by questions regarding what form his career and friendships will finally take and whether he will ever make a truly satisfying life for himself. The lingering impact of his brother's death and an examination of Walter's behavior during his brother's last days are important elements of the story. So is his affection for two beautiful young dancers, Susan and Mitch.

A sense of place is significant in each of Hamilton's books. At the heart of THE SHORT HISTORY OF A PRINCE *is the family's wonderful summer home at Lake Margaret. What role does this big old house play in Hamilton's tale? Why is it so important?*

Walter's response to his brother's impending death is cruel and self-centered. Do you understand his behavior at this point? Are you able to forgive him? Why?

One of the pleasures of this novel is Walter's and Susan's friendship. How does Hamilton manage to show each character at his or her worst in this relationship and still have us believe that they can be devoted friends?

Mariette in Ecstasy, by Ron Hansen, HarperPerennial (paperback)

Do you believe in stigmata, or spontaneous bleeding from the palms, feet, and other areas of the body where Jesus had crucifixion wounds? You may believe that the heroine of Ron Hansen's book, Mariette Baptiste, could be one of the few hundred documented cases of this phenomenon or you may not. It doesn't matter, you can still appreciate Hansen's exquisite novel for its cutting irony and its poetry.

Hansen's tale takes us to the turn of the century in upstate New York, where a lovely young woman dedicates herself to Christ in the most religious of environments. And yet, when Mariette achieves the goal to which many of her sisters at the convent aspire—sharing the suffering of Christ—her success throws the convent into chaos.

The writing is lovely. Hansen frequently feeds us images in short bursts, in a series of words or sentences following one upon the other with little connective tissue, but accumulating into a powerful, larger scene:

> Crickets.
>
> Heat.
>
> Something wriggles in the green stew of algae at the water's edge.
>
> High up on a stark jut of wasted hickory, a hoot owl turns its head completely around and persecutes the night with its stare.
>
> Church windows and song. Matins. Lauds. And then footsteps.

The author of both adult and children's books, Hansen has also written the novels *Hitler's Niece, Atticus, Desperados,* and *The Assassination of Jesse James by the Coward Robert Ford.*

Hansen cultivates between his characters the underlying tension of priory life: the nuns' need for warm, personal relationship versus their dedication to a higher passion. How does this conflict complicate Mariette's story?

Does the author give clues to indicate that Mariette is fabricating or pretending to have stigmata? If you accept that she truly is bleeding spontaneously, do you think it's possible that she has brought this on herself via some form of madness? Where is the line drawn between madness and divine possession?

Hansen's prose provides an ultimate example of the "show, don't tell" admonition often given to writers. Is Hansen so astute at showing that he becomes a witness to events without offering a viewpoint?

Blue Highways: A Journey into America, by William Least Heat-Moon, Back Bay Books (paperback)

If you've ever dreamed of taking a slow drive across the USA, this book may push you to do it. *Blue Highways* is a wonderful, companionable account of one man's travels along the back roads, meeting people in small-town America, reflecting on their lives and his.

The story of William Least Heat-Moon's odyssey in his trusty van, *Ghost Dancer,* from February through June of 1977 is still of interest more than twenty years later, both for the portrait it paints of modern America and the glimpses it gives of how we got to be this way.

On old road maps, the big interstates were delineated in red, and the smaller, less-traveled roads in blue. Heat-Moon took off from Missouri down the blue highways after learning that college cutbacks had eliminated his job teaching English and that his wife had left him for another man. At a loss for what direction his life should take, the former English professor decided that travel and reflection might point the way.

Heat-Moon is the descendant of both Native Americans and early American colonists; his writing shows a sensitivity to the original Americans and newcomers alike. His quiet, bemused reactions to the diverse people he meets, when combined with his offerings of choice bits of historical detail, make the book a special treat. At one and the same time he can savor the loveliness of a small New England town and note that the residents probably don't tell tourists about the child buried beneath the town square whose heart was boiled by early villagers because they thought he was a vampire.

Heat-Moon is also the author of *PrairyErth,* a natural and human history of a single county in Kansas, and *River-Horse,* an account of his journey across the continental United States using waterways.

Robert Penn Warren said of Heat-Moon, "He has a genius for finding people who have not even found themselves." Can you think of examples of this in BLUE HIGHWAYS? *How does Heat-Moon so successfully muster up the essence of these strangers?*

What did you think of the author's technique of searching out unusual town names and using them as a starting point for conversation? In talking with the people he met, what did he learn about differences in quality of life along the back roads?

Into the Forest, by Jean Hegland, Bantam Books/CALYX Books (paperback)

Northern California author Jean Hegland has garnered much attention for her first novel, and rightfully so. *Into the Forest,* published in 1996, is a provocative imagining of what might happen if the physical underpinnings of our culture were to break down. If the power were out and fuel became scarce, what would happen to us? This was a particularly haunting thought at the millennium, when so many people worried about the implications of Y2K computer malfunctions.

Hegland writes of two teenage sisters living alone in a remote rural area. When the electricity goes out, the phone no longer works, their remaining parent dies, their supply of gasoline dwindles, and their pantry empties, Nell and Eva slowly face the fact that they must depend on themselves. A caution: As you begin this story, you may feel that it is bound to be too much of a downer. This is not true; although Hegland provides taut drama, her characters often rise to meet harsh challenge and grow stronger because of it.

Some of the most beautiful writing in this novel—and some of the more breathtaking writing that you are likely to encounter in recent fiction—describes the forest, nature, and its bounty. These lovely passages and the rest of the novel are particularly moving when read aloud; you might want to listen to this book on tape or take turns reading it aloud with a companion.

Nell and Eva's sisterhood evolves through a number of stages, some of them rather surprising. What do you think Hegland is trying to tell us in the successive phases of their relationship?

Eva is poised for a career in ballet; Nell hopes to attend Harvard. At first the postponement of dreams caused by power failure and fuel shortages is excruciating; by the end of the book, how do you feel about these goals?

Hegland points up the fragile nature of our complex society. After reading this book, do you have any ideas as to what you would do if these events came to pass?

The Sixteen Pleasures, by Robert Hellenga, Delta (paperback)

For those used to reading stories about women written by women, this book is a marvel. How did Robert Hellenga create such an authentic female heroine? The answer, said this first-time novelist with some modesty, is that he has a wife and three grown daughters. Others might also say he is a talented writer with the ability to empathize.

In *The Sixteen Pleasures,* a young American woman seeks adventure in Florence in 1966, in the days following terrible flooding that inundated museums and libraries, destroying or threatening to destroy national treasures. Margot Harrington, a book conservator working in the Newberry Library in New York, puts aside her quiet, disappointing life to join the hordes of "mud angels," young foreigners rushing to Florence to help clean and preserve the threatened works of art.

Margot does get her wish for adventure, in an unexpected turn of events. A nun places into her safekeeping a strange treasure, a shockingly pornographic volume bound with a prayer book. A long-lost collection of Aretino's erotic sonnets, it could bring a fortune and help to save the convent from losing its autonomy.

Hellenga's book could simply be an adventure/romance, but he has given it greater depth in a number of ways. He introduces us to a city. He teaches us about book preservation. He explains how an ancient fresco might be removed from a church wall. And he encourages us to think about life and loss and paths chosen.

Hellenga, who is a professor of English at Knox College in Galesburg, Illinois, gained intimate knowledge of Florence during a year spent in that city with a student group in the 1980s. His second novel was *The Fall of a Sparrow.*

Those who know Florence report that Hellenga has captured the essence of that city. Did his characters come to life in the same memorable way?

THE SIXTEEN PLEASURES *wraps together many stories at once. Did the plot ever seem disjointed or lacking in continuity as a result?*

Is it important to know what the sixteen pleasures are?

Dispatches, by Michael Herr, Vintage International (paperback)

Dispatches is one of the best books written about the Vietnam War, in the company of Tim O'Brien's *The Things They Carried.* Author Michael Herr covered the conflict for *Esquire* magazine in the late 1960s and ten years later published this volume of his frontline impressions. He also wrote the narration for the movie *Apocalypse Now* and coauthored the screenplay for another Vietnam movie, *Full Metal Jacket.*

Herr has reported, "I went to cover the war, and it covered me." The brutality, the insanity, and the perverse thrill of life-and-death struggle are all captured in his writing. He is not shy about describing his odd position as an observer, as someone who chose to visit a living hell that many others wished to flee. He is frank about revealing his relish for the dangers of war and his recognition that nothing else in his life would ever match the intensity of these events.

Herr's ability to describe what he saw without preaching makes this a book that involves the reader totally. The dialogue seems entirely authentic and his narration so casual and free-flowing that you feel you are part of a continuing conversation. Furthermore, Herr has a superior journalist's ability to pull you right into the moment with a single sentence: "There were times during the night when all the jungle sounds would stop at once."

Author Robert Stone said of DISPATCHES, *"With uncanny precision [the book] summons up the very essence of [the war]—its space diction, its surreal psychology, its bitter humor—the dope, the dexedrine, the body bags, the rot, all of it. . . . I believe it may be the best personal journal about war, any war, that any writer has ever accomplished." Apparently Herr has admitted that parts of his book are fictional. Does this detract from his ability to convey the gritty, grotesque nature of the Vietnam conflict?*

It appears that many people return to this book again and again over time. Why do you think this is true, especially of a book that has so many repugnant images?

DISPATCHES *reports many outrageous incidents involving our soldiers and war correspondents in Vietnam and Cambodia, from the acid-crazed infantryman who couldn't wait to get back into the field so he could kill Viet Cong to the exploits of photojournalist Sean Flynn. The Vietnam War gave some men a chance to act out their most extreme impulses; do you think that Herr was drawn to stay there because he was fascinated by the chance to see this or possibly to do the same?*

Helen Keller: A Life, by Dorothy Herrmann, Alfred A. Knopf (hardcover)

There are two especially notable things about this book: The author is a gifted storyteller, and she introduces provocative new information on a public figure about whom much has already been published. You may know the "Miracle Worker" story from the theater, film, or schoolroom instruction, but you won't know nearly the whole, engrossing tale of blind and deaf Helen Keller until you read this book.

Herrmann explains the unusual, tightly bound relationships that existed between Keller and the three women upon whom she relied: Annie Sullivan, Polly Thomson, and Nella Braddy Henney. She places the story of Helen Keller within the social and political context of her time, pulling in questions of radical thinking, feminism, sexual mores, and more. This is a big story, well told.

Too often, biographies present far more detail than the lay reader could possibly want, and too many biographies suffer because the author is afraid to take a point of view on his or her subject. Herrmann does not make these mistakes. She builds a case for her portrait of Keller as a woman who might have been a willful and highly sexed southern belle had it not been for her disabilities, and as a person dominated by her sighted companions.

Herrmann is also the author of *Anne Morrow Lindbergh: A Gift for Life* and *S. J. Perelman: A Life.*

Herrmann is not afraid to describe Annie Sullivan as a wonderful, instinctive teacher who had considerable frailties. Sullivan's childhood, she reveals, was punctuated by abandonment and loss. As a result, Keller's utter dependence on her met Sullivan's deepest needs. What did you think of Sullivan when the book was done?

Maddening restraints were placed on Keller, both as a result of her companions' desire to uphold her saintlike image and the widespread belief that the blind and/or deaf should not attempt the same lives as others. Can you imagine Helen Keller having married? Would it have been possible for her to live independently of Sullivan or Thomson?

Second Nature, by Alice Hoffman, Berkeley Publishing Group (paperback)

How can you not like a book in which the middle-aged heroine rescues, on the spur of the moment, a ferocious and mute Wolf Man from incarceration in a state mental hospital?

Alice Hoffman is a knockout storyteller. She proved it in *Seventh Heaven* and *Turtle Moon,* and once more came through in *Second Nature.* Hoffman manages to get everything into a single tale: sensitive portrayal of human relations entwined with questions about truth and integrity and the ways we choose to lead our lives—as well as humor, murder, romance, and passion. The result is a rich, satisfying novel that makes you feel you've been somewhere real, and that leaves you wistful when the visit is over.

The odd thing is that Hoffman often stretches reality so far that, if you allow yourself to consider too long, you won't believe what she's saying. A baby survives a plane crash and is adopted by wolves? He grows to manhood as a member of the pack, learning to communicate without words? It could happen, you tell yourself, because you're having such a good time learning what comes next.

A major delight of Hoffman's writing is her ability to create inviting locales. The main character flees New York with the Wolf Man to her home on a small, rustic island somewhere off the East Coast. The houses are old and well cared for, wisteria droops over garden arbors, and deer amble out of the pine woods to feast on ivy and potted geraniums. There are a few drawbacks, however. Everyone knows everyone else, which makes it hard to hide a grown man. Also, someone has taken to killing brutally the neighborhood pets and deer.

Hoffman is also the author of *Practical Magic,* which was made into a mediocre film, *At Risk,* and *Here on Earth.*

With its magical aspects, SECOND NATURE *could be called a modern fairy tale with lessons about living. What do you think Hoffman is trying to tell us about what it means to be human and how we should live our lives?*

Although her books have wide appeal, Hoffman does not conform strictly to the happy endings school of writing. How did she manage to complete SECOND NATURE *in a satisfying way and still have the conclusion develop logically out of the troubling facts of her story?*

Lost in Translation: A Life in a New Language, **by Eva Hoffman, Penguin Books (paperback)**

In 1959, when she was thirteen years old, Ewa Hoffman fled Poland with her parents and sister to resettle in British Columbia. Contrary to what you'd expect, escape from a communist regime was not a tremendous relief. The first section of Hoffman's memoir, reminiscing about her days in Poland, is entitled "Paradise." Everything that comes after is trauma, until very gradually Hoffman achieves assimilation in America.

Hoffman explains what it means to be suddenly faced with a new language, a new culture, even a new name (Ewa became Eva). Arrival in the West was a profound enough change to stifle her inner thoughts, because she hadn't the English to describe the details of her daily life, and Polish could no longer do the job.

The glimpse of Poland as Hoffman experienced it is fascinating. Her family lived in a three-room apartment in Cracow, and yet they were middle class by Polish standards. In spite of the small space, they had a live-in maid. With her mother and sister, Hoffman attended the theater, opera, and movies. In summer they took monthlong vacations with their friends in the countryside. All of this had to be left behind, along with a promising career for Eva as a pianist, when Poland's leadership cracked down on the Jews in the late 1950s.

Over a period of years, Hoffman came to feel less a pretender and more a participant in her new culture. It is a measure of her success that she has so articulately described the work involved in making the transition. Now a resident of New York City and a former editor of *The New York Times Book Review,* she is also the author of *Exit into History* and *Shtetl: The Life and Death of a Small Town and the World of Polish Jews.*

Did Eva regain herself or create a new identity in America?

As Hoffman portrays them, what are the major differences between Polish culture and American culture?

About a Boy, by Nick Hornby, Riverhead Books (paperback)

This could have been a funny piece of fluff and nothing more, but British writer Nick Hornby has turned out a thoughtful story about a modern single male. Questions about maturity, family life, and commitment weave in and out of his sly tale about Londoner Will Freeman, who hits on a scheme to meet women by attending a support group for single parents.

Will has never been a father and still seems very much a boy himself when he decides to masquerade as the divorced parent of a small child in order to gain entry to SPAT: Single Parents Alone Together. The problem is, a perceptive twelve-year-old named Marcus who is badly in need of a father notices Will and quickly detects that he is childless.

As Hornby portrays him, Will is an ultimate kind of irresponsible young man. Living on family wealth, he need not work. Unconsumed by any passions, he has no interest in a career or hobby. He simply passes the days away with mundane activities until he strikes upon his plan to meet attractive women. It's a real trick for an author to make us care about a protagonist like this, but Hornby does. As the story progresses, Will shows bits of generosity and sensitivity that make us think he may turn out to be a truly decent human being.

The two main points of suspense in *About a Boy* are whether Will can evolve into a responsible adult capable of being a good friend or life companion and whether young Marcus can find family happiness.

Author Hornby is a fanatical soccer fan, as described in his comic autobiography, *Fever Pitch.* His first novel was *High Fidelity.*

Hornby's two main characters are unusually articulate and yet, at the same time, they and their situations seem real. Does Marcus ever seem too wise for a boy his age? Are their problems—and those of the minor characters—resolved in ways that seem believable?

Can you pinpoint the moments in the novel when Will began to be likable?

Cowboys Are My Weakness, by Pam Houston, Washington Square Press (paperback)

Little more than a decade ago, the women in Pam Houston's stories might have seemed like freaks for their adventuresome ways and their physical toughness. Now we're more accustomed to females on the range or on the rapids, but Houston's heroines are still remarkable because they are so very strong and at the same time funny and vulnerable.

And even though we might be less surprised these days by tales of women taking hard knocks in rough work, it is still rather breathtaking to read twelve tales in a row where the heroines are each more like Annie Oakley than Annie Hall.

Set in a handful of western states, Houston's fiction will have you smiling, laughing, groaning, or crying as her heroines tangle their lives with those of heroes and heels. Her women are strong and gutsy but they are still learning, still making mistakes. Most often, they fall for inaccessible men. "I've always had a thing for cowboys," says the narrator in her title story, "maybe because I was born in New Jersey. But a real cowboy is hard to find these days, even in the West." Maybe it's because she's looking for a cowboy that she's sunk from the start; wasn't this always the guy who found his horse more important than his sweetheart? Houston's heroines philosophize as well as wisecrack, and they do point out the incompatibility of the sexes—but they still have fun going after the opposite gender.

Houston is a part-time river guide and hunting guide, although she is most definitely not a hunter. She is also the author of a more recent story collection called *Waltzing the Cat.*

Houston may observe disappointing relations between the sexes and portray men as unknowable, but men as well as women seem to enjoy her writing. What allows a book that often pokes fun at male behavior also to entertain male readers?

What do we like about women who yearn to be loved by wild, hard-to-win men? Even though the book is regional in setting and style, does it have certain universals that make us connect with Houston's characters?

The Bone People, by Keri Hulme, Penguin Books (paperback)

Winner of Britain's Booker Prize in 1985, *The Bone People* was almost not brought to print in the author's native New Zealand because it was such an unorthodox piece of writing. Published finally by Spiral, a New Zealand feminist collective, this astonishing novel concerns a reclusive woman living on the New Zealand coast whose life is forever changed by the appearance of a young blond waif and his Maori foster father.

Reminiscent of *The English Patient* in the way its language becomes music that sweeps over you, *The Bone People* flows not only in narrative but also in sudden bits of interior thought, poetry, and tastes of Maori language. If you are willing to relax and allow the story slowly to emerge, it will carry you away.

Main character Kerewin Holmes is an artist who can no longer create art, and although she possesses enough money to build a dream tower for herself along the beach, she spends much of each day in her magical spire drinking away anguish. Along comes Simon, a child rescued by locals from a shipwreck. He is unable or unwilling to speak, it is not clear which, although it is evident that his silence has much to do with traumatic events in his early childhood. This mystery boy, who has a way of turning topsy-turvy everything in his path, quickly takes to Kerewin, which is an unfortunate choice, as she is not accustomed to being close to anyone.

Curiosity and anticipation will carry you through this novel. Hulme poses a number of intense questions; the answers may not be what you would expect.

THE BONE PEOPLE *focuses on the potential within families for both destruction and healing. What do you think Hulme concludes about loving relationships? If the tower and the spiral structure at the end are symbols, what do you think they mean?*

Each of Hulme's main characters exhibit shortcomings that are displayed savagely at times. It becomes easy to love Simon, but how did you feel about the other two when the book was done?

The Remains of the Day, by Kazuo Ishiguro, Vintage International (paperback)

Ishiguro's novel is likely to dazzle you or offend you. The book has received either rave reviews or cries of disgust for the way it depicts English society. Winner in 1989 of the Booker Prize, the coveted British literary award, *The Remains of the Day* opens in post–World War II England and introduces us to the perfect English butler, who has sacrificed his life in service to his master. It is at once a criticism of British tradition and a sad and funny portrait of a man dedicated to carrying out his job with complete perfection. It is also a love story.

Although the movie based on this book was adequate, it did not nearly convey the bittersweet irony expressed in the narrator's voice. Ishiguro has captured the language and attitude of the old British empire, attacking it on the sly, revealing its particular cruelty and absurdity.

Some critics, many of them British, have dubbed Ishiguro's performance a samurai's approach to English culture, claiming his perspective is unauthentic. However, Ishiguro is far more English than Japanese. Born in Nagasaki in 1954, he became a resident of Great Britain at age six. After graduating from the University of Kent, he worked as a social worker until a career as an English novelist and TV film writer beckoned. It's possible that a short stint as a grouse beater for the Queen Mother at Balmoral Castle in Scotland when he was nineteen helped shape his views of the British ruling class.

He is also the author of the novels *The Unconsoled, A Pale View of Hills,* and *An Artist of the Floating World.* The latter won England's Whitbread Book of the Year Award.

Stevens has tried to give his life meaning by following his father's example and working hard to keep Darlington running smoothly. Do you think he succeeded on any level?

Did you notice the bit of dialogue from which Ishiguro took the book title? What moral do you think he is offering about lost opportunities?

La Mollie and the King of Tears, by Arturo Islas, University of New Mexico Press, (paperback)

Arturo Islas was a professor of English at Stanford University when he died of AIDS at age fifty-three in 1991. Author of *The Rain God* and *Migrant Souls,* this gifted author wrote a third novel of great liveliness, pain, and humor but did not complete it. Thanks to the editing and persistence of Paul Skenazy, a professor of American literature at the University of California, Santa Cruz, we now have *La Mollie and the King of Tears.*

Louie Mendoza sits in a San Francisco emergency room pouring out his heart about one of the worst days of his life to a stranger with a tape recorder. The stranger is looking for examples of American dialect; Louie is waiting anxiously for a companion to be treated and takes the opportunity to sort out the events of his life and talk away his fears. It is a tribute to Islas's ability as a writer that one long monologue can grab us and play on our emotions for the entire length of a book.

As real as Louie seems, it's intriguing that Islas created him in response to an assignment he'd given his own students: Write a story in a voice as unlike your usual style as you can imagine. As Skenazy reports, "When he did the assignment along with the students, Louie Mendoza started talking and wouldn't stop." Louie emerged as a saxophone player and street-smart philosopher in love with an Anglo lady of dubious intellectual merit.

There is only one thing that might be criticized about the book: The afterword by Skenazy, although at times illuminating, needn't have taken thirty-one pages to explain a novel that stands quite well on its own.

Islas uses Louie to comment on the Chicano condition, with his fast-talking, unstoppable character a man of insight and some sensitivity; a man not afraid to laugh at himself as well as everyone else. As a person positioned between two cultures, did he surprise you with any unusual insights?

How does the author initially create sympathy for Louie so that you are willing to stay with him as it becomes clear that the book will consist mainly of his commentary?

Ground Rules: What I Learned My Daughter's Fifteenth Year, by Sherril Jaffe, Kodansha International (hardcover)

Don't make the mistake of relegating this book to the narrow genre "how I coped with my teenager." Jaffe's *Ground Rules* reads almost like a novel as she leads us through the trauma and suspense of trying to understand, discipline, and help her older daughter and at the same time hold their family together.

An important part of the book's appeal is the author's humor. The wife of a San Francisco rabbi, she not only has an unruly teenager with whom to contend but also must face an entire congregation as their family scenario unfolds. Jaffe is able to laugh at her own ineptitude as a puzzled mom, her husband's threatened public image as a wise man and counselor, and her daughter's contradictory behavior as she vacillates between child and woman.

The result is a memoir that anyone who has ever been a parent is likely to appreciate. Your child may not have run away or skipped school as Jaffe's did, but he or she is likely to have caused worry and confusion in your household. Jaffe asks herself hard questions that most of us ask in the course of raising children. Her honesty in portraying her own confusion and possible mistakes is refreshing and valuable. Her description of the beginning of a solution for her own family is downright encouraging.

Jaffe is the author of both fiction and nonfiction, including *The Unexamined Wife* and *Scars Make Your Body More Interesting and Other Stories*. She is now at work on a nonfiction book, *The Zen Rabbi*.

KIRKUS REVIEWS *criticized Jaffe for not thoroughly examining why the child of two apparently loving parents would steal from them, lie to them, shoplift, disappear for days on end, and fail in school, saying this is not "run-of-the-mill teen rebelliousness." Although your children probably don't exhibit all of these behaviors, do these problems seem like only remote possibilities?*

Do you think it might have been detrimental to Rebekah to have her mother reveal their problems so thoroughly in a book?

King & Raven, by Cary James, Tor Books (paperback)

Instead of a sequel to Marion Zimmer Bradley's unforgettable *Mists of Avalon,* how about a parallel story, this time from the point of view of a teenage boy? In the Camelot legend there's room for numerous interrelated stories, and in his extremely rewarding first novel James has given us the pleasure of revisiting the Arthurian legend with a fresh perspective.

In thirteenth-century Britain, Micah of Greenfarm, the fourteen-year-old son of impoverished English farmers, sets out to seek revenge for the rape and murder of his sister at the hands of four of King Arthur's knights. To do so, he must slip the bonds of peasant life and attempt to gain access to the world of chivalry, courtly love, and deadly revelry. He leaves his family farm near Camelot, finds a way to gain entry to the castle, and from there ends up traveling across the sea to Normandy and Anjou, where finally he is dubbed a knight. When he returns to Camelot, it is near the end of Arthur's quest for the holy grail. Close to achieving revenge, he finds that his oath may be impossible to uphold, as he is now torn between his loyalty to the ideals of chivalry and his desire to save Camelot and a hatred for the men who destroyed his sister.

Although marketed as fantasy genre, with an eye to the young adult market, this novel is also serious adult fiction. James's writing is no more otherworldly than Alice Hoffman's *Second Nature* or *Turtle Moon,* no more youth-oriented than Ella Leffland's coming-of-age story, *Rumors of Peace.* The narrative and dialogue of *King & Raven* are steeped in the language of ancient England. The characters roam through a carefully researched medieval landscape. When there is magic, it pops up in the midst of sweaty, detailed reality.

Choosing the perspective of a peasant boy lends the Arthurian legend a feeling of authenticity that other versions of the legend don't offer. Can you think of examples of gritty realism that made James's story seem based in a real time and place?

In Cornish legend, Arthur's soul entered a raven's body upon his death. Do you see a tie-in with Micah's choice of the name Raven?

A Very Long Engagement, by Sebastien Japrisot, translated from the French by Linda Coverdale, Plume (paperback)

Do not start reading this book in the bookstore; the suspense is such that you might not leave until the lights are turned out. A runaway best-seller in France and winner of the 1991 Prix Interallie, *A Very Long Engagement* is an odd, provocative combination of fairy tale and war story. Set during World War I, the book is one more testimonial to the reasons the conflict should never have been dubbed "The Great War." Japrisot has made his account of the madness palatable by mixing in romance, mystery, and humor.

Mathilde, a lovely young woman confined to a wheelchair since childhood, refuses to believe the official notice that her fiancé has been killed in the line of duty. Unfortunately for the authorities, she is wealthy and can pursue the truth for as long as it takes. Although disabled, she is not weak, and her spunky nature adds to the suspense, for you are never quite sure what she will do or say next.

Why does Mathilde mistrust news of her lover's death? She has heard a strange tale from a dying veteran: Five soldiers were tried by the French military for their attempts to flee service, and their punishment was to be thrown over the French line at a spot called Bingo Crepuscule, where presumably they would die in German crossfire. Mathilde's fiancé was one of the five. She pieces together numerous accounts of the events at Bingo Crepuscule, trying to make sense of conflicting stories, attempting to dig up what has been hidden, searching for explanations that will fill in the gaps in a severely fragmented puzzle.

As a comforting counterpoint to the brutality of this war tale and its cast of unsavory accomplices, Japrisot surrounds Mathilde with colorful, likable family and friends and gives her a sense of integrity that cannot be compromised.

Japrisot has also written *One Deadly Summer, The Lady in the Car with Glasses and a Gun, The Sleeping Car Murders,* and *Women in Evidence.*

This book has been called a latter-day WAR AND PEACE. *Do you think this is an appropriate comparison? Does the playful quality of the narrative diminish the seriousness of Japrisot's implicit criticism of war and official corruption?*

Le Divorce, by Diane Johnson, Plume (paperback)

C'est fantastique! Divorce may not seem like a particularly amusing topic or the source of much suspense, but Diane Johnson has devised an exceedingly witty tale of intrigue based on the circumstances of one young woman's broken marriage and the conflict between the two cultures involved.

Le Divorce is recounted by the perky, insightful Isabel Walker, a California film school dropout who has volunteered to come to Paris to assist her older sister as she awaits the birth of her second child. Isabel arrives in Paris to find that her sister Roxanne has been jilted by her French husband, Charles-Henri, who claims that he has fallen completely and passionately in love with another woman.

One dilemma follows another, with sister Roxanne refusing to divorce, Charles-Henri's family urging Roxanne to overlook her husband's indiscretion and stay married to him, a suddenly valuable painting owned by the Walkers getting in the way of a possible divorce settlement, and Isabel falling into an unsettling love affair of her own.

All along the way, we are treated to Isabel's reflections on the differences between French and American culture and her own growing attachment to the Parisian way of life. Her delight in gradually learning to understand French, her combined disdain and affection for Gallic customs, and her reflections on human behavior in general, all add wonderful layers of interest to Johnson's amusing story.

Johnson, who lives in both San Francisco and Paris, is the author of numerous other books, both fiction and nonfiction. Her novels include *Burning, Persian Nights, Lying Low,* and *Lesser Lives.* She has been a two-time finalist for both the Pulitzer Prize and the National Book Award.

Does the Hollywood-style violent action toward the end of the book undo the sly, witty flavor of Johnson's social comedy?

Some have compared Isabel Walker in LE DIVORCE *with Henry*

James's innocent aboard, Isabel Archer. Do you think this is a fair comparison?

Perhaps the strongest elements of Johnson's writing in this book are the establishment of setting and her ability to capture the experience of living in a new culture. What do you think of her characterization and plot structure?

Geography of the Heart, by Fenton Johnson, Pocket Books (paperback)

Granted, there are plenty of published love stories in the world, but this one is different from most because it involves two men. In *Geography of the Heart,* Fenton Johnson tells, with a professional author's acuity and eloquence, the true story of his love affair with Berkeley high school teacher Larry Rose, and how, in spite of Larry's eventual death from AIDS, Johnson came to see himself as a lucky man.

Johnson is not afraid to meet difficult questions head on. Why would a man who is not HIV-positive allow himself to become involved with one who was? How did it happen that he, one of nine children of a devoutly Catholic rural Kentucky family and unused to a possessive kind of love, fell in love with the only, indulged child of German Jews who were Holocaust survivors? How was it that Larry, in the midst of his suffering, could teach Johnson about feeling fortunate?

Larry cheerfully and relentlessly pursued Johnson, who just as stubbornly resisted entanglement. Johnson feared Larry's HIV-positive status, he feared having to take care of Larry once he developed AIDS, and he feared having to bear the loss of someone he allowed himself to love. When he finally gave in, Johnson discovered that the experience of loving Larry enlarged his life.

The AIDS aspect of this story does not control it. *Geography of the Heart* is an enjoyable, positive story that details how two souls who differ greatly could meet, fall in love, and have a relationship that endured.

Johnson is also the author of *Songs of the Soil, Crossing the River,* and *Scissors, Paper, Rock.*

GEOGRAPHY OF THE HEART *does make us cry but manages to avoid sentimentality. How does Johnson achieve this?*

There have been many memoirs published in recent times; Johnson's has gone beyond the usual life story to offer certain lessons. What special ideas do you think he had to offer?

Shooting the Boh: A Woman's Voyage Down the Wildest River in Borneo, by Tracy Johnston, Vintage Departures (paperback)

Early on it becomes clear that this will be an unusual adventure. On the morning of departure, the natives standing alongside the shore, having failed to persuade Johnston and the other river rafters not to go, begin to cry.

The Boh River in Borneo was not known to be navigable, and the country it penetrated was not hospitable. Longtime traveler Tracy Johnston explains that her decision to take this particular journey rose primarily out of a need to prove herself as she felt her youth slipping away—and that the decision was foolhardy. Things began to go wrong almost immediately.

For all of us concerned about saving the rain forest, here's a good lesson in what the rain forest actually is. It's full of slimy leeches, dangerous insects, poisonous snakes, and unrelenting moisture. You can't sit on a log for a moment without being attacked by something or other. Not only should we save the rain forest, we should stay out of it.

There are also high points to this passage down the river, and Johnston conveys them with wry humor and pleasure.

Her fellow crew members are two high-fashion models, a wealthy Italian, a Florida couple, a Chicago attorney, and two young Australians. Our anxiety for them builds as they take themselves farther and farther along the perilous route. Clouds of sweat bees swarm them, wild rapids toss them, Tracy enters menopause, and a certain amount of romance manages to blossom. It's a thrilling ride, especially since you get to experience it as a reader and not as a rafter.

Although Johnston shows a bravery and sense of daring that make her seem unusual, the reader is able to identify with her. What kinds of things does she reveal about herself that make it possible for us to identify and even imagine that we are there with her, experiencing this wild ride?

Savages, by Joe Kane, Vintage Books (paperback)

Joe Kane has given us a rare gift by introducing us to a nomadic tribal culture that for thousands of years fiercely guarded its home and its privacy in the Ecuadorian rain forest. We come to know the Huaorani people of *Savages* and learn of their heroism as Stone Age people fighting the corporate oil interests of a twentieth-century world.

One of the amazing things about the research for this book is that the Huaorani were just as likely to murder Kane as to befriend him. The spear-carrying Amazon warriors had killed a missionary they didn't trust and routinely killed others they identified as enemies, but they seemed to sense that Kane was both a sincere friend and an expert communicator, someone who could tell the larger world about their struggle to save their land.

Winner of the Bay Area Book Reviewers Association Award for nonfiction in 1995, *Savages* details Kane's time spent traveling with the Huaorani in their territory as well as in urban Ecuador and Washington, D.C.

Kane's admiration and love of tribe members comes through in a series of memorable vignettes. In the same way that tribe members lost their warrior stance and became vulnerable and childlike in an urban setting, he would become dazed and confused when faced with the harsh rigors of their jungle life. While the Huaorani were used to going for days without eating and then bingeing when they caught a monkey, Kane came close to starving to death between meals. In the same way that they shared the bounty of the hunt, the Huaorani would leave Kane's apartment wearing his backpack, tie, shirts, and sunglasses, which, of course, now had become theirs.

Kane is also the author of *Running the Amazon.*

Did Kane maintain adequate arms-length distance from the Huaorani to be termed an objective observer? Does this matter?

The search for oil seems to bring inevitable environmental destruction. What can we do about it?

A River Town, by Thomas Keneally, Plume (paperback)

Australian Thomas Keneally is the author of *Schindler's List,* winner of Britain's Booker Prize in 1982 and the basis for Steven Spielberg's award-winning film. His novel *A River Town* is another, quieter story about displaced people, this time based on Keneally's grandfather's experience as an Irish immigrant in Australia at the turn of the century.

Although not written on the same epic scale as *Schindler's List, A River Town* is powerful in its own right, telling many stories simultaneously. First, there is the account of an Irish family trying to make a go of it in the Australian frontier. Second there is the moving story of a husband's imperfect, and very real, love for his plump wife. Third, there is the tale of an immigrant's prejudice against other minority newcomers in his adopted country. And fourth, there is a murder mystery involving an unidentified girl. Keneally threads these stories together with mastery into a satisfying whole.

Other books by Keneally include *The Great Shame: And the Triumph of the Irish in the English-Speaking World, Bring Larks and Heroes, The Chant of Jimmie Blacksmith, A Family Madness, Woman of the Inner Sea,* and *To Asmara.*

Keneally has sometimes stirred controversy by basing his stories closely on real people and events. When SCHINDLER'S LIST *was first published, the literary world argued at length whether Keneally had written fiction or nonfiction. The events were true, while the dramatized scenes were Keneally's creations. Here again, in* A RIVER TOWN, *there is a blending of history and dramatization. Does the use of fictional characters and events diminish the accuracy of the historical backdrop or the importance of his grandfather's experience as an immigrant?*

Tim Shea is eager to be rid of the restrictive social mores of his native country, but he finds the rowdy ways of the Australians hard to accept. What do you think Keneally is trying to say about the dreams and struggles of immigrants and the baggage they carry with them from the old country?

Green Grass, Running Water, by Thomas King, Bantam Books (paperback)

This is a funny little book. At first it seems incomprehensible. King jumps from one peculiar scene to another, taking us from an offbeat creation myth that includes pizza and television and the irrepressible Coyote, to four old coots on the lam from a mental lockup, to the romance problems of a female college professor. Gradually, if you're patient, *Green Grass, Running Water* coalesces into a moving tale of Native American life in modern America and culminates in an elaborate joke honoring the Columbus Quincentennial.

In recent years, books by Native American authors have begun to fill the gap for that ethnic group in this nation's literature. Accomplished writers like Louise Erdrich, Michael Dorris, and Greg Sarris have written about their people with affection and realism. What makes King's book so interesting—and different—is its wacky humor and irreverence. Like Sherman Alexie, he isn't afraid to poke fun at Native Americans or at white culture, but he distinguishes himself from Alexie with unconventional story structure and characters that are truly eccentric.

Although his story seems surreal at times, King is good at down-to-earth dialogue. Listening to the exchanges between his characters, you feel you are eavesdropping on real conversations. Sarcasm, irony, frustration, and misunderstanding abound.

The chair of American Indian studies at the University of Minnesota, King is also the author of the highly acclaimed novel *Medicine River.*

King's wicked sense of humor is often aimed at men, satirizing their phallus-centered myths. Can you recall any other male authors who are willing to take potshots at their gender's macho hang-ups this way?

Apart from being extremely amusing, what does King's book tell you about being a Native American in Canada?

In throwing together two strong, sassy women with three hard-luck men, what does King suggest about Native Americans finding a middle ground between their old ways and the modern world?

Animal Dreams, by Barbara Kingsolver, HarperPerennial (paperback)

The novel *The Bean Trees* earned Barbara Kingsolver recognition in the American literary world when it was published in 1988. For many readers, her next book, *Animal Dreams,* was the real winner. However, there are now a lot of Kingsolver fans, and each time a novel of hers is published, they pronounce it the best, so you may well be told that *Pigs in Heaven* or *Poisonwood Bible* is tops. Read them all; you'll have a great time, and you'll also be a better person for it, as Kingsolver always conveys important social messages in her writing.

"Animals dream about the things they do in the daytime, just like people do. If you want sweet dreams, you've got to live a sweet life," says Lloyd, the Apache love interest in *Animal Dreams.* And this is what this novel is about, finding a sweet life among good people, even if it means coming home to a small town you thought you'd outgrown.

Codi returns to Grace, Arizona, a young woman without a career or attachments of any kind, save a passionate bond to her younger sister, who has gone off to war-torn Nicaragua. Codi discovers that her life finally takes on meaning amidst the closely knit population of this tiny southwestern community. Grace saves Codi, and, in a surprising turn, she helps to save Grace.

Kingsolver tells her story in a voice that blends Hispanic, Native American, and modern American culture in a distinct rhythm. The writing is lush and at the same time refuses to take itself too seriously, with frequent infusions of wit and gentle sarcasm.

Kingsolver is also the author of excellent nonfiction: *High Tide in Tucson,* a collection of essays regarding life in the Southwest, and *Holding the Line: Women in the Great Arizona Mine Strike of 1983.*

Although both social and political awareness are extremely important to Kingsolver, she manages to incorporate her issues into fiction that can be read by those looking purely for entertainment. How does the author manage to be so sneaky, getting across important messages without standing on a soapbox?

The Woman Warrior: Memoirs of a Girlhood Among Ghosts, by Maxine Hong Kingston, Vintage Books (paperback)

Well before Amy Tan's novels hit the best-seller lists with stories of modern young women confronting the ghosts of an Asian past, Maxine Hong Kingston won both literary and popular acclaim for her nonfiction writing about growing up Chinese American.

Winner of the National Book Critics Circle Award in 1976, *The Woman Warrior* traces Kingston's childhood in California's Central Valley, where she attended both American school and Chinese school, worked in the family laundry, and listened to the instructive stories her mother pulled from the past to scare her into good behavior.

As a little girl, Kingston had to figure out the multiple contradictions in her life, including a partial picture of the culture that her parents left behind. As she was not purely Chinese, her mother could not confide completely the stories of her past in China. However, there were "talk stories" she could share, where women were warriors. Yet these stories also illustrated that women were slaves and had to be clever and strong to fight their way to what they wanted.

Kingston's memoir is intense, introspective, and full of the unexpected. The American laundress who had been a Chinese doctor, the trip across the state to find a husband not seen for thirty years, and the mentally retarded boy who follows Maxine home after class are all part of a rich montage that beautifully illuminates a life lived between two cultures.

Kingston is also the author of *China Men, Tripmaster Monkey,* and *Hawaii One Summer.*

For Kingston's family, anyone who is not Chinese is called a "ghost." And yet in China, ghosts are supernatural beings. Does this mean that the non-Chinese hold unusual power over the Chinese immigrants, or is this term cast only as an aspersion?

As she attempted to explain her dual world, young Kingston created stories of her own, filling in the blanks her mother left. Did her new stories help her to adjust to the facts of American life, or did they have their own blanks?

The Fisherman's Son, by Michael Koepf, Broadway Books (paperback)

This is such a strong, uncomplicated novel that there's a danger in writing too much or too complexly about it. Michael Koepf has crafted a deeply stirring ode to the ocean and the way of life of the men who fish upon it, as experienced by a young boy growing up in Half Moon Bay, on the foggy, rugged, and beautiful coast just south of San Francisco. Koepf's novel is also a family drama and a coming-of-age tale that illuminates the conflict between the oceangoing life and the world back on shore.

The Fisherman's Son opens with Neil Kruger adrift in a lifeboat in the midst of a raging storm. As he struggles to stay alive and to maintain hope, he summons up memories of his fisherman father and his father's membership in that isolated group of men who earned their living pulling fish from the sea. Kruger also slowly recalls the events that led him to his current predicament.

Koepf's prose is both eloquent and poetic. Underlying it is the immense power of the ocean: a constant threat and yet a tantalizing mistress to the men who float upon it. The writing in this book is spectacular in its precise, accomplished nature, particularly since Koepf has not spent a lifetime writing. He has, however, put in nineteen years as a commercial fisherman, worked some as a journalist and teacher, written one other published book *(Save the Whale),* and served as principal of a one-room schoolhouse. At present he lives in a tiny town on the northern California coast, where he is writing a screenplay about Lewis and Clark for Steven Spielberg's Dreamworks SKG.

Neil's father is a single-minded man, willing to plunge his family into debt because he refuses to give up the fishing life as it becomes clear the trade is dying out. Is Ernie Kruger a man we respect?

Neil remembers again and again his mother's request that he promise never to make his life on the sea, and the way she violated her own words by sending him out with his father. This is a pivotal moment in the book; what do you think Koepf is trying to say with this contradiction?

Ishi in Two Worlds: A Biography of the Last Wild Indian in North America, by Theodora Kroeber, University of California Press (paperback)

When Ishi stepped out of the woods and into the world of white people near the town of Oroville in northern California in 1911, he believed he was headed for death. The last of the Yana tribe, he had seen his people slaughtered by whites over the five decades of his life. Now he assumed that the white people would murder him, too.

Fortunately, when local headlines about "The Wild Man of Oroville" being held for his own protection in the local jail spread to the San Francisco papers, anthropologists Alfred Kroeber and T. T. Waterman at the University of California at Berkeley took note. They were among the few people in the country at the time equipped to understand his predicament and to help. They brought him to the university, tried to make him comfortable, and gradually uncovered the story of who he was and how his people had lived.

Theodora Kroeber, wife of the famed anthropologist, tells the story with sympathy and understanding, giving it historical context and relating Ishi's experiences as a Stone Age man adjusting to the modern world. Ishi lived—and died—at the university's Museum of Anthropology in San Francisco, and while he readily learned the language and customs of trolley-car modern America, he never gave up the dignity of his own people.

Theodora Kroeber's very moving book was first published in 1961, a year after her husband had died, and in the introduction, Lewis Gannet called it "one of the great American stories, a contribution not only to our history but to our literature." Perhaps one reason Kroeber's account has become a classic is that she did not whitewash the behavior of the white people who worked with Ishi. If Ishi's emergence could be repeated today, how would you hope his treatment would differ? Is it possible to study people of other cultures and at the same time allow them to preserve their dignity and the integrity of their ways?

***Bird by Bird: Some Instructions on Writing and Life*, by Anne Lamott, Anchor Books (paperback)**

In spite of Lamott's subtitle, this is not just an instruction book for writers. You can merely be an avid reader and love this book. There are two reasons: (1) Lamott, who is a very amusing woman, tells a lot of entertaining stories, and (2) she helps you to understand what it is that makes you like any piece of writing.

An example of the first: what Lamott's friends have to say when she makes a point of having her three-year-old view a dead person.

An example of the latter:

> The climax is that major event, usually toward the end, that brings all the tunes you have been playing so far into one major chord, after which at least one of your people is profoundly changed. If someone isn't changed, then what is the point of your story? For the climax, there must be a killing or a healing or a domination. It can be a real killing, a murder, or it can be a killing of the spirit, or of something terrible inside one's soul, or it can be a killing of a deadness within, after which the person becomes alive again.

Of course, there's also the strong possibility that, after reading her book, you might also end up doing writing of your own, since Lamott has led you so engagingly through the process.

If you haven't looked at *Operating Instructions,* Lamott's hilarious and sad account of her son's first year of life and her best friend's last year, do so (see next entry). Lamott has also written a number of novels, including *Crooked Little Heart, Hard Laughter, Rosie,* and *All New People.* Her most recent nonfiction book is *Traveling Mercies: Some Thoughts on Faith.*

Lamott tends to offer writing lessons that are also life lessons. Give yourself short assignments, she says. Just get it out, she advises; expect a "shitty first draft." Can you think of any other advice of hers that could help with completing all sorts of tasks?

Operating Instructions: A Journal of My Son's First Year, by Anne Lamott, Fawcett Columbine (paperback)

With this book Anne Lamott hit her stride as a humorous writer. Lamott already had a loyal following for her novels *Hard Laughter, Rosie, Joe Jones,* and *All New People* when she chose to chronicle the first year of her only child, Sam, letting loose with neuroses, bliss, and self-mockery that can be appreciated best by those who've experienced the wild highs and lows of beginning parenthood.

Lamott has the courage to say what many think when they are annihilated by weariness from caring for a newborn: She wants to send the child back to wherever he came from. There's an odd comfort in these words. Said aloud, they voice our own worst thoughts and render them ridiculous; Lamott exposes our most depraved parental moments and helps us to put them past. She also provides fair warning to anyone who has not yet experienced them.

The writing in *Operating Instructions* combines the best of Lamott: witty sarcasm, tender moments, loving portraits, and glimpses of a funky, hip life thrown together unpredictably. Lamott can give us a heavenly interval resting under a tree with a baby Sam or abruptly recount how she warned him that Nixon was a bad president. She's not shy about the fact that she's newly sober and newly religious. Woven into her tale of Sam's arrival in her life is the story of the departure of Lamott's dear friend Pammy as she died from breast cancer. The mix is bittersweet.

Lamott's other nonfiction includes *Bird by Bird: Some Instructions on Writing and Life* (see previous entry) and *Traveling Mercies: Some Thoughts on Faith.* Her latest fiction is *Crooked Little Heart.*

Lamott captures our attention because she is a single mother living in an offbeat community with an unusual group of family and friends who lend support. On top of that, she's a recovering alcoholic and a suddenly devout Christian. As unusual as this combination may be, she reaches us by communicating certain universal experiences. What are the aspects of her new motherhood that ring true for most new parents?

Breath and Shadows, by Ella Leffland, William Morrow (hardcover)

The latest book by the well-loved, reclusive San Francisco author Ella Leffland proves that she has incredible breadth as an author, both in her ability to create a diverse cast of characters and in her graceful handling of a new historical backdrop. If you relished the classic *Rumors of Peace* (see next entry) or *The Knight, Death, and the Devil,* both set in the World War II era, be prepared for something equally memorable but much different.

In *Breath and Shadows* Leffland traces a Danish family's history by spotlighting three generations, each separated by a century. Although they know little or nothing of each other, we begin to see the connections and the influence of each on the other. A misshapen dwarf living in the 1700s manages to win our sympathy and our disgust at the same time. A lovely, affluent couple residing with their children in a comfortable country home in the 1800s catch our attention with ominous hints of downfall. A brother and sister living in modern-day Switzerland and America suffer a strange ennui in spite of their relatively privileged lives—an ennui that perhaps can be alleviated if they uncover the stories of the people who preceded them. A sense of history, Leffland seems to be saying, is essential to forming a satisfying identity in the present.

Speaking of diverse characters, this is the only novel I can recall where a cat becomes a serious figure. Leffland manages to reveal his reasoning without becoming cute or disingenuous.

One of many themes in BREATH AND SHADOWS *is the idea that all of us need to believe in something greater than ourselves. As Leffland pointed out in a recent interview, even Olaf the cat feels a hunger greater than that for food. Can you identify that need for each of the main characters?*

Leffland seems to indicate that none of her characters are ever truly known to each other, and some of them are not known to themselves. Did any characters strike you as having a particularly good understanding of themselves?

Rumors of Peace, by Ella Leffland, HarperPerennial (paperback)

Here's a book that has beaten the odds in modern publishing. While most novels come and go from the bookstores after a few seasons, *Rumors of Peace* has been available for two decades. It is quietly becoming an American classic.

Leffland's novel is a sensitive and sometimes droll coming-of-age story combined with a revealing view of small-town America during a terrifying period in U.S. history. The setting is the San Francisco Bay area during World War II, and the main character is a young girl traumatized by screaming headlines and threats of bombing in her own backyard.

The characters are an intriguing, unpredictable group, beginning with Suse, the heroine. A bright, attractive child who has made the decision that school is a waste of time, she has been placed in the class for troublesome and backward children. There she meets Peggy, who becomes her best friend and who inadvertently provides entry to the world of the intellect.

That the war terrifies her, that she feels seething hatred of the immigrant Japanese living nearby, that she believes she may die at any moment, Suse keeps to herself, suffering tremendously over her private worries. By the time the book ends and the war is over, both the conflict and her curiosity about it have transformed her.

Other books by Leffland include *Breath and Shadows* (see previous entry) and *The Knight, Death, and the Devil.*

What is the effect of having a sympathetic character like Suse experience strong, ugly prejudice toward Japanese Americans? Do you like the character less?

Leffland portrays the classic struggle between growing up and retaining the innocence of childhood. As Suse develops emotionally and intellectually, are you sorry to see her let go of innocence?

It's tempting to think of RUMORS OF PEACE *as factual memoir. Does it make the story more powerful if you believe that it is entirely true? Why would an author choose to write a novel rather than nonfiction in telling a story based on fact?*

Postcards from France, by Megan McNeill Libby, HarperPaperbacks (paperback)

Megan McNeil Libby was a spirited sixteen-year-old high schooler when she went off to France as an American Field Service student for the 1994–95 school year. Her "postcards" are a series of informative and often amusing columns she sent back home for the local paper in her Connecticut town, describing the humbling experience of becoming a newcomer in another culture.

As her editor at *The Ridgefield Press* points out in his introduction, Libby is a talented writer whose work became progressively more accomplished and engaging as the months in Valence, France, went by. Her accounts of difficulty in actually speaking French with French people after diligently studying the language for two years are valuable for anyone who might plan to do what she did. Her description of the moment, when it finally arrived, that she could understand clearly and even think in this other language is exhilarating.

Sections of this book are downright comic: for instance, Libby's articles on the attitudes of the French toward their dogs and the difficulty of cooking a Thanksgiving dinner in a Gallic setting. On the other hand, she effectively tells of heartaches, as in her descriptions of feeling isolated on the first day of school, or of her continuing frustration over her failure to communicate adequately.

Although she has not yet authored another book, it's clear that Libby is likely to become an accomplished professional writer. Hopefully, she's continuing to do creative writing as a college student.

Is this a guide for travelers only? Would you recommend Libby's POSTCARDS *to someone as a worthwhile read for other reasons?*

Is Libby's account of cooking venison for Thanksgiving dinner entirely funny? At moments does it reveal how narrow the expectations of Americans can be? Would we know how to celebrate Bastille Day?

After reading Libby's POSTCARDS, *would you be more likely to send a child of yours to live abroad? Does Libby display a certain sophistication and readiness for adventure that particularly qualify her for this kind of experience?*

Cleopatra's Sister, by Penelope Lively, HarperPerennial (paperback)

Watch out—it's easy to become a Penelope Lively addict. This witty and thoughtful prize-winning British author has written an awful lot of novels and short stories, and if you like her as much as some of us do, you can make a career out of reading her work.

In *Cleopatra's Sister* she spins a tale of two improbable lovers, Howard and Lucy, who meet in the midst of crisis when their plane is suddenly forced to land in modern-day North Africa. The tiny nation of Callimbia where they touch down is obviously the creation of the author, but her love story rings with such wonderful moments of truth—and satire on Third World politics—that the entire drama becomes real.

Lively has a way of creating delicious moments that engender conflicting and unexpected emotions. Her two main characters, along with the rest of the plane's passengers, are filled with fear when their plane is forced down, and their terror increases as events unfold. Yet, at the same time, Howard and Lucy begin to feel sparks of pleasure as gradually they come to know each other.

The country of Callimbia could be considered a third important character in *Cleopatra's Sister.* It is meant to represent many small countries in upheaval, and although Lively takes seriously the problems and the resulting conflicts of its people, she does not let Callimbia escape the touch of her humor.

Lively is also the author of *Heat Wave* (see next entry), *Spiderweb,* and *Moon Tiger,* winner of the Booker Prize in 1987.

When you were done with CLEOPATRA'S SISTER, *did you feel you'd read a light romance about star-crossed lovers, or did Lively create a strong enough sense of danger to make you take her political backdrop seriously and understand all the possible outcomes?*

Clearly the author had fun creating a national history. What do you think she was trying to say about the real historical record?

Heat Wave, by Penelope Lively, HarperPerennial (paperback)

This apparently quiet little story gains momentum with each page, as step by step Lively throws open the romantic lives of a mother and her grown daughter. By the end, the mild tale has turned stunning.

Winner of the Booker Prize for *Moon Tiger,* Lively is a prolific English author. Why her name isn't widely known in the United States is a mystery; if her stories are all like this one, it could be that we Americans have trouble holding still long enough to let her narratives creep up on us. At the opening of *Heat Wave,* there is no immediate conflict, violence, or obvious problem to draw the reader in. However, do yourself a favor and read on.

Fifty-five-year-old Pauline is a book editor spending the summer in a glorious bit of English countryside. Staying there, too, are her daughter, tiny grandson, and son-in-law. As she gets a closer look at her daughter's relationship with her husband, certain questions begin to gnaw at Pauline, and she is filled with dread.

Telling observations of lovers, reflections on modern life compared to the good old days, and musings on nature are all laid out by Lively in a lovely, crisp prose style, in the voice of Pauline, who does not suffer fools gladly. The dialogue is sparse but perfect. We come to like Lively's people a lot, except for the ones she hates.

Lively's other novels include *Cleopatra's Sister* (see previous entry), *Spiderweb, Pack of Cards, The Road to Lichfield,* and *Passing On.*

In her quiet setting, Lively lays the groundwork for all kinds of tension. In addition to Pauline's longtime distrust of Maurice and her daughter's obvious love for him, what other threads of conflict crisscross to create massive tension?

Lively uses relatively muted language to convey simmering, intense emotions. How does she do it? Are there certain gestures and words spoken along the way that contribute to the sense of threat?

Foreign Affairs, by Alison Lurie, Avon Books (paperback)

Winner of the Pulitzer Prize for fiction in 1985, *Foreign Affairs* is a deceptively simple story about two professors on sabbatical to do research in London. Each finds a lover, but with unexpected results, and the two accumulate more knowledge about love than they do about their fields of study during their six months abroad. In relating the stories of fifty-four-year-old Vinnie and young Fred, Alison Lurie takes the opportunity to poke fun at social mores and to play with the boundaries between illusion and reality.

Vinnie has decided that, although she's been married, she has never truly been loved, probably because she is not pretty. When she meets Chuck Mumpson on the plane to England, he does not seem to be the answer to her dreams. A loud, retired waste disposal engineer dressed in Oklahoma cowboy garb, he is repellent, if anything. However, against a backdrop of glittering English society, this unsophisticated American teaches a supposedly suave intellectual that goodness is more important than beauty or social finesse.

Alternating with the chapters about Vinnie are those involving Fred, who takes up with a titled British actress and gains entry to her privileged circle of friends. All the while, the story is told in the voice of an omniscient narrator who provides wickedly sarcastic and amusing commentary.

Lurie is also the author of *Imaginary Friends, The Last Resort, The Truth About Lorin Jones, The War Between the Tates,* and *Love and Friendship.*

What is the source of drama in FOREIGN AFFAIRS*? What is the conflict or dilemma you hope will be resolved? In fiction, the story usually comes to a climax when the main character has taken action that intensifies his or her situation, often making it worse. What would you call the climax of Lurie's novel?*

How does Lurie hold your interest without introducing sensational situations or the threat of violence?

Palace Walk, by Naguib Mahfouz, Anchor Books (paperback)

In 1988 Naguib Mahfouz was awarded the Nobel Prize for literature, the first Arab author to be so honored. His success as a fiction writer led to the popularization of the novel and short story in the Arab world, where poetry was long considered the only serious literary medium.

Mahfouz's work translates well into English, and this gifted Eastern author has captured his exotic culture within a story form long enjoyed in the West: the good old-fashioned family saga. *Palace Walk* is the first book in Mahfouz's Cairo trilogy, which follows three generations of a middle-class Egyptian family beginning in the early 1900s. In particular, if you have always wanted to know what it is like to be a female living in the Arab world, *Palace Walk* will provide plenty of insight. The title refers to the street upon which the family lives, and over which the mother is able to view the male population freely coming and going.

Al-Sayyid Ahmad, a Cairo shopkeeper and the father in this saga, leads a dual life: that of a harsh authority figure at home and of a bon vivant on the town. His dutiful wife Amina may seem like a mouse in a cage at first, but be prepared for a few surprises.

Mahfouz's political leanings in favor of peace with Israel have made him the target of death threats, and his book *Children of Gebelaawi,* an allegory about the world's monotheistic religions that ends with the death of God, has inflamed Arab fundamentalists. In 1994 the eighty-two-year-old author was stabbed outside his home in Cairo but survived the attack.

Books by Mahfouz published in the United States include *Arabian Nights and Days* and *Children of the Alley.*

An important backdrop for PALACE WALK *and the two following books,* PALACE OF DESIRE *and* SUGAR STREET, *is Cairo in the 1950s, when a military coup overthrew King Farouk, ended Egyptian monarchy, and made way for the rise of power of Colonel Gamal Abdel Nasser. Can you recall examples of political change and inklings of social change that come to light in Mahfouz's powerful writing?*

***Dreams of My Russian Summers,* by Andrei Makine, translated from the French by Geoffrey Strachan, Scribner (paperback)**

Andrei Makine was born in Siberia in 1957 and was granted political asylum in France in 1987. This lyrical description of his childhood, which was strongly influenced by his French grandmother, is a memorable account of life in Communist Russia and an ode to the woman who gave him other worlds of which to dream.

Makine and his sister visited their grandmother Charlotte at the edge of the vast steppes each summer, looking forward to evenings in which she spun tales of long-ago Paris, sang Gallic songs, and read poetry and news clippings that told of a fantastical land where people might attend the opera or elegantly protest the policies of a visiting czar. Trapped in Soviet Russia just after the revolution, the French-born Charlotte had married a Russian and become a hardworking Soviet wife and mother, but she never was transformed into a dowdy babushka or lost the special qualities that linked her to another nation.

Although laced with harsh accounts of Soviet life and wartime brutality, Makine's book has a dreamy quality. He unfolds his childhood in impressionistic bits and pieces alternating with the facts of his grandmother's history. This is not a memoir to gobble up quickly, but rather to muse over, in the same way that Makine and his sister sat on their grandmother's flower-laden balcony on lazy summer evenings, imagining scenes of high theater thousands of miles and years away.

Winner of both of France's top literary prizes, the Prix Goncourt and the Prix Medicis, *Dreams of My Russian Summers* is an unexpected combination of sentimental reminiscence, unflinching insight into the Russian character, and, finally, jarring surprise.

Makine more recently authored the novel *Once upon the River Love.*

DREAMS OF MY RUSSIAN SUMMERS *has been called a love letter to an extraordinary woman. Charlotte Lemonnier's voice is the predominant one in this autobiography, but of course the character of the young boy comes through as well. Compared to his grandmother, how does his character fare? Do you like him? Do you care about him?*

Makine's impressive, romantic use of language conveys the differences in sensibility between his French and Russian heritages. Can you find passages in the book that illustrate these cultural differences?

An Imaginary Life, by David Malouf, Vintage Books (paperback)

In the first century A.D., the popular and prolific poet Ovid was banished from Rome and sent to live on the edge of the known world. His ancient exile inspired modern Australian novelist David Malouf to write a brilliant little novel about civilization and its relative merits. Malouf imagines the sophisticated Ovid living with barbarians near the Black Sea, at first unable to converse with his primitive hosts and appalled by the loss of what he considers very advanced Roman society and its amenities.

Into this picture comes a feral child, a young boy who apparently has grown up only in the company of deer. During a hunting expedition, Ovid is drawn to this elusive creature and tries to befriend him, thereby pulling him into the primitive circle of civilization of his hosts. The results are dangerous for both him and the child.

Malouf summons superb tension and suspense without using much dialogue. Ovid's first-person narrative is simple and eloquent, so that we see clearly his new, stark home and slide with him through an intense scale of emotions. As he works to communicate with the child, the haughty man of words gains a new form of language and insight.

Malouf is also the author of the novels *The Great World,* which won the Commonwealth Prize, and *Remembering Babylon,* which was shortlisted for England's Booker Prize.

You might call AN IMAGINARY LIFE *a spiritual journey. Ovid is transformed from an apparently amoral being into one who acts in a fatherly role. Do you think Malouf is saying that it's easier to be a decent human being away from the temptations of civilization?*

Malouf takes us to a world where language is not a necessity but communication is still essential. There's irony in the fact that the author uses lyrical, poetic prose to create this nonverbal realm. How does he appear to divest Ovid of language and at the same time communicate this transformation?

West with the Night, by Beryl Markham, North Point Press (paperback)

Reading Markham's memoir is like breathing pure air, a bit of heady atmosphere trapped from an earlier time and exotic place. Set in East Africa, where Markham grew up to become, in the 1930s, the continent's first female bush pilot and first female thoroughbred trainer, *West with the Night* is a poetic, invigorating account of Markham's adventures.

Ernest Hemingway said of Markham, "she has written so well, and marvelously well, that I was completely ashamed of myself as a writer . . . she can write rings around all of us who consider ourselves writers." Whether describing wildebeests tripping over their own feet, a zebra going after a bottle of beer, or a downed pilot dying of thirst and coming to life with a grin, Markham takes us to a domain few have seen and savored as she has.

If you've read Isak Dinesen's *Out of Africa,* you'll find that their stories collide at times; both Dinesen and Markham lived in the same locale and loved Bror Blixen and Denys Finch-Hatton. However, while Dinesen was a woman of letters, Markham was more a woman of action. In 1936 she became the first person to fly the Atlantic alone the most difficult way, against the headwinds, traveling from England to North America.

Markham describes three major phases in her life: growing up on her father's farm, staying on in Africa as a horse trainer after the farm was lost, and flying across land and water as the first woman in East Africa with a commercial pilot's license. Of these changes, she said, "I have learned that if you must leave a place that you have lived in and loved and where all your yesterdays are buried deep—leave it any way except a slow way, leave it the fastest way you can. Never turn back and never believe that an hour you remember is a better hour because it is dead." Does it appear Markham was able to live according to this creed?

Praisesong for the Widow, by Paule Marshall, Plume (paperback)

If you had high hopes for *Waiting to Exhale* but found the writing shallow, try this. Paule Marshall's story about a recently widowed African American woman doesn't have the same romantic fireworks, but is rich and deep.

A few days into a Caribbean cruise with two of her friends, Avey Johnson decides to jump ship. The sedate, middle-aged widow feels strangely ill and doesn't understand why, but she does know she must get off the luxury liner.

As she waits for a plane home, Avey is slowly pulled into a series of events that turn her life around. Lost in memories of her marriage, which took her from Harlem to the affluent New York suburbs, she wonders if her strivings for material success were made at a cost of personal happiness. In the midst of her queasiness and her strangely dreamy state, she meets up with a jovial group of people who are traveling to the island of Carriacou for an annual reunion.

The events that follow on the small Caribbean island pull Avey back to her childhood and to the ways of her people. Instead of a coming-of-age novel, this might be called a returning-to-the-pleasures-of-youth story. As Avey loosens the tight, white, urban fetters in which she's bound herself, Marshall evokes the thrilling feeling of letting go, of remembering and reexperiencing what is delicious and true.

A former magazine writer and researcher and the recipient of a MacArthur Fellowship, novelist Marshall is also the author of *Brown Girl, Brownstones; Daughters;* and *The Chosen Place, the Timeless People.*

Marshall returns repeatedly to images of Avey's forebears. Summers with her grandmother, the Shout Ring, and the slave ships from Africa seem to figure importantly in PRAISESONG. *What is the connection between these stories and Avey's personal redemption?*

As she experiences a spiritual rebirth, does it seem important for Avey to leave behind entirely her relationships with the friends she has known? Do you get the feeling that she will reject all aspects of her recent past?

We don't often encounter sixty-five-year-old heroines in contemporary fiction. In the film world, a mature heroine is often regarded as an oxymoron. Do the facts of her age and her disappointing prime make it hard to identify with Avey?

The Color of Water: A Black Man's Tribute to His White Mother, by James McBride, Riverhead Books (paperback)

On Mother's Day in 1981, journalist James McBride published a piece on his mother in *The Boston Globe;* readers were so moved by his essay about this powerful, eccentric woman that they wrote him to suggest he do an entire book on Ruth McBride Jordan. It took him more than a decade to get the headstrong, private lady to agree to such a thing.

As a teenager in Virginia, Ruth Jordan broke away from her Orthodox Jewish family and became "dead" to them, as far as they were concerned, to move to New York City, where she married an African American and helped to found the New Brown Memorial Baptist Church. Living in poverty, she managed to raise twelve children, send them all to college, and even see most of them through graduate school. However, she refused to tell them about her past.

As a youngster, James McBride knew that his mother was different from most people in their black community. When he asked her if she was white, she would reply, "I'm lightskinned." When he asked what that made him, she snapped, "You're a human being. Educate yourself or you'll be a nobody!"

The Color of Water, more than anything else, expresses the singular voice of an unusual, spirited American woman who would not let adversity bring her down. Her recollections, sprinkled with Yiddish words and accented with black idiom, are unforgettable and unique.

A former staff writer for *People* magazine, *The Washington Post,* and *The Boston Globe,* James McBride is a freelance writer, composer, and saxophonist.

In alternating chapters, McBride presents his mother's voice and then his own as they reconstruct the past. As he slowly learned his mother's story, McBride reports that he began to take pride in his Jewish heritage and to open his heart to people of all kinds outside his own community. Are his chapters a match for his mother's bracing style?

Ruth McBride Jordan's personal story is highly unusual. However, certain truths emerge in McBride's book that give it universal appeal. What would you say they are?

Spinners, by Anthony McCarten, HarperPerennial (paperback)

Have you read any books by New Zealand authors? Start with this one. Written by one of that country's leading playwrights, *Spinners* is Anthony McCarten's first novel and is an amusing, thought-provoking, one-of-a-kind experience.

A teenage girl living in a small New Zealand town reports quietly to the local policeman that, while out walking one night, she was intercepted by a group of aliens and had sex with them in their spaceship. Shortly thereafter she turns up pregnant. So do two other girls who are friends of hers. All of them claim not to have had sex with any human male. All three believe themselves to have been impregnated by beings from another planet. The news causes an uproar in the small town, the three are ostracized for their apparently flagrant lies, and there are a number of interesting ramifications to all of this, including, of course, the arrival of a big-city reporter seeking a sensational story about space aliens.

McCarten structures his tale with a number of intriguing subplots. The weary policeman, who so badly needs to confide his job difficulties to a sympathetic soul, is further burdened by his wife's inability to keep her mouth shut. Delia, the girl who first claims to make contact with spacemen, lives with an abusive father and has lost her mother to suicide. The mayor's nephew Phillip, who arrives in town looking for a chance to start life afresh, reopens the small library and thereby gains surprising entry to the secret life of the town.

Vic Young, the journalist, goes through a number of stages in his reaction to Delia's reported close encounter. Based on his behavior at the end of the book, what do you think he has learned from this entire episode?

The library takes on a luminous quality as Phillip revives it, and as he does so, he becomes an increasingly attractive person. At the same time, McCarten gives us bits of tantalizing interaction between him and Delia. How does McCarten capture our attention and hold it in developing their relationship?

That Night, by Alice McDermott, Delta (paperback)

In the hands of award-winning writer Alice McDermott, a suburban story of teenage love and loss of innocence on Long Island in the 1960s takes on the feeling of *Romeo and Juliet,* with an offbeat twist. The unlikely narrator is a ten-year-old girl who is a neighbor to the teenage heroine, Sheryl.

In tackling the star-crossed lovers theme, McDermott offers a somewhat unconventional look at the issue. While so many of us worry over the various implications of teenage love in modern times, our worries don't often include the emotional trauma of young love thwarted. McDermott dares to add humor to this perspective by using as her vehicle the innocent commentary of a child.

When teenage Rick discovers that Sheryl's mother won't let him see her daughter anymore, he and his friends gather in a drunken group at the woman's house to threaten her with violence. The events leading to this moment and the story that follows are evoked with vivid, unorthodox imagery: Men out at night walking dogs seem huge and foolish, like fullbacks on tricycles; an exiled daughter drives past shuttered houses with damp lawns and purring window fans; children watch as teenage boys with chains in their hands shake neighborhood fathers from their legs and arms.

McDermott's book won the PEN/Faulkner Award for fiction in 1988 and was nominated for a National Book Award. She was praised for lyrical writing that is almost nineteenth-century in its lushness and for her original way of handling an often-told story.

McDermott is also the author of *A Bigamist's Daughter, At Weddings and Wakes,* and *Charming Billy,* which won the 1999 National Book Award.

By choosing to tell her story from the point of view of an innocent young girl, does McDermott achieve a fairly unbiased view of Sheryl and Rick's romance? Why do you think she chose to have a grown woman look back on these events, recalling them as she observed them when ten years old?

Do you ever get an inkling of how the author feels about the teenagers' plight?

Enduring Love, by Ian McEwan, Anchor Books (paperback)

On an idyllic spring day, Joe Rose is pulled from a picnic with his lover to aid in the rescue of a little boy, and his life is forever altered. When the Englishman runs toward a wayward helium balloon, he has no idea that a glance at one of the strangers who join him in the rescue will ignite an obsessive love.

This could be a downer of a story. There's suspense, fear, and crumbling relationships. However, Ian McEwan is a master at balancing mania and reason, so he gives you good cause to believe that Joe can fight off this weird blight. Meanwhile, he illuminates a number of lives with such clarity and erudition that you empathize easily with the characters and their weird situation.

One of the pleasures of this novel is the masterful way in which McEwan portrays his characters' thinking, uncovering surprisingly different takes on the same incidents. His ability to reveal opposing views, whether by a crazy man, a distraught widow, a harried spouse, the police, or the sensible but desperate main character, creates a world of mirrors, in which the reader asks repeatedly, "But who is right?" The letters written to Joe by Jed Parry, the madman, are particularly clever in the articulate way they misinterpret reality.

Another satisfying aspect of *Enduring Love* is the main character's intelligent response to his crazy pursuer. Each step of the way, you may feel that Joe is doing exactly what you might have done in this situation. McEwan feels no need to throw in ridiculous mistakes on Joe's part to jack up the suspense.

McEwan's novel *Amsterdam* won Britain's Booker Prize in 1998, while his novels *Black Dogs* and *The Comfort of Strangers* were finalists for that award. *The Child in Time* won England's Whitbread Novel of the Year award.

Is McEwan's novel a parable about the delicacy of every marriage or relationship?

Did you ever doubt Joe's sanity? Do you think McEwan wanted you to?

Does the author make a case for the strength of reason and logic in confronting the vagaries of human emotion?

Taming It Down, by Kim McLarin, William Morrow (hardcover)

What is it like to be a young, professional black woman today? Everyone has expectations of you. You are a representative for your race . . . you are the hope of your race . . . you are responsible to your people—and, of course, to your family. On the job, you must prove yourself both as a woman and as an African American, which means you must work harder than others who do the same work. And who is the modern man who can be your partner and accept your modern role?

Kim McLarin touches on all of these issues and more in her first novel, *Taming It Down,* the story of a young black reporter working for a Philadelphia newspaper. She makes the story entertaining and makes it move by creating the character of Hope Robinson with a voice that is sarcastic and true. She also captures our attention by introducing Hope just as she is beginning to crack from the pressure of being caught between two worlds.

Hope is living a life in transition. She grew up in a black, southern working-class community and then, as a scholarship student, struggled to adjust to the alien environment of a New England prep school. Now she attempts to prove herself as a journalist on the staff of a mostly white newspaper. Cut off from black culture, uncomfortable in the white world, she begins to flip out. How she will fight her way to some sort of resolution for herself is the question at the heart of this engaging book.

McLarin is a graduate of Phillips Exeter Academy and Duke University and is a former journalist at the Associated Press, *The Philadelphia Inquirer,* and *The New York Times.*

Hope is not without friends and family. As she begins to crack, why doesn't she reach out to anyone she knows?

What is it about Malcolm that makes him attractive to Hope? Is this relationship believable?

What do you think McLarin is saying is the right path for a minority group person struggling as Hope is?

Fugitive Pieces, by Anne Michaels, Vintage Books (paperback)

Anne Michaels has written an elegant, magical, after-the-Holocaust book about a young boy's journey to healing and redemption through love. Winner of six Canadian literary awards, her work is a first novel but reflects her clearly established talent as a poet, as demonstrated in her two award-winning collections of poetry, *The Weight of Oranges* and *Miner's Pond.*

Seven-year-old Jakob emerges eerily from the mud in an excavation site in Poland where he has been hiding from the Nazis since they attacked his family. Digging nearby is a Greek geologist named Athos who watches this strange manifestation, uncertain whether he is observing the rising of a strange bog creature or a boy. When he learns that Jakob has witnessed the murder of his parents, Athos recovers enough to quickly hide the boy, then sneak him out of the country and home to his native Greece, where he conceals him until the war is over.

Athos is a lover of paleobotany. Multilingual, he is an extremely well-educated man used to living a solitary existence. Michaels's prose glimmers with affectionate enthusiasm as it reveals how Athos distracts Jakob from his terrible memories by teaching him about the flora and fauna of ancient eras. The growing connection between the young boy and noble man, the attempts to conquer the recent past by studying the distant past, and Jakob's heartsick memories of his sister Bella emerge in stunning imagery.

FUGITIVE PIECES *is not a history of the Holocaust. Michaels has taken a rather free-form approach to crafting her story, concentrating more on emotion and memory than historical fact. Not every step in the story was outlined. Were you frustrated by the author's approach, or did you find it appropriate?*

Did you condemn Athos for being at work in Poland while the Nazis occupied it? How would you explain his being there?

Michaels seems to be saying that we can save our souls from misery through the power of language and learning. Did becoming a poet enable Jakob to place painful memories behind him?

Martin Dressler: The Tale of an American Dreamer, by Steven Millhauser, Vintage Books (paperback)

Winner of the Pulitzer Prize in 1997, *Martin Dressler* is a mesmerizing fable about a humble New York boy who makes it big as the creator of extravagant hotels. Millhauser's saga has a strange duality: As it becomes increasingly fantastical and out of control, it seems more and more calculating and accurate as a description of an obsessed American dreamer.

Set in the late 1800s, in a New York where farmland is sprouting into tall buildings and commerce is king, *Martin Dressler* surrounds you with the sights and sounds of the emerging modern city. The workings of hotels and the philosophy behind creating a successful luxury establishment are explored in fascinating detail. (A note for those accustomed to West Coast architecture: Many hotels in New York actually were built with numerous subterranean levels—as many as thirteen. This part is not bizarre fantasy on the part of the author.)

If you find yourself reading this book as if it were a typical novel, watch out. Characterizations of Martin and the two sisters who become important in his life are developed well enough, but Millhauser feels no qualms about abruptly leaving behind others as Martin moves ever onward toward his American dream. This is a statement about who Martin is, rather than an oversight on the part of the author.

Millhauser is also the author of the novel *Edwin Mullhouse: The Life and Death of an American Writer 1943–1954 by Jeffrey Cartwright,* which is another book club favorite.

In this parody of the American entrepreneurial spirit, does Millhauser take a totally negative view of his protagonist? Do you think he feels an affection for him? Which was the character for whom you most cared?

Martin creates all kinds of recreational environments for his hotel patrons to enjoy. Do you ever see him enjoying or engaging in life the way he hopes his customers will?

A Fine Balance, by Rohinton Mistry, Vintage Books (paperback)

"Monumental." "Astonishing." Usually blurbs on the covers of a book are a bit over the edge. Not in this case. Rohinton Mistry has written a piece of fiction that seems to encompass the entire scope of modern India, both explaining its sorrows and degradation and acquainting us fully with four of its citizens, who at least briefly experience happiness together.

Ishvar, Om, Maneck, and Dina meet during the state of emergency declared during the reign of Prime Minister Indira Gandhi in the 1970s. Although the two tailors, the young student, and the widowed woman initially seem to have little in common except a distaste for each other, they are eventually forced by circumstance to live together in Dina's small apartment in an unnamed city.

As he introduces each of his main characters, Mistry places them against clearly defined backdrops. We learn about Maneck's mountain home, Ishvar and Om's small village, and Dina's city, becoming well acquainted with many aspects of India in the process. Mistry clearly wants us to know about the political, social, economic, and religious forces at work in his country of birth, and the picture is not complimentary. *A Fine Balance* provides the reader with serious education, and you may be surprised to learn about the extent of corruption and violent misdeeds in that country as late as the 1970s and 1980s.

A Fine Balance won the Los Angeles Times Book Prize in fiction and was a finalist for Britain's Booker Prize, as was Mistry's first novel, *Such a Long Journey*. He is also the author of a collection of short stories, *Swimming Lessons*.

Ishvar says that the secret to life is "to maintain a fine balance between hope and despair." Does Mistry manage to do this in his novel? In the end, at least one of his characters is unable to; did you have trouble believing that this particular person would choose the course he did?

Riverwalking: Reflections on Moving Water, by Kathleen Dean Moore, Harvest Books (paperback)

Expect more than rivers here. Expect more than advice on what it means to truly stop and observe nature. Look for children going off to college, parents dying, and the old lady across the street demanding a visit to pick up a banana. The love of rivers is central to Kathleen Moore's life, and she's willing to spread that life out before you just as much as she does the Deschutes, the Rogue, or the Willamette. In the best tradition of Annie Dillard or Terry Tempest Williams, this is naturalist writing with poignant human history intertwined.

Moore's credentials include essays for *The New York Times* and literary reviews plus a childhood filled with Sunday afternoons spent wading the Rocky River in Cleveland while her naturalist father took visitors on nature walks through Rocky River Park. Now chair of the Department of Philosophy at Oregon State University, Moore is married to a biologist who loves to walk, boat, and hike alongside rivers as much as she does. *Riverwalking* is a reminiscence of their family's time on rivers, both rain-swollen and desert-dry.

If you daydream about rafting on white water or hiking over sand dunes but never seem to get around to it, Moore's accounts of her family's outdoor reveries allow you to savor them vicariously. If you do spend time among streams and mountains, you're likely to relish her descriptions of moments when all seems right with the world—or when a sudden storm or the appearance of a rattler puts one to the test.

Riverwalking won the 1996 Pacific Northwest Booksellers Association Award. Her next book was *Holdfast: At Home in the Natural World,* a collection of essays that examines our connections to the things we hold most dear.

In a relaxed, conversational style, each essay tells of a trip down a different river. Moore's writing style is simple, but she examines certain bits of philosophy that can be quite profound. What were some of the messages you took away from this book?

Someone else, in trying to speak of the complexity of the natural world, could have overwhelmed us with words and technicalities. How does Moore convey the vast, complicated world of nature without losing us?

In Babylon, by Marcel Möring, translated from the Dutch by Stacey Knecht, William Morrow (hardcover)

Best-selling, award-winning Dutch author Marcel Möring has finally come to print in the United States, with a novel that Erica Wagner in *The London Times* described as a masterwork that reminds you what an extraordinary contraption a book is. Ghosts, rich family history, fairy tales, suspense, romance, humor, eroticism, intriguing characters—they all stream together on the pages of *In Babylon* to create a complex story that seems to live and breathe on its own. Möring's ability to raise provocative questions makes this a novel that you won't simply put down when you're done. You'll want to hash it over with friends.

In the present-day Netherlands, Nathan Hollander and his niece Nina barely make it through the snowbound forest to the former hunting lodge of Nathan's uncle Herman, where the two had planned a vacation. A man in his sixties, Nathan is an accomplished writer of fairy tales. His niece is his literary agent. Stranded without electricity and frightened by an extremely odd situation they have found at the grand lodge, Nathan helps to pass the hours by slowly unfurling their family history for Nina.

A major theme for Möring is the importance of having a sense of family history, especially when one has no national history. The author quotes Isaac Deutscher at the outset: "Trees have roots. Jews have legs." The Hollander family has taken its name out of gratitude for its relatively new home in the Netherlands; as the Levis, they had, like many other Jews, been tossed around during centuries of upheaval and violence in Russia, Lithuania, and Poland.

Möring is the author of two other novels: *Mendel* and *The Great Longing*.

The author suggests that our world is composed of story fragments that we struggle to fill in. At the end of his book, a number of questions go unanswered. Did you find this frustrating, or were you willing to come up with your own answers? For example, who is Nina? What was real, what was fantasy? What was the meaning of Zeno's story?

The Bluest Eye, by Toni Morrison, Plume (paperback)

Toni Morrison, who won the Nobel Prize for literature in 1993, here tells the nightmare story of a black child who prays for blue eyes in the belief they will solve her problems. This was Morrison's first novel, and it is a potent account of abject misery in one child's life and of the adults who helped to make it that way.

In the 1940s in Lorain, Ohio, eleven-year-old Pecola Breedlove is rejected by both her family and her peers on the basis of her looks and her extreme poverty. Sexually abused by her father, she prays for salvation in the form of blue eyes, which have become for her a symbol of all that is admired and loved. Gradually we watch her descend into insanity.

What is particularly interesting about the nightmare of *The Bluest Eye* is that each contributing adult is seen as a human being and not a monster. Each person's story is told, and in the telling there is some sympathy and understanding. The description of what it's like to be a black maid in an affluent white household is one of the more notable sections of the book.

While many of Morrison's adults are culpable, the true villain in *The Bluest Eye* is, of course, racism. Throughout the novel runs a refrain from the story of Dick and Jane, the two white children who served for decades as the heroes of every American schoolchild's primer. The black youngsters in *The Bluest Eye* seem to inhabit a different planet than Dick and Jane; the contrast between what they read at school and what they see at home is, in itself, insanity-inducing. As she did in her Pulitzer Prize–winning *Beloved,* Morrison has once again skillfully shown us the long-lasting effects of slavery and racism.

Morrison is also the author of *Paradise, Song of Solomon,* and *Jazz.*

When first published in 1970, THE BLUEST EYE *was acclaimed as an eloquent indictment of certain subtle forms of racism. Three decades later, does the racism seem so subtle in this book?*

Is Pecola a passive victim throughout the novel? Are there ever wisps of hope that she might speak on her own behalf? What is the climax or turning point in this novel, when we see a main character significantly changed?

Northern Borders, by Howard Frank Mosher, Delta (paperback)

Although *Northern Borders* is too new to be an American classic, it is bound to become one. Mosher has written a staggering, epic novel encompassing New England farm life, an unforgettable family, frontier exploration, and the anatomy of a marriage. He presents all of these stories through the eyes of a young boy growing to manhood and does so with wit and eloquence.

The "borders" of the title refer not only to a farm at the edge of the United States in Vermont's remote Kingdom County but also to the borders of human existence and the distances people may be willing to go to find love and satisfaction.

There is hardly a character in this novel who is not noteworthy and eccentric. Austen, who is six years old when he comes to live with his grandparents in Vermont in 1948, is perhaps the most ordinary person in the book. The surprises that befall him as he becomes part of the strong-willed Kittredge family seem all the more extraordinary because they are seen from his conventional point of view.

Mosher is a multitalented author. As he gradually reveals the cogs in the marriage between Austen's feuding grandmother and grandfather, he demonstrates an empathy with both genders. He takes time with character development so that every major player is human and real. His description of the daily, weekly, and yearly demands of farming come through as integral parts of the story, and his knowledge of both farming and nature feels authentic and passionate. He also has a wonderful ability to unfold an amusing yarn.

A resident of Vermont, Mosher has also written the novels *A Stranger in the Kingdom, Marie Blythe, Where the Rivers Flow North,* and *Disappearances.* His nonfiction work includes *North Country: A Personal Journey Through the Borderland.*

What is the tie between Austen's grandmother's obsession with Egypt and the difficult events of her youth?

Was there one person to side with in the forty-years war between Austen's grandparents? What do you think of Mosher's portrayal of this marriage?

The Holder of the World, by Bharati Mukherjee, Fawcett Columbine (paperback)

Read the description on the book jacket and you've got to know more: A twentieth-century woman who makes her living hunting for collectible treasures stumbles on information about a relative who lived 330 years earlier in New England. This ancestor, astonishingly daring given the mores of Puritan society, sailed off to India with her adventurer husband and then took a Hindu raja as her lover. Do you want to know the details, or what?

Berkeley English professor Bharati Mukherjee has written more than a bodice ripper. Her rhythmic, opulent language drips with details of sixteenth-century New England and India, creating an impressive, well-researched historical backdrop. Her novel becomes not only a cross-cultural study but an across-time drama as well. Colonialism and war come under her magnifying glass as do the power of romance and the will to survive.

While tracking a legendary diamond in modern-day America, a young New England woman named Beigh Masters pieces together the story of Hannah Easton, born in the American colonies in 1670. Hannah does not fit comfortably into Salem society. Harboring the secret that her mother ran off with a native lover during the French and Indian War and possessing an independent spirit of her own, she jumps at the chance to marry the dashing traveler Gabriel Legge. He takes her first to England and then to India.

Mukherjee was born in Calcutta, attended college in both India and the United States, and is now an American citizen. Her other fiction includes *Jasmine* and *The Middleman and Other Stories,* which won the National Book Critics Circle Award.

Mukherjee offers up a number of astounding ideas, including the romp of a Protestant woman from seventeenth-century New England in southern India and connections between King Philip's War in Massachusetts and a Muslim-Hindu holy war in India. Does the author go too far when she introduces the virtual reality program employed by an MIT researcher? If you accepted all of these ideas, what made you agree to participate in the willing suspension of disbelief?

The Love of a Good Woman, by Alice Munro, Vintage Books (paperback)

Winner of the 1998 National Book Critics Circle Award in fiction, Alice Munro's book is a masterful collection of short stories centering on themes of love and passion. Each story turns on an act of fervor, sometimes with drama that will take your breath away. Furthermore, each of these eight stories is a satisfying read and each can easily be finished in an evening. Not a bad idea: one thought-provoking tale per night.

Munro has been called one of the best short story writers in the English language. Other writers praise her wildly for her purity of style and technical know-how, including the complex way in which she layers her stories with multiple subplots and themes.

Munro lives in rural Ontario, Canada, where most of her stories are set. In *The Love of a Good Woman,* her title story opens near a small Canadian town just after the drowning of a local optometrist. The mystery of his death, however, is only a starting point. The local boys who discover his body, a hateful dying woman, her husband, and the nurse who cares for his wife are all caught in Munro's web. She has a gift for getting inside each person's head, revealing thoughts that range from idyllic to disgusting, and doing it with such finesse and honesty that her characterizations ring out with immediate truth.

Munro's novel *Lives of Girls and Women* is another book club favorite. *The Beggar Maid* was a Booker nominee.

Love relationships in Munro's stories involve more than romance . . . parents and children, friends, and in-laws are included as well. The slowly revealed understanding between father and daughter in "Before the Change" takes the reader by surprise with its impact. What is the emotional turning point in this tale?

Munro likes to look at what she calls "a new kind of old woman." Her favorite story in this collection is "Save the Reaper." Can you guess what in particular she likes so much about the grandmother?

The Green Knight, by Iris Murdoch, Penguin USA (paperback)

Is this a melodrama focused on murder and romance? Is it a philosophical study of good and evil? Is it a clever portrayal of the inner thoughts of adults and teenagers? Is it good storytelling?

Yes on all counts. The late Iris Murdoch, prolific novelist, poet, playwright, and philosopher, was a Commander of the Order of the British Empire as well as a winner of the Booker Prize and other British literary awards. She deserved the accolades.

In *The Green Knight* it takes a while for Murdoch to set the trap that will snag you. Slowly she introduces her characters in all their curious variety, and just when you are wondering why you've been invited to join them, BAM!, the story takes off. Basically, the novel concerns an extended group of families and friends living in contemporary London. All of their lives are touched by an attempted murder perpetrated by one of them.

Murdoch is especially clever at revealing human thought in all its neurotic, self-centered glory. Her characters very often love each other, bounce up against one another, and yet completely misconstrue each other's actions. This makes them seem quite believable.

The Irish-born Murdoch began her writing career in 1953 with a study of French existentialist Jean-Paul Sartre. A year later, she published *Under the Net,* the first of more than twenty novels. *The Sea—The Sea* won the Booker Prize in 1978; her more recent fiction includes *Jackson's Dilemma, The Message to the Planet,* and *The Good Apprentice,* which was a Booker Prize nominee in 1985. After her death, her husband, John Bayley, wrote a touching account of their last days together and of their marriage in the book *Elegy for Iris.*

Murdoch was pleased to point out that her novels have a beginning, a middle, and an end. Do you think she was too eager to wrap things up nicely at the end of THE GREEN KNIGHT*?*

Do you think it's fair to compare this story to that of Cain and Abel? If so, is it awkward to mingle both biblical and medieval references in the same work of fiction?

Blanche Among the Talented Tenth, by Barbara Neeley, Penguin USA (paperback)

You don't have to love mystery to fall for Barbara Neeley's stories of a cleaning lady who becomes a detective-by-default in *Blanche Cleans Up, Blanche on the Lam,* and *Blanche Among the Talented Tenth.* Neeley has created a gutsy, thoughtful character who lets us know what it's like to be a very black-skinned African American working in the homes of whites and living in a world where rules about power and beauty have been laid down by whites. In fact, the mystery is really secondary to the portrait of Blanche.

W. E. B. Dubois's comment that the "talented tenth" of the Negro race would be its salvation is a sore point with Blanche, because black educator and author Dubois was apparently referring to the light-skinned elite among the descendants of African slaves. In *Blanche Among the Talented Tenth,* she finds herself in a New England resort frequented by wealthy, mostly pale African Americans and must cope with snobbish behavior as well as an unexplained death.

Blanche is an easy character to like. She is plump and middle-aged and not ashamed of either. An obviously bright woman, she doesn't complain about what might have been. She deals with the present as best she can, making astute and sometimes amusing observations along the way. She is so accustomed to handling difficulty and living on her own that when she becomes involved in a romance, we worry a bit at the tough Blanche letting down her guard to have some fun.

The special joy of reading *Blanche Among the Talented Tenth* is in coming to know a strong, intelligent woman with her own special take on American life.

Blanche comments on "heart talk," the way that women becoming acquainted exchange bits of personal information as a means of expressing good intentions toward each other. Is it uncommon for an author to focus on feminist sensibility for an African American character rather than having her concentrate on race-related concerns?

Is this as much a tale of the working-class woman as it is a story of an African American woman?

The Dogs of Winter, by Kem Nunn, Washington Square Press (paperback)

This may be a book about surfers, but it's not necessarily one that surfers will like. Nunn paints a dismal picture of both old heroes and newcomers to the sport. However, he does deliver an enthralling story dripping with atmosphere that involves murder, lost glory, and redemption. And for those of us who are not surfers, there are vicarious thrills from reading Nunn's description of surfers riding gigantic mountains of water.

In *Dogs of Winter*, a big-wave photographer fallen on hard times gets one last chance to prove his mettle. A surfing magazine hires Jack Fletcher to capture all-time surfing great Drew Harmon riding thirty-foot waves at the mythical Heart Attacks, California's last secret surfing spot. When photographer Fletcher arrives north with two young surfer champs to include in the footage, he finds Harmon and his wife living a rather strange existence in the trailer of a recently murdered Native American woman.

Okay, so this sounds like action-adventure with murder thrown in. It is, but there's more to it than that. Nunn has done something odd and wonderful with his language. The dialogue, especially that of the two young surfers, is appropriately modern and crude. The narrative, on the other hand, has a genteel quality, an elegance almost reminiscent of knights and castles. Nunn makes this combination work, rarely exaggerating either style. Also, Nunn's descriptions of the California north coast do it justice, his eloquent prose bringing to life the harsh but beautiful cliff-lined beaches, the dark forests, and the damp climate. For all those in the rest of the country who imagine the California coast to be one long, warm, and gentle Malibu, Nunn corrects the impression.

The author of three other novels, Nunn was nominated for an American Book Award for *Tapping the Source,* which was also a surf-related tale.

One of Nunn's themes relates to the search for an ultimate experience or state of being. Most of his characters, even the less likable ones, are absolutely determined in their pursuit of that dream. What do you think Nunn is saying about this kind of obsession?

Nunn's fiction has a noir quality, a bleak atmosphere that permeates almost every scene and plot twist. Do any of the characters escape this desolate attitude enough to make you like them? What makes you care about the story and want to stay with it?

In the Lake of the Woods, by Tim O'Brien, Penguin Books (paperback)

Tim O'Brien is a superlative writer, and if you've not yet read any of his work, it's time to begin. *In the Lake of the Woods* will hold you in thrall with the quality of its writing and the questions the author raises. The central issues of O'Brien's novel make it curious and painful: What is evil? How does it happen? Who is responsible?

On the face of it, *In the Lake of the Woods* is a mystery story about the marriage of John and Kathy Wade. John has recently lost an election, and the two retreat to a lakeside cabin to recover from his defeat. Then one morning, Kathy is gone.

Has John's wife run away from the lack of honesty in her marriage? Has she been murdered? What has brought the couple to this point? O'Brien lays out the lives of his characters to raise more questions and reveal horror lying just beneath the surface.

The main narrative, written in the voice of John Wade, alternates with other people's viewpoints in the form of interview quotes and newspaper clips. Since this is such a desperate, personal story, the effect of reading other people's reactions is welcome relief and sometimes even comic.

O'Brien, who has written much about the war in Vietnam, uses that experience once more, bringing in the details of John's time there with fierce and agonizing exactitude.

O'Brien won the National Book Award in fiction for *Going After Cacciato,* and his novel *The Things They Carried* was widely recognized as definitive writing on the soldier's experience in Vietnam.

As the character of John Wade emerges, we gain a picture of a young boy who loved sorcery and grew to be a man who tried to make terrible problems magically vanish. Do you sympathize with his desire to make difficulty disappear with sleight of hand? Dose he become despicable or tragic for building his life on deceit?

O'Brien never resolves the mystery of Kathy's disappearance, but offers a number of possibilities. What do you think of the way he handled the end of this book?

***The English Patient*, Michale Ondaatje, Vintage Books (paperback)**

Don't assume you know the book if you've seen the movie. It was a wonderful film, but a different version of Ondaatje's novel. For more of Ondaatje's exotic story, take a look at this consummate piece of work, which won England's Booker Prize in 1992.

First, it's important that you let the words of Ondaatje's novel wash over you like music. They are meant to be absorbed loosely rather than read carefully, one at a time, for meaning. His language is a kind of poetry that gathers force as the story builds.

Second, keep in mind that the love story between the nurse Hana and the bomb diffuser (or bomb sapper) Kip comes more to the fore than that between the English patient and his love.

Although poetic, Ondaatje's novel is gritty and strange. World War II has just come to a close, and we find ourselves at an abandoned villa in the Italian countryside, where a burn victim is attended by a devoted Canadian nurse. Who is this patient scorched beyond all recognition: war hero or villain? On the lawn of the elegant old building camps the Indian soldier Kip, a member of the Allied forces, searching for bombs to dismantle in the ravaged countryside. He and Hana fall in love, and yet the strangeness of the time threatens their romance. A fourth character who appears at the villa, Caravaggio the thief, raises disturbing questions about the burn victim and stirs memories of Hana's past.

Born in Ceylon, Ondaatje has lived in England as well and now makes his home in Canada. Recollections of life in Ceylon appear in his *Running in the Family;* Canada is the setting for *In the Skin of a Lion;* and New Orleans is the locale for *Coming Through Slaughter,* the story of jazz musician Buddy Bolden.

The war has left Hana embittered and unwilling to move on. She finds a certain solace in caring for the mysterious, terribly damaged Englishman. Kip meanwhile tries to undo the munitions left behind in battle. Caravaggio cannot let go of rage over his own injuries.

What themes about war surface in Ondaatje's complicated postwar tableau?

The Englishman may be a villain or an innocent. By the end of the story you have enough information to decide. Does it matter that the historical record seems to show that the real person Ondaatje used as inspiration for his character was guilty of evil acts?

My Year of Meats, by Ruth L. Ozeki, Penguin Books (paperback)

If you're looking for offbeat, provocative, and funny fiction, this is it. A debut novel by Ruth Ozeki, *My Year of Meats* tells the story of an American named Jane Takagi-Little who is hired to produce a Japanese TV show, *My American Wife!* Her documentary shows are supposed to promote the consumption of imported meat among the Japanese by displaying archetypal U.S. families in a variety of settings enjoying their favorite meat recipes.

The only problem is that Jane is a true documentary filmmaker, not a maker of commercials. She leans toward unusual, telling bits of reality rather than bland stereotypes. As a result, she can't resist leading her crew to film an unexpected assortment of Americans who don't meet the standards of her Japanese bosses—for example, a lesbian couple who are vegetarians.

Also, Jane begins to uncover disturbing information about beef raised in this country. When her documentary work veers toward an investigation of hormones given to cattle, not only is her job threatened, her life is endangered.

Ozeki manages to raise a number of serious questions concerning food consumption, media influence, and commerce and still engage us in her characters' personal dramas. Jane emerges as a distinctive, independent character with dilemmas of love and career, while across the world, we follow the contrasting story of a terribly mistreated housewife, Akiko Ueno, whose submissive relationship to her husband is disrupted by watching *My American Wife!*

Be sure to check out the interview with the author at the end of the novel.

MY YEAR OF MEATS *offers a highly disturbing indictment of the American meat industry. Did you see this coming? Did you get the impression that Ozeki wrote her book only for this reason? Have your meat consumption habits changed any since you finished reading the book?*

Ozeki draws her characters beautifully, giving them imperfections that make them seem like real people. Are her portraits of men as fully realized as her portraits of women? If not, does this mean her book is flawed?

The Magician's Assistant, by Ann Patchett, Harvest Books (paperback)

What is magic, what is not? In this sparkling novel, Ann Patchett shows us mundane aspects of life and makes them magical, even as she tosses out moments of unreality and makes them seem normal. The elegant use of language, the fully realized characterizations, and the adept play of tension and conflict all combine in *The Magician's Assistant* to create a wonderful read.

Sabine is the widow of a successful magician, Parsifal. As his onstage assistant for more than twenty years and his wife for one, she has an odd story to tell about their life together. While still reeling from his untimely death, she is dealt another surprise: Parsifal, who had said his family died long ago in an accident, is survived by a mother and two sisters. When they visit her unexpectedly in Los Angeles, their presence seems to fortify her. Sabine finds herself traveling from her beloved Los Angeles to rejoin them in their Nebraska hometown, as she begins to uncover other secrets of her dead husband's past.

(This novel is also remarkable because it delivers a wholeheartedly loving portrait of Los Angeles; Patchett's approach is refreshing and certainly unexpected, adding to the offbeat flavor of her story.)

Patchett has a talent for picking out tiny, telling details that make an entire scene come alive. She also has a fine ear for dialogue and handily interjects mild, wry humor throughout her tale.

Patchett's other novels are *Taft* and *The Patron Saint of Liars;* the latter was also recommended as a book club favorite.

Sabine is suffering terribly when Dot and Bertie Fetters arrive on the scene. How do they begin to help pull her out of her depressed state?

THE MAGICIAN'S ASSISTANT *is, in its own way, a display of wizardry in that it addresses age-old questions about the nature of love and makes them seem fresh. How does Patchett pull this off?*

Patchett places believable characters in improbable situations. What techniques does she use to help us accept the verisimilitude of her story?

***Winterdance: The Fine Madness of Running the Iditarod,* by Gary Paulsen, Harvest Books (paperback)**

You don't have to care about dogsledding or even be a fan of adventure books to enjoy this one. The writing is great, the author is hilarious, and his book might be called a classic. Some folks list this among their top ten books of contemporary writing.

Paulsen isn't kidding when he uses the word *madness* in regard to his participation in the Iditarod, the annual 1,180-mile race by dogsled across remote Alaskan terrain. When he first trains for the race, he is simply a guy living in Minnesota who likes to hunt and trap with a few dogs. By the time he has finished seventeen days in the Alaskan wilderness, following fifteen wild and crazy canines across canyons and over frozen rivers, braving moose attacks and frostbite and blinding snowstorms, he has taken your breath away with the audacity of his dream and the endurance with which he has achieved it.

Paulsen writes with clarity and high spirits. Relating his misadventures during preparation for the race and the running of it, he is not afraid to mock himself. One of the more memorable interludes in *Winterdance* is a training session in which the dogs pull him across his snow-free yard, raking him through the gravel and creating enough friction to ignite a book of matches in his pants pocket. Time and again he is chewed by dogs and wrapped around trees, and yet he never loses his sense of humor or his sense of wonder at the beauty of his more successful interludes in the wild.

A popular and extremely prolific children's writer, Paulsen has also authored a number of other books for adults: *The Madonna Stories; Clabbered Dirt, Sweet Grass; Eastern Sun, Western Moon;* and *Zero to Sixty: The Motorcyle Journey of a Lifetime.*

Critics have called WINTERDANCE *both a contemporary classic and an unassuming masterpiece and have compared Paulsen favorably to*

Jack London and Ernest Hemingway. What are the features of this book that make it seem classic?

The author offers a fair amount of technical information about dogs and sledding. How does Paulsen appeal to the armchair traveler or adventurer and avoid directing his book only to those with expertise about his subject matter?

An Instance of the Fingerpost, by Iain Pears, Berkley Publishing Group (paperback)

This is one of those very big books you feel grateful for. Iain Pears's seventeenth-century murder mystery is so engrossing and such a page-turner that you won't want the experience to be over too quickly.

British author Pears has taken the *Rashomon* approach to a crime, having four different characters give their take on the events surrounding a murder in the late 1600s in England. As you plow through their accounts, you'll be rather amazed at the different translation each participant gives to the very same details. One of the major pleasures of the book is the way Pears toys with the question of determining what is really true.

In addition to creating four very singular, lively characters to tell his tale, Pears illuminates the extremely tumultuous time in which they live. The 1660s in Britain were marked by political unrest, religious conflict, and the continued blossoming of scientific experimentation and discovery that had begun during the Renaissance.

The first of the four characters to explain the events leading to murder is an Italian visitor to Britain's shores. His take on English customs and particularly the primitive practice of medicine is a hilarious mixture of informative and bizarre. Through him, Pears somehow conveys English ineptitude in treating illness and injury without making his Italian foreigner look too smart himself.

The multitalented Pears has worked as an art historian, journalist, and TV consultant and is the author of six detective novels, including *Death and Restoration: A Jonathan Argyll Mystery* and *The Raphael Affair.*

AN INSTANCE OF THE FINGERPOST *has been compared to Umberto Eco's* THE NAME OF THE ROSE *because, in addition to being an intricate period piece, it displays the same intellectual complexity. As a book of ideas, what are some of the major themes or philosophies that Pears's novel conveys?*

Were you able to figure out exactly what the words "an instance of the fingerpost" mean?

Pears appears to provide four gospels and the appearance of a new messiah in the figure of Sarah. Do you think this is pure literary artifice, done only for fun, or is he saying something deeper in this construction?

Here Be Dragons, by Sharon Kay Penman, Ballantine Books (paperback)

If history were taught only with books like this one, we'd remember every word. There are no dragons in the historically accurate *Here Be Dragons,* but there's plenty of suspense, drama, and romance.

Penman's book is a portrayal of royal intrigue in the 1100s and 1200s in England and Wales. Written as a novel, it is a painstakingly researched account with none of the dryness of historical record. The characters come to life; they have intense longings and human frailties, they are hungry for power, and yet they undo themselves.

The only real problem with this book is that it is seven hundred pages long, and you won't want to let go of it until the seven hundredth page.

How did Penman achieve such successful storytelling? It seems that much of the work was done for her by the people who actually lived the story. Given the tendency of European royalty to marry off their daughters to their enemies in attempts to avert war, there was ample potential for family conflict and broken hearts. Given the political instability of the region, there was often occasion for bloodshed and opportunity for both heroes and villains to grab power. In *Here Be Dragons,* Joanna, the illegitimate but beloved daughter of England's King John, weds her father's enemy, Llewelyn, Prince of North Wales. Joanna is not thrilled with the marriage but comes to love her husband as he pursues the noble goal of uniting Wales. Unfortunately, her husband's goal is diametrically opposed to her father's interests, and Joanna loves her father as well.

Here Be Dragons is the first book in a trilogy that includes *Falls the Shadow* and *The Reckoning.* Penman is also the author of the novels *Cruel as the Grave: A Medieval Mystery* and *When Christ and His Saints Slept.*

"Here be dragons" are the words that medieval mapmakers would

write across any part of a map that was unknown. How has Penman used this phrase as a metaphor?

It's not easy to write a historical novel that dramatizes at length the psyches of the long-dead. Many have called Penman's writing seamless in the way it blends fact and dramatization. Were there ever any times when you became aware that the author was taking liberties with her material or overdoing the fictional aspects?

Zen and the Art of Motorcycle Maintenance: An Inquiry into Values, by Robert M. Pirsig, Quill (paperback)

Did you read this meaty book when it was a best-seller twenty-five years ago? Quill's anniversary edition (available in Fall 2000 from HarperCollins as a Perennial Classic) is definitely worth a refresher look, especially with the new, enlightening introduction by the author and a Reader's Guide that includes fascinating excerpts from correspondence between Pirsig and his editor during the years the book was being written.

It's easy to remember Pirsig's masterwork only as a philosophical inquiry that challenges the reader and requires slow, thoughtful reading. However, there are two other very immediate stories unfolding here as well, each with its own high drama.

Pirsig, who is taking his son on a motorcycle trip from Minnesota to California, has been treated for mental illness and has almost no recollection of the person he was before electroshock therapy. Slowly, as he travels over vaguely familiar territory, the old self, whom he calls Phaedrus, begins to emerge. Will this alternate persona burst loose and destroy him? What did Phaedrus do that warranted electroshock treatment?

Pirsig's young son Chris has been having problems of his own. He recognizes that this man piloting their motorcycle is not the father he once knew and loved. As Chris begins to show signs of emotional disturbance, we worry about him as well. His awkward attempts to express his worries are met with little understanding by Pirsig, and further suspense builds as we wonder how this father-son relationship will be resolved.

Pirsig is also the author of *Lila,* the sequel to *Zen and the Art of Motorcycle Maintenance.*

Applauded by many critics as complex and ambitious in scope, Pirsig's book was also dismissed as the self-absorbed ranting of an egotistical rhetorician. How did you feel about the author's Chautauqua format? Did it put you off or intrigue you? If it put you off, was it perhaps meant to tell you something important about the narrator?

Why do you think this intellectually formidable book attracted so much attention when it was first published? Did it have to do only with the tumultuous times in which it appeared, when the status quo was repeatedly questioned?

The Hot Zone: A Terrifying True Story, by Richard Preston, Anchor Books (paperback)

Richard Preston may be a science writer, but he tells his story like a master of suspense. *The Hot Zone* is an edge-of-your-seat thriller about an actual outbreak of the ebola virus in Virginia in 1989.

Ebola is the same tropical filovirus that starred in the movie *Outbreak,* but here the details are all accurate and the events actually happened. Filoviruses kill most of their hosts in rapid, grotesque ways. In fact, you might want to begin reading the book in the daytime only; you probably don't want to fall asleep and dream just after learning what ebola can do to the human body.

Preston builds his story carefully, first outlining what is known about ebola and its appearance in Africa. Slowly he introduces the Americans who will be called upon to combat the outbreak in a "monkey house" just outside Washington, D.C. As we get to know them, we begin to worry about each of these scientists.

Approximately sixteen thousand wild monkeys are imported annually to the United States for use as laboratory animals; they are held in quarantine for a month to prevent the spread of infectious diseases they may have carried from their origins in the tropical regions of the world. The monkey house at Reston, Virginia, was one such quarantine unit.

Preston also details his visit to Kitum Cave on Mount Elgon near the edge of the Rift Valley in Kenya. This is the location that many scientists believe is the source of all four identified filoviruses: the Marburg, the Sudan, the Zaire, and the Reston strains of ebola. His entry into this cave is spine-tingling.

Preston is the award-winning author of *First Light* and *American Steel,* both nonfiction. He has also written a novel: *The Cobra Event.*

Some of the scientists at the laboratory were lax in their handling of samples from the Reston Primate Quarantine Unit. How do you think this could happen in a laboratory set up specifically to handle biohazards?

Preston argues that a number of viruses and other rain forest agents are likely to emerge as we destroy the tropical biosphere. What can each of us do now to slow and prevent this destruction?

One True Thing, by Anna Quindlen, Delta (paperback)

What does it mean to be part of a family? How much should you be asked to sacrifice for the other members? As close as you are to your parents, do you truly know them? These are some of the questions Anna Quindlen raises and skillfully pursues in *One True Thing.*

Pulitzer Prize–winning *New York Times* columnist Quindlen apparently had no trouble making the switch from journalism to fiction. Her spectacular novel *One True Thing* is a gripping story of a modern mother-daughter relationship, a quiet salute to women who are full-time mothers and wives, and an appreciation of the conflicts that young working women face.

Quindlen pulls us into the story immediately when the main character informs us at the outset that she's in jail for the death of her mother. Ellen's mother Katherine, it turns out, was dying of cancer, and Ellen has been accused of shortening her suffering.

Although Kate's death remains an enigma until the end of the book, this is not a murder mystery. Instead, it is a finely tuned portrait of a family and all the forces that have led it to this moment in time. Ellen's life as a professional woman and her mother's role as a nurturer of her family are compared and contrasted with sympathy. Even Ellen's father, the egotistical professor and unfaithful husband, seems human in the end.

Quindlen's other novels are *Object Lessons* and *Black and Blue.* Her columns are available in two collections: *Thinking Out Loud* and *Living Out Loud.* She has also written a nonfiction book, *How Reading Changed My Life.*

How is Ellen transformed in the course of caring for her mother? What are the moral lessons that Quindlen is offering here?

Would this story have pulled you in if it hadn't begun with the high drama of Ellen in jail? Does this seem like transparent technique to catch your attention, or does Quindlen's choice to begin toward the end of the story and then leap back work well for you?

Did you find it hard to believe that Katherine had chosen to stay with her seriously flawed husband for so many years?

If you saw the movie, did you find it was entirely faithful to the book?

Ishmael: An Adventure of the Mind and Spirit, by Daniel Quinn, A Bantam/Turner Book (paperback)

A story told by a gorilla may sound too cute, but this piece of fiction is in no sense adorable. Rather, *Ishmael* provides a clever framework for a proposal to change world order. Although written as a novel, Daniel Quinn's book is more a series of Socratic dialogues between a wary man and a brilliant gorilla who suggests new laws for behavior in the modern world.

The best thing about Quinn's book is all of the debate and controversy it has stirred. When *Ishmael* was declared the winning entry from among twenty-five hundred submissions for the Turner Tomorrow Award, and Quinn was awarded $500,000 in the ecology-oriented contest, there was a revolt by some of the contest judges. The author has now attracted something of a cult following.

Rather than give away his ideas about human beings' proper place in the world, I'll simply say that an unnamed man answers a newspaper ad stating, "Teacher Seeks Pupil." The professor is Ishmael, who then leads his startled applicant through a series of logical conclusions about the destructive effects that certain human attitudes and behaviors have wrought on the planet. The amazing ape suggests how the course of human activity can be reversed and the future of the world protected.

Quinn has written an autobiography, *Providence: The Story of a Fifty-Year Vision Quest,* as well as the fictional *Dreamer, The Story of B,* and *My Ishmael: A Sequel.*

Does the author provide us with absolutely new information? Is this a rewrite of evolutionary theory? If he is rethinking existing material, does Quinn present his concepts in a way you hadn't considered before?

Quinn purposely does not suggest specific actions that the reader can take to move the planet toward the type of arrangement he envisions; he wants others to generate ideas. Do you have any?

"With gorilla gone, will there be hope for man?" What do you think?

Bad Land, by Jonathan Raban, Vintage Books (paperback)

Bad Land is a horror story about the American West that has particular impact because it is true, but Jonathan Raban's stirring book also contains a certain amount of inspiration and uplift. The author explains how the Milwaukee Road Railroad, in league with the American government, drew thousands of settlers to eastern Montana in the early 1900s with the promise of free, rich farmland. The railroad wanted people living along its newly established route; what these unsuspecting homesteaders discovered was a great American desert that went antarctically cold in the winter and often bone-dry in the spring and summer.

Not everyone failed here, however, and not everyone moved away. As Raban's story unfolds, it's clear there will be devastating misfortune, but there's also suspense as to how some settlers survived and made a decent home for themselves.

Bad Land was the winner of the National Book Critics Circle Award for nonfiction in 1996, the Pacific Northwest Booksellers Award, and the PEN West Creative Nonfiction Award.

Raban spotlights the personal stories of a number of the Montana settlers, effectively bringing alive a jumble of immigrants that included heroes and bums, titled Europeans, and a woman photographer who would make a name for herself by recording the misfortune of eastern Montana as well as misrepresenting it.

Raban is the author of numerous books, including *Old Glory: A Voyage Down the Mississippi*, *Soft City*, and *Hunting Mister Heartbreak*.

Rather than following a strict chronology, Raban chooses to tell his story via conceptual chapters and portraits of a number of the people who lived in eastern Montana. Does this approach seem less scholarly and more subjective than that of traditional history books?

Some have argued that Raban reinforces the stereotype of Montana as a wasteland and the idea that its inhabitants are lacking in intelligence. Do you come away with this impression? Can you find any portions of the book in which Raban paints a radiant picture of the Montana landscape? Would you guess that Montana is one of the largest wheat-producing regions of the world? Is it important that Raban doesn't mention this?

Rocking the Babies, by Linda Raymond, Penguin USA (paperback)

Winner of the Bay Area Book Reviewers Association Award for fiction in 1995, *Rocking the Babies* is a distinctive first novel that will grab you and not let go. Set in the neonatal unit of a Dayton, Ohio, hospital, Raymond's story follows two African-American women hired as "grandmas" to give gentle attention to the tiny patients in intensive care.

From the outset, Nettie Lee and Martha don't like each other. Outspoken, poverty-stricken Nettie Lee has faced many of the crises that wallop single moms living in the ghetto. Martha is educated, tense, and middle class, indelibly scarred by the loss of her only child and unwilling to reveal her pain to anyone. However, as the two strangers sit rocking crack babies, abandoned preemies, and other tiny infants in peril, they begin to lay their lives open to each other.

Much of the richness of Raymond's novel lies in its revelations of family history. Slavery days, more contemporary times of happiness and passion, and tragic turns taken by the women or their children accumulate to give the story both drama and warmth.

Suspense is created by the dilemma of Nettie Lee, who has come to the neonatal ICU secretly to be close to Baby X, the crack-addicted, premature newborn that her daughter Yolanda has abandoned. Although Raymond could easily have wrapped up Nettie Lee's and Martha's stories in a pat ending, she instead concludes in a way that seems both satisfying and believable.

The story really starts moving when the two women finally begin to communicate with each other. When did this turning point come? Can you see how Raymond led up to this breakthrough?

Each character in ROCKING THE BABIES *is well drawn, including the minor ones. What techniques does the author use to reveal personality and physical appearance? Does she state these things directly in narrative, or does she use indirect methods?*

The Rapture of Canaan, by Sheri Reynolds, Berkley Books (paperback)

Why would you want to read about a young girl trapped by birth into a small, strange religious enclave in the South? This could have been too much to bear, but in Sheri Reynolds's hands the story becomes a tender, human tale of what it means to be part of a close-knit, extended family, even if the price is high. *The Rapture of Canaan* is as much a story about family love as it is an explanation of how a religious cult might evolve.

Ninah Huff's Grandpa Herman has founded the Church of Fire and Brimstone and God's Almighty Baptizing Wind, and as you might gather, the rules that he has laid down are a strange combination of the austere and the bizarrely comic. Often in this story, you don't know whether to laugh or cry, and maybe that's a good indication that Reynolds has adequately captured the reality of a situation like this.

Although pious and reconciled to living in the relative isolation required by her grandfather, fifteen-year-old Ninah struggles against strong impulses that oppose her religious training. Falling in love, feeling the sort of desire that most teenagers experience, she must fight to avoid the church's dire punishments. Fortunately for her, she has a loving grandmother who provides some solace and who isn't entirely afraid to be critical of her husband Herman. Ninah's likable, gutsy teenage character and her grandmother's soft and wise soul make it possible for you to traverse a landscape that is at times horrific.

Reynolds is also the author of *Bitterroot Landing*, another southern coming-of-age tale, and *A Gracious Plenty*.

Ninah is not the only one to wrestle with her grandfather's odd brand of theology. Are the other family members sympathetic as they try to figure out the contradictions in the rules for living and worship handed down to them by Herman? Does the way Reynolds portrays them affect the way in which we view Ninah?

Did you have trouble believing that Nanna would remain with Her-

man, given her skepticism about his beliefs? What does she teach Ninah about love?

The author explains that she plucked a number of Herman's religious guidelines from her readings on the rules and punishments of medieval societies. Does this seem an inappropriate choice in writing about a modern-day southern cult?

The Mummy, or Ramses the Damned, by Anne Rice, Ballantine (paperback)

If you're curious about Anne Rice and the power of her writing but can't stomach vampires or witches, this is the book to try. It's great storytelling and great adventure, with the added bonus of skillful narrative and dialogue.

Why include the incredibly popular Rice here? As the author of eighteen books, most of them best-sellers, she might be overlooked by those on a serious search for good literature. If that means you, break out of your narrow rut. Reading *The Mummy,* you can soar along on a roller-coaster ride of emotion and adventure and at the same time trust that you are in the hands of a master.

In *The Mummy,* you'll discover Ramses the Great of Egypt, who has not really been dead for centuries; he has only been asleep in the wrappings of a mummy. He awakens in Edwardian London, fittingly as an Egyptologist, and when he travels back to his homeland seeking his lost love Cleopatra, all hell breaks loose. Along the way, Rice blends historical detail, social commentary on modern technology and modern mores, and a great deal of romance and suspense. How can you knock that, if it's well done? One question, though: What ever happened to the sequel to *The Mummy* promised at the end of the book?

Rice's preoccupation with horror is very possibly linked to certain traumatic events in her life. When she was fifteen, her mother died of acute alcoholism. When the author and her husband, poet Stan Rice, lost their eight-year-old daughter Michelle to leukemia, Anne Rice first turned to drink, as her mother had, and then found salvation in writing dark tales of vampires and eternal life.

Rice's first two vampire tales are often cited as her best: *Interview with the Vampire* and *The Vampire Lestat. Cry to Heaven,* the story of a fourteenth-century castrato, is another favorite. She is also the author of *Vittorio the Vampire, The Vampire Armand,* and *Servant of the Bones.*

Some critics say that Rice has wasted her superior talents as a writer by dealing in the supernatural. Why not write what you love, and make it as good as you can? Is "good literature" confined to a narrow spectrum that excludes mystery, science fiction, and fantasy?

Miss Julia Speaks Her Mind, by Ann B. Ross, Harper Perennial (paperback)

If someone has not already optioned his book as a movie, they should. Whoever makes that smart move ought to retain Miss Julia's narration. When Miss Julia speaks her mind, which she does repeatedly through this romp of a book, it is with a distinctly southern flavor and a good dose of unexpected humor and sarcasm.

Miss Julia Springer is a proper southern lady with all kinds of improper impulses lurking beneath the surface. Recently widowed and the recipient of a large estate, she suddenly finds herself dealing with the pressures that money can bring—for instance, the desire of her husband's favorite church to appropriate her inheritance for their building campaign.

And then there's the little matter of her husband's bastard son. One morning a young woman rings her doorbell, announces that the child beside her is Wesley Lloyd Junior Springer. She has not been left a penny by Wesley Lloyd senior, announces Hazel Marie Puckett, and she's not going to ask for anything, except that Miss Julia watch the child for six weeks while she finds a way to support the two of them by learning to manicure nails at a beauty school.

Miss Julia has no children of her own and at this point in her life, her early sixties, she doesn't have much use for them. Especially not one who represents a more than decade-long affair that, until now, Miss Julia had no knowledge of.

This is not a one-idea book. All sorts of complications arise for Miss Julia, and you'll have fun and feel concern for her as she musters the strength to do what is right.

Ross is the author of one previous novel, *The Pilgrimage.*

Supporting Miss Julia or sabotaging her is an intriguing cast of characters, including her confidante and housekeeper, Lillian. What do you think of the way Ross handles Miss Julia's relationship with her black employee? Do you detect any signs of racism? Does this seem like a believable friendship?

Miss Julia displays a healthy ability to take things with a grain of salt. Does this include issues regarding her sex life? Did you accept her feelings of doubt about her behavior?

Patrimony: A True Story, by Philip Roth, Vintage Books (paperback)

This compelling nonfiction account by American literary phenomenon Philip Roth of his father's last days won the National Book Critics Circle Award in 1992. Herman Roth was eighty-six years old when he was diagnosed with a brain tumor. His son, who stayed by his side as he learned his fate and then faced it, here honors his father's life and his bravery in meeting death.

Surprisingly, Roth's book offers a fair amount of comedy and uplift, both as a result of Herman Roth's eccentric character and of his son's ability to tell a good anecdote. Roth's engaging, conversational style pulls you right into the story, revealing intimate bits of his own life as well as confiding personal details about his father. This candor about himself is particularly surprising, since Roth usually avoids interviews, author appearances, and media coverage.

Patrimony is property inherited from one's father. Roth makes it clear that his own inheritance amounted to far more than a collection of material goods. Herman Roth was a fiercely independent man who held everyone around him to tough, uncompromising standards. As he accompanied his father through each medical ordeal, the author recollected his father's lifelong tenacity and ability to persevere, and at the same time met staggering tests of his own.

A prolific novelist, Roth authored *American Pastoral*, which won the Pulitzer Prize in 1998, and *Goodbye, Columbus* and *Sabbath's Theater*, which won the National Book Award for fiction in 1960 and 1995, respectively. *The Counterlife* won the National Book Critics Circle Award in 1987. He is also the author of *I Married a Communist* and *Portnoy's Complaint*.

Roth gives us two hardheaded men facing a terrible situation. Is he also successful at showing each in vulnerable moments? What wins us to the author's side as he deals with his father's illness?

At first it seems that Roth and his father are two very different souls in terms of personality and life history. By the end of the book, do you see strong similarities between the two?

Fields of Glory, by Jean Rouaud, translated from the French by Ralph Manheim, Arcade Publishing (paperback)

In 1990 the French awarded *Fields of Glory* their highest literary honor for a work of fiction, the Prix Goncourt, and the book has been widely read in that nation. Before he won literary acclaim, Jean Rouaud was a newsstand vendor who'd never before been published. His fame is well deserved, as he has written a novel that offers fond, evocative portraits and the opportunity for a brief, tantalizing visit to a small French town called Random in the Loire Valley.

Written in a fresh, playful voice, Rouaud's exceptional prose offers up a memorable cast of characters living in the shadow of the First World War's "fields of glory." His work reads more like a memoir than a novel as he introduces us to Grandfather, Grandmother, and Aunt Marie, three elderly characters whose antics and odd habits are given greater meaning when seen finally in the context of youth scarred by World War I.

The novel's jocular tone gives welcome comic relief against the somber background events. Grandfather smoked a rare brand of cigarettes that "we never saw anyone else smoking. Once when we asked him, he claimed to order them from Russia, but on another occasion he said, with the same deadpan expression, from Rangoon beyond the moon. Production, I am certain, was stopped at his death." Aunt Marie, a maiden schoolteacher who depended on the saints to remedy any problem that life might present, kept a card file on the blesseds and soon-to-be blesseds and also had statues of them in every nook and cranny of the garden wall. However, when her plea to a saint seemed to go unanswered, she was not above turning its statue's face to the wall.

Rouaud is also the author of a work of nonfiction, *Of Illustrious Men.*

The author chooses to take the perspective of a child in recounting the antic foibles of three crotchety old people. Why do you think he made this choice in unfolding a war story?

The three main characters are trapped in a kind of time warp of their youth. Although the setting is very specifically French and related to World War I, do you find certain universals in Rouaud's story?

Straight Man, by Richard Russo, Vintage Books (paperback)

You may have seen the movie *Nobody's Fool*, staring Paul Newman. The best thing about that film is the multidimensional, sensitive portrait of Newman's character: You keep watching him, seeing that he isn't what he first appears to be, and wondering what he'll do next. Richard Russo, author of *Nobody's Fool*, has done the same thing again with *Straight Man*, only this time making his main man, William Henry Devereaux, Jr., an extremely funny guy.

In fact, if this book has any real flaw, it's that you might often sit back from the story and think, "I can't believe he's this amusing on every page." Told in Devereaux's voice, *Straight Man* is beguilingly sarcastic. Devereaux is the head of an English department at a small Pennsylvania college, where budget cutbacks and political infighting threaten most of the staff. Devereaux's inability to resist the clever remark and his impatience with stuffy behavior cause him to escalate the brewing crisis into a maelstrom.

The suspense in this story lies in character development, which is a tricky thing to pull off in a novel. We become concerned for Devereaux and wonder whether he will behave like an immature jerk or will rise above the squabbling to be a good leader, good husband, and good father.

Russo is also the author of *Mohawk* and *The Risk Pool*.

Devereaux tries to apply William of Occam's philosophy to each ridiculous situation that comes his way: Choose the simplest approach. Is Russo deriding the philosophy or making fun of Devereaux for failing to live up to it?

The English department staff are loathsome. Do these individuals come alive as authentic characters, or do they seem to be caricatures?

It's difficult to create a protagonist whose main challenge is overcoming his own pronounced shortcomings. Do Devereaux's high jinks ever alienate you to the extent that you have trouble caring about him?

An Anthropologist on Mars: Seven Paradoxical Tales, by Oliver Sacks, Vintage Books (paperback)

Oliver Sacks was the neurologist portrayed in the movie *Awakenings* by actor Robin Williams, and given both Sacks's writing style and his demeanor in appearances before literary audiences, the warmth of his screen persona as portrayed by Williams seems entirely accurate. Sacks has written a number of books in addition to *Awakenings* about the people who have been the objects of his scientific study, including *The Man Who Mistook His Wife for a Hat, The Island of the Colorblind,* and *An Anthropologist on Mars.* Two characteristics distinguish his writing: the strangeness of the afflictions and the humanity with which Sacks approaches the afflicted.

The seven stories in *Anthropologist* include an account of an autistic woman named Temple Grandin, who emerged from oppressive childhood symptoms to become an inventor, professor, and writer in her own right. She is the one who coined the phrase "anthropologist on Mars" to try to explain what it feels like to live among people so mentally different from herself.

Sacks also includes a doctor with Tourette's Syndrome who is able to perform surgery and pilot aircraft in spite of his uncontrollable jerking and verbal outbursts; a blind man whose life is thrown into chaos once his sight is restored; a man whose memory is so damaged that for him it is always 1968; and an artist who stops painting, eating, and relating to those around him when he becomes colorblind.

Using terms the layperson is likely to understand, Sacks allows the fascinating aspects of each story to emerge, asking us to understand sensory problems we may have never imagined, and treating each subject with dignity and compassion.

In analyzing brain malfunctions, Sacks helps us to gain a better understanding of the normal workings of the brain. Most of us are probably attracted to his work because of the strangeness of his subjects' symptoms; does Sacks create a feeling of empathy with his patients, so that we regard them as more than interesting cases?

Would you say that neurological disease is different from other forms of illness, in that the former becomes part of the persona of the patient?

The Catcher in the Rye, by J. D. Salinger, Little, Brown and Company (paperback)

Here's a book you may have read decades ago. Then, it was a hallmark work of disillusioned youth, written in the wise, unpredictable voice of sixteen-year-old Holden Caulfield. Pick it up now, and you'll be amazed at just how fresh it seems.

Salinger's forty-five-year-old novel exudes humor and pathos as Caulfield relates the story of his recent past and how he came to be on the lam in New York after leaving his Pennsylvania prep school. His confiding tone and his funny, sarcastic commentary will pull you in from the very first page.

Caulfield's heartsick comments on teachers and phonies aptly convey the angst at the heart of adolescent alienation. Very possibly, it is this aspect of the novel that keeps it on banned book lists.

Salinger, who was born in 1919, has written numerous short stories and until recently was known for only two novels in his long career: this one, and *Franny and Zooey.* (It took him ten years to write *The Catcher in the Rye.*) His most recent book, *Hapworth 16, 1924,* was published in 1999 with much controversy as to the quality of the writing. The author, who shuns media attention, lives on the East Coast and writes stories for *The New Yorker.*

Is Caulfield emotionally ill, or is he simply exhausted from having to deal with depressing reality?

Does Salinger's protagonist seem too wise? Is Salinger simply using him as a vehicle to vent his own frustration with society, or does Caulfield's articulation of his confusion, intense emotions, and dismay at phoniness seem authentic for someone his age?

Caulfield displays strong feelings of affection and concern for his younger sister. Is it possible that the author inserted her in the book to give his protagonist significant, positive personality traits that counterbalance his complaints and ennui? Or is she an important element of the story for other reasons?

What did you think of the ending of Salinger's novel? Did it leave too many questions unanswered, or did it pave the way for you to create your own ending? Was the open-ended approach in keeping with the style of the rest of the story?

The Soloist, by Mark Salzman, Vintage Books (paperback)

If you read *Iron and Silk*, you know Mark Salzman can write. His captivating description of time spent in China teaching English to college students and learning martial arts from a master was both comic and telling. In *The Soloist* he proves he can also write fiction, and write it beautifully.

Salzman introduces us to Renne Sundheimer, whose ability to play the cello as a child led the musical world to hail him as possibly the greatest cellist who had ever lived. Unfortunately, Renne's talent failed him when he turned eighteen, and ever since he has made his living as a cello teacher in southern California. We join thirty-six-year-old Renne as two events are about to jolt him again: a summons to jury duty and the request to serve as mentor to a nine-year-old Korean cello prodigy.

Although *The Soloist* is not a comedy, Salzman's irrepressible humor sparkles through in many wonderful little moments. "Judge Davis had a huge head. At first I hadn't realized it because the rest of him was so big as well, but when either of the lawyers approached the bench you could compare more easily. His head looked like one of those heroic Roman busts of Caligula or Nero or Brutus that at first look life-sized, but gradually you see as you get closer that they are really about half again as big. During lulls in the trial, I enjoyed picturing him with a little crown of olive leaves on top of his head, presiding over events at a marble coliseum."

Salzman has also written a memoir, *Lost in Place: Growing Up Absurd in Suburbia*, and another novel, *The Laughing Sutra*.

Renne is forced to participate more fully in life when he accepts Kyung-hee as a student and participates as a juror in the murder trial of a Zen student accused of killing his master. How does this cause Renne to gain a new sense of himself?

What did you think of Renne's relationship with Maria-Teresa? How did this contribute to the protagonist's growth? Did it give you hope that Renne would be capable of rewarding, intimate connection?

Is Salzman saying the artist's life is one that requires terrible sacrifice?

The Reader, by Bernhard Schlink, translated from the German by Carol Brown Janeway, Vintage Books (paperback)

A best-seller in Europe and the United States and translated into fourteen languages worldwide, *The Reader* is unfortunately the only one of Bernhard Schlink's books currently available in English in our country. This German professor of law and practicing judge is also the author of a number of prize-winning crime novels.

Actually, *The Reader* is a kind of crime novel, but on a much larger scale than you'd expect. Michael is a fifteen-year-old student recovering from hepatitis when he first meets Hanna, an unpredictable and attractive woman twice his age who works as a streetcar conductor in Berlin in the years following World War II. They have a secret, torrid affair, which very often includes Michael reading aloud to Hanna at her request. When their union is over, Hanna disappears. Michael grows from a gangly youth into a young law student who is taken by surprise one day to find Hanna on trial for war crimes in the courtroom where his professor has brought him and other students.

Schlink raises questions of morality in a number of ways that makes this piece of fiction a prime topic for discussion. Sin and innocence: Are they absolutes? Does understanding the cause of apparently inexcusable behavior make it any more excusable? When is it appropriate to fear guilt by association, and does humane treatment toward a criminal make one somehow criminal?

In addition to teaching constitutional law and philosophy at Humboldt University in Berlin, the author is also a justice at the Constitutional Law Court in Münster and has written papers on collective guilt. As a member of the generation born just after the war, he says he bears a "second guilt," or feelings of guilt by association that plague those whose parents complied with the Nazi regime.

With Hanna, Michael begins to blossom as a young man, gaining confidence and ease. Yet, after their breakup, it seems that Michael remains frozen in time, awkward in intimate relationships years after the fact. What do you think would have allowed him truly to grow up and break out of this frozen state?

The Golden Gate, by Vikram Seth, Vintage International (paperback)

Treat yourself to a truly unusual experience: Read a contemporary novel in verse. *The Golden Gate* is not at all difficult; in fact, it's a lot of fun. Poet, novelist, and travel writer Vikram Seth has fashioned a tale of love and Bay Area living using sonnets in iambic tetrameter. The structure is Shakespearean, but the language is modern, including a fair amount of slang and references to an iguana named Schwarzenegger.

As you read his novel, you'll be amazed at the ease with which Seth's characters and setting emerge within a disciplined framework of rhyming verse. From Silicon Valley to San Francisco to the Sonoma wine country, he follows three men and two women (a computer expert, philosopher/peace protester, advertising executive, sculptor, and attorney) as they seek love and meaning in their lives.

Although *The Golden Gate* may seem more a literary stunt than anything else, Seth was acclaimed as a technically solid poet by the literary world when his book was first published. The novel won both the Quality Paperback Book Club New Voice Award and the Commonwealth Poetry Prize in 1986. Seth explained that he had patterned the work after Russian author Alexander Pushkin's *Eugene Onegin.*

Not one to shy away from the difficult, Seth's next novel was *A Suitable Boy,* at 1,349 pages the longest novel to be published in the twentieth century. He has also authored the novel *An Equal Music,* two books of poems, and *From Heaven Lake: Travels Through Sinkiang and Tibet.* The latter is an account of his 1981 hitchhiking adventure from Nanjing University in eastern China through Tibet and Nepal to his home in Delhi, India.

Born in Calcutta, Seth earned both a bachelor's and a master's degree at Oxford, a master's at Stanford University, and a graduate diploma at Nanjing. He was also a Guggenheim Fellow.

Apart from frequent use of the word yuppie, *does Seth's novel set in the 1970s seem at all dated?*

Do you think the author is saying that passionate love cannot withstand the institution of marriage?

The Dancer Upstairs, by Nicholas Shakespeare, Nan A. Talese/Doubleday (hardcover)

This thought-provoking thriller is less about a dancer and more about the single-mindedness that creates political martyrs. Set in an unnamed country in South America, *The Dancer Upstairs* follows a humble police officer named Agustin Rejas whose job it is to track down the terrorist Ezequiel, the killer of thirty thousand and torturer of many more.

Although Rejas becomes a likable, admirable man in the hands of Nicholas Shakespeare, it soon becomes clear that both his government bosses and the revolutionaries are equally deranged and cruel. Walking the line between these two fronts, Rejas tries to carry out justice and at the same time to have some sort of personal life. Both endeavors are almost impossible. It's interesting that the author lets us know from the outset that Ezequiel will be captured; the suspense comes from our worry over Rejas and the eventual impact of these events on him.

Shakespeare based his novel on his time as a journalist reporting on the hunt for Abimael Guzman, leader of Peru's Shining Path guerrillas. He has framed his fiction with a story about a journalist searching for information on Ezequiel's capture, although it's not clear that this other plot is essential to the core drama.

The Dancer Upstairs is brushed with unexpected strokes that lend the writing authenticity, including the portrayal of Rejas's wife, whose concerns about selling cosmetics seem stunningly prosaic compared to the life-and-death questions posed by her husband's work.

Shakespeare's novel *Elena Silves* won Britain's Somerset Maugham Award.

In THE DANCER UPSTAIRS, *nothing is ever safe and people are rarely what they seem to be. The tension builds until you can barely stand it. Is this tension more a function of the political situation Shakespeare is hoping to portray, or is it typical of the thriller genre?*

What would justice looks like in this twisted situation? How could it be achieved?

Hula, by Lisa Shea, Delta (paperback)

Two little girls in the backyard in summertime, having adventures, dressing their dog in a hula skirt and lei, keeping one eye out for a half-crazy father: Could this be the makings of an entire novel?

Shea pulls it off with ease. Each scene portrays a moment of childhood with all the right intense flavor. The dialogue feels like the very real talk of children. Their Vietnam vet father lurks on the horizon, a metal plate in his head, someone who might grab and burn their toys in the front yard ditch, or someone who might come to their rescue when they are stuck in the sump pump mud. You want to know what will happen next, and while you are waiting, you savor two summers of childhood in a Virginia backyard.

There are odd gaps in this first novel, but they appear to be calculated. The dog and rabbit are called repeatedly by name, Mitelin and Lily, but the family members are only "my sister," "our father," and "our mother." Mom is not a threat, and yet she is largely left out of the narrative, an elusive and ineffectual presence, except at key points where she takes decisive action. What happens in the lives of the sisters during the school year? It's not mentioned. All we see is a child's close-up view—two little girls in a backyard, often having fun, sometimes making their way around scary obstacles—and it is more than enough.

Hula won a $30,000 Whiting Writers Award in 1993, which put Shea in the company of authors like Tobias Wolff, Mona Simpson, and Alice McDermott.

Why did Shea choose HULA *as the title of this book?*

Of their father, the younger sister says, "My mother says something happened to our father in the war, but my sister says he's just mean." This sentence captures a dual feeling that we develop about the father as the story unfolds. Is it fair to blame him for his actions? Are there clues as to how Shea feels about him?

The Stone Diaries, by Carol Shields, Penguin (paperback)

Winner of the 1995 Pulitzer Prize and the National Book Critics Circle Award, *The Stone Diaries* is a deceptive book. As you travel along through the characters' lives, following love affairs, catastrophes, proud achievements, and personal failures, it feels as though you are part of an epic story with beginning, middle, and end. And yet, there is no such structure here. The book is simply a tapestry of lives woven together in such an exceptional way that they all seem important.

Designed mainly as a fictional biography of the likable and impressive Daisy Goodwill Flett, born in 1905 in Manitoba, *The Stone Diaries* bears an ironic title. Shields in fact appears to be saying that our lives are anything but written in stone. Daisy's history is marked by a number of phases in which she assumes entirely new roles. Her father, Cuyler, the stonecutter who builds a tower in his wife's memory, turns from being a timid, awkward young man in one chapter of his life to popularity as a public speaker in another.

Shields has a wonderful ability to create flashes of intense, exotic emotion in otherwise commonplace settings. Single moments in these pages stand out, their passion or pain shimmering with clarity. Cuyler's pronouncement of love to his wife, as overheard by a third person, or the moment of Daisy's first husband's death will probably stay with you long after you've read the book.

Shields has authored a number of novels, including *Larry's Party, Swann, The Orange Fish, Happenstance, The Republic of Love,* and *Various Miracles.*

Is there a consistent point of view in this novel? Is Daisy the only character through whose eyes we see?

Perhaps Shields provides a clue to the meaning and intent of her novel when Daisy says, "When we say a thing or an event is real, never mind how suspect it sounds, we honor it. But when a thing is made up—regardless of how true and just it seems—we turn up our noses. That's the age we live in. The documentary age." Is the author urging us to examine the role of the storyteller and in particular the dynamics of a well-wrought piece of fiction?

The Weight of Water, by Anita Shreve, Back Bay Books (paperback)

What a knockout book. A true, nineteenth-century murder story lies at the heart of *The Weight of Water,* a novel crafted with such beautiful precision in both language and storytelling that it will hit you between the eyes.

In 1995 a photojournalist arrives at Smuttynose Island off the coast of Maine to cover two axe murders committed more than a century before. With her, Jean has brought her husband, small daughter, her brother-in-law, and his girlfriend. As they travel around the island on their boat, the small group is threatened by suspicions, jealousies, and betrayal almost as dramatic as those that tormented the Norwegian immigrants Jean has come to research.

Author Anita Shreve has no fear of leaping from one story to the other, back and forth in time, with little or no connective tissue to soften the way. She manages to accomplish this without confusion, making it clear when Jean is piecing together the past and when she is puzzling over the present.

Shreve provides a contrasting narrative within her own, which serves as a comfortable counterpoint to her stark style: a retelling of the 1873 tale by one of the participants. Maren's account written years later of the awful events is much fuller and opinionated than the narrative seen through Jean's eyes, and although the details are ghastly at times, it is satisfying to have them so thoroughly explained.

Shreve is also the author of the novels *Eden Close, Strange Fits of Passion, Where or When, Resistance,* and the best-seller *The Pilot's Wife.*

In both Jean's and Maren's worlds, there is an exquisite tension deriving from what is imagined rather than fully explained. For both women, there is a single moment that changes their lives forever. What do you think Shreve is trying to say about the nature of happiness and the human psyche?

Maren's relationship with her brother takes on unusual significance for her because of lack of parental affection. Shreve does not clarify certain events that happen between them. Do you think her brother misinterpreted her love when he defined it as sinful?

Lost Lake, by Mark Slouka, Alfred A. Knopf (hardcover)

These powerful, connected short stories almost make a novel as they re-create a boyhood spent in a tiny Czech community on New York's Lost Lake. While book clubs often shy away from short story collections, maybe because they seem like hors d'oeuvres rather than a full meal, Slouka provides a feast in *Lost Lake,* and it would be a huge mistake to miss it.

Although Slouka's narrator begins by describing his youth as ambiguous and undramatic, he is overly modest. Scenes of an old man with a terrible grudge against all the lake's turtles or memories of a grandfather escaping death in the old country will imprint themselves in your memory. So will lighter moments, like the highly inconvenient loss of an expensive watch by an obnoxious visitor. As with other tales of ordinary life, these anecdotes about a lakeside community become noteworthy in the hands of this superlative storyteller.

Slouka's twelve stories share the upstate New York setting, many of the same characters, and a fishing motif. However, unlike Norman MacLean's *A River Runs Through It,* the people are what you'll remember more than the outdoors and the fishing. Slouka's prose is carefully spare and his characters one-of-a-kind. When added to moments of drama, these ingredients add up to a tour de force.

"The Woodcarver's Tale," the fifth story in this collection, a heartbreaking gem centered on the narrator's father, won a National Magazine Award in fiction for *Harper's* in 1995. Now a southern California resident, Slouka has taught at Columbia, Harvard, Penn State, and the University of Virginia. *Lost Lake* is his first book of fiction.

Slouka cultivates a rich, melancholy view of love, memory, and yearning from a male perspective. Is it unusual for a male writer to show this kind of sensitivity and to strike so many emotional chords? Can you think of other men whose writing flows in this same vein?

LOST LAKE *lulls us with the dreamy, idiosyncratic details that make up the narrator's summers on the lake, but also staggers us with certain images of death or betrayal. Are the former necessary to make the latter palatable? What would you say are his themes?*

The Age of Grief: A Novella and Stories of Love, Marriage, and Friendship, by Jane Smiley, Fawcett Columbine (paperback)

If you haven't already read *A Thousand Acres,* Smiley's Pulitzer Prize–winning blockbuster, you may not want to now. In recent times, there have been so many books involving incest and abusive parents that you may not be willing to digest one more story about that kind of dysfunctional family, no matter how well it's written.

So here's *The Age of Grief.* As gloomy as the title sounds, the stories in this collection are uplifting and humorous, with touches of tragedy. Smiley is a portrait artist who with great talent paints human lives and souls. Published well before *A Thousand Acres,* these tales display the potency of her writing, although the magic doesn't really appear until the third story. Then watch out.

In "Jeffrey, Believe Me," the narrator's authoritative voice takes on a half-evil, half-comic tone as she explains to poor Jeffrey why she has used him to make a baby . . . how she chose him, how she plotted. You won't know whether to laugh or cry, but you'll want to read on. In "Dynamite," Smiley rivets you with a lead sentence that begins, "I used to not call my mother or my brother and sister because their phones were being tapped . . ." In the other stories, she climbs inside the souls of her characters, revealing weaknesses as well as strengths, causing you to like these people and at the same time to root for them to behave a lot better than they have.

Smiley is also the author of a mystery, *Duplicate Keys;* two novellas, *Ordinary Love* and *Good Will;* the novels *The Greenlanders, Moo, At Paradise Gate,* and *The All-True Travels and Adventures of Lidie Newton.*

A number of these stories often end without a clear resolution but rather with a strong emotion or a quiet revelation on the part of one of the characters. Is the story less satisfying without a resolution? Is it enough to have only a feeling about what might or might not happen?

Who or what is the villain in the novella THE AGE OF GRIEF*? What do you think of the husband's search for the "ironic middle," the state of being in marriage that will enable him and his wife to hold together their shaky alliance?*

Saving Grace, by Lee Smith, Ballantine Books (paperback)

Somehow popular southern author Lee Smith has pulled off telling a story about the child of a snake-handling fundamentalist minister without making fun of religious extremists. Smith unfurls with slippery dexterity and compassion the tale of Grace, a southern girl who loves her parents but who also has the good sense to question their behavior.

Grace's daddy, Virgil Shepherd, minister of God, moves his family from town to town in Appalachia, sets up tent meetings, heals the sick, and faces run-ins with the law for handling venomous snakes and drinking poison to illustrate the strength of God's love for those who believe. His wife and children accept his mission, to a point. How each responds is part of the drama of Smith's story, with Grace's narrative the main thread.

Secretly, Grace hates Jesus and feels hardly better toward her insensitive father, who seems to care little about his family's suffering. At the first chance, she leaves home, but marries the Reverend Travis Word, improving her lot only by small degree. It's not until she arrives at Uncle Slidell's Christian Fun Golf Course, after a number of side paths, that her spirit truly soars. From her days in the relatively idyllic setting of Scrabble Creek, North Carolina, to her years as an adult in Tennessee, Grace takes a journey marked by suspense, romance, and a good dollop of humor.

A prolific author, Smith has eleven books to her name. Among them are *Fair and Tender Ladies, Black Mountain Breakdown, Family Linen, Fancy Strut, Oral History, Me and My Baby View the Eclipse,* and *The Devil's Dream.*

Smith conjures up a number of spellbinding scenes involving a bizarre religious cult. Instead of making the serpent-handling and poison-drinking purely grotesque, the author manages to get at the humanity of those involved. How does she do this?

There is an impressive range of voices in SAVING GRACE. *How does Smith duplicate the sound of hill-country and other dialects without weighing down her dialogue with broken speech?*

What did you think of the ending? Did you see this as a successful culmination of Grace's travails or a disappointment? Did it seem likely?

Rose, by Martin Cruz Smith, Ballantine Books (paperback)

Martin Cruz Smith is not just a wonderful mystery writer, he is a wonderful writer period. The northern California novelist is a master at building story, using language simply and beautifully, developing fascinating characters, and re-creating other times and places.

If you think Smith is solely an expert writer about Russia because of his novels *Gorky Park, Polar Star,* and *Red Square,* think again. *Rose* is set in the coal mining town of Wigan in Victorian England, with the mines and their workers emerging full-blown from Smith's pages.

Jonathan Blair, an explorer and mining engineer who would much rather be back at his old job in Africa, has been sent to Wigan to find a missing young minister. The young curate is engaged to Blair's patron's daughter. If Blair is successful, there's a chance the wealthy mine owner will send him back to the Gold Coast—that is, if he can stop his heavy drinking.

In the course of Blair's search, we come to know tunnels one mile beneath the surface of the earth and the dark existence that miners of the 1800s led around the clock, as well as the elegant life of the privileged class living nearby. As Blair begins to gather clues, he becomes serious about his quest, and with us is snared by the romance, violence, and mystery of this drizzly, perverse environment.

Smith is also the author of *Havana Bay* and *Stallion Gate,* two other novels not set in Russia.

It could be said that Blair is a hero and a jerk. Smith has given him the challenge of both solving a mystery and overcoming his own limitations. Does he achieve the latter? How has his character improved by the end of the book? What has caused this development?

Smith has been praised for his ability to create exceptionally vivid scenes, transporting his readers to foreign locales. ROSE *drips with the dark atmosphere of England's coal country. Did the realism of his setting and the expert construction of his novel trick you into accepting an amazing denouement? What did you think of the ending?*

The Knowledge of Water, by Sarah Smith, Ballantine Books (paperback)

Here's another book that's been labeled "mystery" but is really so much more. The puzzle at the heart of Sarah Smith's novel, set in Paris at the turn of the century, is whether a young American aspiring to a career as a concert pianist can withstand pressures to marry and settle down to domesticity, and whether the man she loves will kill her artist's dream.

The secondary mystery, as to who murdered a crazy homeless woman and who is stalking the two main characters on the streets of Paris, seems not nearly as puzzling, although that question does lend further ominous overtones to Smith's tale.

Although Smith's book is the second in a trilogy, *The Knowledge of Water* stands on its own as a novel. However, members of my book club did read the first book in the series, *The Vanished Child,* and found that many details were clarified for them.

The Knowledge of Water is written in overlapping layers, and it does require patience to wade through them, meeting a number of new characters, waiting to see the connections among them. The payoff is worth it. Smith raises questions of truth, art, love, sexism, and class discrimination, building toward a climax that coincides with the great flood that submerged much of Paris in 1910. As the novel culminates, you'll feel swept along in a tremendous flow of events.

Smith, a university professor of film and literature, was formerly a Fulbright Fellow in London. The paperback includes an informative interview with her as well as a thought-provoking set of questions to serve as a reader's guide.

Although set in Paris almost a century ago, Smith's novel addresses questions women still grapple with today concerning the conflicting demands of career and family. Why do you think the author added an additional burden for Perdita in the form of near blindness?

Baron von Reisden is ensnared in questions of murder, art forgery, and natural disaster that distract him from his pursuit of scientific research. While Smith's heroine seems like a thoroughly decent person, the baron has a certain shadowy quality. How do you think Smith wanted us to feel about him?

Crossing to Safety, by Wallace Stegner, Penguin USA (paperback)

Wallace Stegner has a place among modern American literary giants. Stegner founded the highly respected creative writing program at Stanford University, won the Pulitzer Prize for *Angle of Repose* in 1972, and was awarded the National Book Award for *The Spectator Bird* in 1977. He was a prolific writer of both fiction and nonfiction before his death in 1993.

However, there was something about Stegner's style that invited literary praise but made him less than accessible to the public. He was a writer of deep emotion and romantic enthusiasm for people and for nature, but his work can have a slower, more meandering pace than the typical work of fiction.

If you are willing to hang out with Stegner and take the story at his tempo, it's possible to have a deeply satisfying experience. In *Crossing to Safety,* you'll become part of a friendship between two couples who meet in a small college town. The story of their love and companionship has a fairy-tale quality, involving both amazing good fortune and terrible crisis. There is not so much a traditional rising and falling structure to this novel as there is revelation about the alchemy of friendship and how it has enriched four lives.

Once you've read *Crossing to Safety,* you may find yourself returning to incidents in the book in the same way you'd muse over events in your own life.

Stegner is also the author of *The Big Rock Candy Mountain, Where the Bluebird Sings to the Lemonade Springs,* and *Joe Hill.*

The character of Charity is both appealing and repugnant for her liveliness and her ability to create a good time and for her damaging criticism of her husband. Is it really possible to be the close friend of someone who wants to squash artistic talent and be so controlling? Did this reflect poorly on the other characters?

Stegner's book begins quietly. At what point does he snag your interest? What are the elements in his writing that cause you to read on?

Old Books, Rare Friends: Two Literary Sleuths and Their Shared Passion, by Leona Rostenberg and Madeleine Stern, Main Street Books (paperback)

Here's a remarkable memoir about a friendship and lust for learning that has propelled two women through almost a century of life. Leona Rostenberg and Madeleine Stern have devoted themselves to finding and selling rare books and also to solving literary mysteries. In the course of these pursuits, they have traveled the world and have lived happily together as partners, each encouraging the other as they've turned out scholarly books of their own.

In 1995, an article on the two in *The New York Times* inspired editors at Doubleday to ask Leona and Madeleine if they would do a joint autobiography. Although their literary accomplishments make for an unusual story, the two women realized that a number of other facts about them set them apart. Although each had been courted by various men, neither had ever married. (They are quick to point out that their relationship is not a sexual one.) Furthermore, both lived at home with their parents long after the time that children usually do and both pursued higher education when women were discouraged from doing so.

One of the joys of this book is the description of searches for antiquarian books. Their accounts of their trips to Europe, in which they discover little-noticed books of great historical impact among stacks of old tomes, are highly satisfying. So, too, is their description of Madeleine's investigative work on Louisa May Alcott, in which she uncovers the steamy romance writing with which Alcott anonymously helped to support her family.

Given the times in which they've lived, do you think it's likely that either of these women would have accomplished as much as they did if they had been married?

In alternating chapters, each woman tells her life story and provides a great deal of information about rare books and literary sleuthing. What did you learn about antiquarian books that was particularly interesting?

***I Been in Sorrow's Kitchen and Licked Out All the Pots*, by Susan Straight, Anchor Books (paperback)**

Don't let the title fool you. This surprising story has its highs as well as lows. Novelist Susan Straight introduces us to the unforgettable figure of Marietta, a poor black teenager who ekes out a living selling baskets to tourists along the highway on the South Carolina coast, and by book's end we've arrived with her in California to find a new world of possibilities.

Along the way, Marietta must cope with the death of her mother, find her way in the big city, and try to support twin boys on her own. Most important, as a tall, big-boned black woman who has been made to feel ugly and invisible, she must come to terms with who she is.

Much of the beauty of the book lies in its language, which has two aspects: a very rich, evocative narrative and the rough dialect of the coastal low country. At first the Gullah dialect is hard to wade through, but stay with it, you'll get used to it.

Whether Marietta is working in the fields of a pseudo-plantation or suffering stark suburban isolation as a football mom on the West Coast, we feel respect for her dignity and cheer each achievement. Straight creates a fresh, genuine character and gives us a taste of an existence many of us have never known.

A graduate of Amherst College, Straight is a white woman who grew up in the black community of Riverside, California, and continues to live there today. She first wrote her stories of African Americans as part of her doctoral thesis. Much of her work, she reports, is based on tales passed along in her neighborhood.

Straight is also the author of *Blacker Than a Thousand Midnights, The Gettin' Place,* and *Aquaboogie.*

Does it matter to the reader that Straight is a white woman writing about black Americans? How does this influence your view of the authenticity of this book? Taking a broader perspective, how do you feel when a male author depicts a female heroine (as in THE SIXTEEN PLEASURES, *for example) or a woman dares to draw a male main character (as in* FUGITIVE PIECES*)? Does the ability to cross racial, gender, age-based, or cultural lines make an author's work seem suspect or even more magical?*

Darkness Visible, by William Styron, Vintage Books (paperback)

At the height of his writing career in 1985, William Styron was overcome with depression so crippling that he seriously contemplated suicide. His melancholia was not the result of any immediate events in his life but rather, he came to learn, of a collection of circumstances that went all the way back to childhood and before.

Having survived his struggle with madness, Styron wrote this slim volume to help the many others who face it in one degree or another.

Depression, Styron learned, is very often genetically determined. It can also be caused by emotional trauma in childhood, particularly unresolved grief, or incomplete mourning at the loss of a parent. The abrupt cessation of years of excessive drinking can also bring it on, as it seemed to do in Styron's case, and, ironically enough, the use of certain antidepressant drugs can encourage suicidal thoughts.

In his lucid, thorough explanation of his experience with the disorder, Styron makes depression something tangible, a force to be battled with intelligence, rather than a hazy concept of emotional distress. By laying open his own condition, he helps to make depression an affliction more likely to be acknowledged by those who suffer it and others who bear the brunt of it.

Styron is also the author of *Lie Down in Darkness, The Long March, Set This House on Fire, The Confessions of Nat Turner, Sophie's Choice,* and *This Quiet Dust.* His work has been awarded the Pulitzer Prize, the National Book Award, the Howells Medal, and the Edward MacDowell Medal.

As a renowned wordsmith, Styron was able to elucidate with great effectiveness the sensations and experiences associated with severe depression. Can you pinpoint passages that were particularly vivid in communicating these feelings?

Were you satisfied with the ending of DARKNESS VISIBLE, *in which Styron indicates that he got better? Did you want more detail? Was this the place to give more information, or was it better that he left that to medical experts?*

Styron pays homage to his wife for her patience and resilience during his weeks and months in the depths. Do you wonder how she managed? Would you have liked more information on their interaction while he was experiencing depression?

Follow Your Heart, by Susanna Tamaro, translated from the Italian by John Cullen, Delta (paperback)

Winner of Italy's coveted Premio Donna Citta di Roma in 1994, *Follow Your Heart* was a best-seller in that country and then throughout Europe. A short, bittersweet novel written in the form of a grandmother's letters to her estranged granddaughter living in the United States, Susanna Tamaro's uncommon story deserves a less clichéd English title; the original Italian was *You Must Go Where Your Heart Takes You.*

An elderly woman who knows that death is near sits down at her desk to write letters that will be read by her granddaughter only after she is gone. The loss of her daughter and of her granddaughter weigh heavily on her. Her task is a hard one, as she hopes to break through to the girl with her letters in a way she could never do when they were still talking, and this will mean confessing to a secret that she had planned to take with her to the grave.

As the dying woman divulges her story and that of her mother before her, her underlying message is that if you can truly understand the past, you can face the future with strength. She hopes her granddaughter will see that, although one's mistakes can be costly, the choice of a path in life does not have to be immutable.

The writing in this novel is breathtakingly simple; the first-person narrative is immediately engrossing. The Italian landscape as well as several generations of mothers and daughters emerge on the page full-blown as the frail woman remembers. If you are won over, you're likely to read this small gem in a matter of hours.

Tamaro was born in Trieste and is now a resident of Rome. She is also the author of a novel, a collection of short stories, and a children's book published abroad.

Often critics will greet with a sour-grapes attitude a successful, simple, eloquent piece of fiction that expresses deep passion, as if to distrust the widespread public excitement it has evoked. What is it about this book that distinguishes it as good literature rather than merely popular writing?

Do you agree with Tamaro's proposition that knowing your family's history can help you control your own destiny?

The Kitchen God's Wife, by Amy Tan, Ivy Books (paperback)

If you complained about the difficulty of following multiple characters in Amy Tan's elegantly written and incredibly successful *The Joy Luck Club*, you'll want to look at this book. It is the rousing tale of a single, valiant character making her way in China from the 1920s through late 1940s, at the mercy of a culture that victimized its women and under the domination of a cold, brutal husband.

Although *The Kitchen God's Wife* is labeled a novel, it is based on the life of Tan's immigrant mother, Daisy. That it is a true account lends the epic story even more impact and also makes the protagonist's ordeals more bearable, as you know eventually she will escape and prosper. When Tan completed the book and asked her mother what she thought of the portrayal of her monstrous ex-husband, Daisy replied, "You didn't make him mean enough."

Tan has a gift for telling her stories in the rhythms and imagery of Chinese and Chinese American people. The author has explained that she prepared to write the novel by videotaping interviews with her mother, and this technique helps to explain Tan's ability to evoke so thoroughly the sights and sounds of pre-Communist China.

Tan is also the author of *The Hundred Secret Senses* and has produced two children's books with illustrator Gretchen Schields: *The Moon Lady* and *The Chinese Siamese Cat.*

THE KITCHEN GOD'S WIFE *is framed within a taut mother/daughter relationship and a friendship between the mother and her oldest buddy. Lifelong friend Helen believes that Winnie is dying and that it's time for Winnie to reveal a number of terrible secrets about her past to her adult daughter, Pearl. Meanwhile, Pearl has a confidential matter of her own that she is keeping from her mother. What messages is Tan offering about mother/daughter relationships? Was this mother/daughter conflict framework crucially tied to the China story at the heart of the book?*

What lessons does Winnie teach her daughter about hope, love, and the contradictions inherent in one's life?

Imagining Argentina, by Lawrence Thornton, Bantam Books (paperback)

Amazingly enough, Lawrence Thornton really was imagining Argentina when he wrote this, his first novel. Although the California native has lived in France, Spain, and England, he had never been to Argentina when he chose to write a story about the "disappeareds," the thousands of Argentinians who were tortured and killed or imprisoned by the generals in that country during the 1970s.

In his inspiring tale, a man whose wife has disappeared suddenly finds he can "see" what has become of other people's missing loved ones but not his own. Thornton's book was proclaimed an instant classic for the way he seemed to capture the voice of Argentinians in pain and at the same time emblazoned the message that hope can ennoble the spirit. Although some have found controversial his lack of personal contact with the country that was his subject, his novel won numerous awards when it was published in 1987.

In addition to telling the story of Carlos Rueda as he strives to learn what has become of his wife, the novel is also a beguiling account of a person with no political interest who finds himself drawn into the heart of politics. As Carlos takes action, even though of a mystical nature and consisting of relatively small effort, the effects ripple outward to stir the emotions of many others . . . and to threaten the authorities.

Imagining Argentina is the first in a trilogy; it was followed by *Naming the Spirits* and *Tales from the Blue Archives.*

Thornton offers lessons in how to cope with political repression without turning into a villain yourself. Are his suggestions practical?

The narrative in IMAGINING ARGENTINA *has a lyrical quality that suits the passion between Rueda and his wife, their love for their daughter, and the affection he feels for his country. However, how is it possible to use delicate, crystalline prose to highlight the awful violence of the Argentinian regime? Does this perverse contrast heighten the effect of the book?*

The Samurai's Garden, by Gail Tsukiyama, St. Martin's Press (paperback)

What seems to be a serene tale about a young man recovering from illness opens up into a novel of stark drama and romance in Gail Tsukiyama's *The Samurai's Garden.* Set mainly in Japan on the eve of World War II, the novel follows a Hong Kong college student who must leave his university when he is felled by tuberculosis. Sent to recuperate at the family summer home in a tiny Japanese beach town, he quickly feels cut off from all those close to him.

The narrative catches fire once Stephen comes to know the unassuming old man named Matsu who is the beach house caretaker. Matsu is the gateway to certain powerful hidden knowledge, and as the young Chinese student grows strong physically, he also gains spiritual strength from the older Japanese man. Matsu introduces Stephen to two local people who have played crucial, tragic roles in his life, and as he does so, teaches Stephen lessons in dealing with the cruel and arbitrary events that fate might throw one's way.

The Samurai's Garden is a story as simple as the strong, lucid prose Tsukiyama uses to tell her tale of love and sacrifice. With it, she binds a number of compelling subplots into one, placing all of them against the foreboding backdrop of a nearby invading army.

Tsukiyama is uniquely equipped to write this cross-cultural fiction: Born in San Francisco, and now a resident of the Bay Area, she is the child of a Chinese mother and a Japanese father. Her books include *Women of the Silk* and *Night of Many Dreams.*

At times, the fact that Stephen is residing quietly in Japan and slowly regaining his health while Japanese troops are raping Nanking and conquering one Chinese city after another seems incongruous. His growing attachment to Japanese locals seems a very strange contrast to the events threatening his family and friends back home. What is Tsukiyama trying to tell us about the realities of war?

The author is expert at conveying sensations, whether the smell of ocean air or the heat of a steaming bath. Can you find passages in the book that are good examples of Tsukiyama's ability to stir our senses?

The Accidental Tourist, by Anne Tyler, Berkley Books (paperback)

You may have seen the movie version of this story; it is one of those rare films that does justice to the original novel. Read the book anyway, for the pleasure of seeing the characters emerge more fully and of falling completely under this whimsical writer's spell. The premise is enticing: Macon Leary is a travel writer who hates travel and who has managed to arrange his life into a bleak routine. He meets up with a dog trainer named Muriel whose snappy obedience techniques and curious personal style jar loose Macon's dreary persona.

Tyler wrote eight novels before capturing the popular spotlight with *Dinner at the Homesick Restaurant* in 1982. Her next book was *The Accidental Tourist,* which won the National Book Critics Circle Award in 1985. *Breathing Lessons* followed and won the Pulitzer Prize in 1989. More recently she has written *A Patchwork Planet, Celestial Navigation, Saint Maybe,* and *Ladder of Years.*

Perhaps the most winning feature in all of Tyler's books is the way she draws her peculiar characters, people with failings and eccentric habits so lovable that you can't help but care about them.

Like filmmakers Barry Levinson and John Waters, Tyler favors Baltimore as the setting for her stories. The city is her hometown, and by the time you have read one of her novels, you will feel you know it and a number of its residents intimately.

While Tyler's characters are weird, they are capable of a certain amount of change. Was Macon Leary's major character development that he loosened up, or was it more complicated than that?

Tyler's novel seems to say that we stumble through life, experiencing loss and pleasure by accident. Does the character of Muriel stand for an opposing, positive force, or is she simply another accident?

Families tend to exert a strong influence in Tyler's books. Her family members often seem inescapable, and they also have odd habits. What do you think the author is trying to say about family relationships?

Morality Play, by Barry Unsworth, W. W. Norton & Company (paperback)

The enchantment of this book lies not only in the murder mystery at its core but in the fact that you are so thoroughly transported to England in the 1300s, traveling with a group of hungry actors. Your host and narrator is a young priest who has three times run away from his church because of spring fever. His quirky outlook sets the tone for the events that follow, and in the hands of master writer Barry Unsworth, the novel builds to spellbinding theater. In fact, *Morality Play* would make a great movie.

As young Nicholas tells us about his problems and about the acting troupe's visit to a rural village, the behavior code and beliefs of the day are vividly revealed. For example, six hundred years ago it was thought that all plays should be religious in nature; there were stock figures such as Satan and God the Father and the Devil's Fool that the audience expected to see on stage.

When the impoverished, desperate actors in Unsworth's tale decide that they will draw a larger crowd—and more ticket money—by abandoning their stock characters and dramatizing a real incident in the life of a village, we see history being made. And the results are far more than just good box office. The actors barely understand what they have gotten themselves into until they begin to investigate the local murder and try to do it justice on stage. In the course of carrying out their new project they put their lives in danger. Unsworth blends humor, drama, romance, and mystery in a delicious mix as the troupe tries to find its way out of its predicament.

Morality Play was a finalist for Britain's prestigious Booker Prize in 1995. Unsworth earlier won the prize with the novel *Sacred Hunger.* His other works of fiction include *Stone Virgin, Mooncranker's Gift, Pascali's Island,* and *After Hannibal.*

How does Unsworth transport you so thoroughly to Britain six centuries ago? There isn't much exposition; Nicholas assumes you are familiar with the times and simply confides his difficult adventure.

Did you have trouble caring about a main character who seems so inept? Would you have read past the third chapter if you hadn't been told this was a great book?

My Own Country: A Doctor's Story of a Town and Its People in the Age of AIDS, by Abraham Verghese, Vintage Books (paperback)

Abraham Verghese is an accomplished author as well as a compassionate physician. In *My Own Country,* he has written two edifying stories: One tells of his dream to become an American doctor despite the barriers presented by his status as a member of a foreign-born minority. The other is an account of the AIDS virus's arrival in small-town America, the first written history by a physician of his experience with patients infected with HIV.

The weaving of these two stories is achieved with care so that the doctor, his Indian American family, his new friends, and his patients all come to life and their fates, in the path of the virus, become crucial.

When Verghese saw his first AIDS patient in Johnson City, Tennessee, in 1985, there was no test for AIDS, no way of determining whether the virus was present apart from looking for certain symptoms. The young man he examined was but the first of eighty people Verghese would treat in that town for the virus; together they were eighty-one more than Johnson City expected or was prepared to acknowledge.

The homosexual son, the factory worker who had caught it from her husband, and the devout older couple who refused to tell their own family were all at first disconcerting to the doctor, but in time they became his calling. Simultaneously, they threatened to become his undoing. The emotional demands of fighting a virus that seemed unconquerable took a dramatic toll on Verghese's personal and social life, and you'll find yourself rooting for this young man who cares so deeply about the people he treated.

Verghese has since authored another critically acclaimed nonfiction book, *The Tennis Partner: A Doctor's Story of Friendship and Loss.*

Verghese explains his feelings of displacement as an Indian born in Africa and a minority immigrant to this country. Did he especially identify with the newly diagnosed AIDS patients because their disease dislocated them socially?

Verghese's brand of tenderhearted treatment and concern for patients has been discouraged in the practice of modern medicine. Since it played havoc with his life, do you think there's justification for doctors to remain distant from those they treat?

Winter Wheat, by Mildred Walker, University of Nebraska Press (paperback)

We're extremely fortunate that this book is still in print, as the once-popular name Mildred Walker has fallen into obscurity. Written in 1944, *Winter Wheat* was one of thirteen novels by this American author, of whom the *Philadelphia Inquirer* said, "You are either a Mildred Walker enthusiast or you are missing one of the best writers on the American scene."

Winter Wheat was a Literary Guild selection in 1944, and her fictional *The Body of a Young Man* was nominated for a National Book Award. Why Walker is not better known today is a mystery, as her writing is elegant and timeless in its appeal.

The only child of farmers in the dryland wheat country of Montana, Ellen Webb makes a pivotal step away from the home she loves and toward the more sophisticated world of college when she travels off to school in urban Minnesota. Almost immediately she falls in love. When she brings her fiancé home during a school break, Ellen views her family's modest existence amidst the arid landscape through his unsparing eyes, and her feelings about herself and her parents are forever altered. Heartbreak, revelations about her mother and father, and discoveries about the nature of love follow.

Walker's fiction may sound modest in scope, but she repeatedly shakes us with powerful insights and dramatic complications. Ellen's voice is deceptively uncomplicated and humble; her observations and her questions hit hard. In between the novel's dramatic incidents, Walker's descriptions of farm life and nature provide lovely, lyrical interludes and conjure up a moving portrait of rural Montana.

An introduction by the author James Welch seems mostly unnecessary, but he does include an interesting biography of Walker.

In assuming new, critical opinions of her parents, Ellen decides that their coolness is a sign that they barely tolerate each other. Is this true or are they still in love?

Walker offers no easy solutions for Ellen's heartbreak; her protagonist goes through a series of trials that toughen her. As it describes initiation into adulthood, what particular themes does the novel express?

Montana 1948, by Larry Watson, Washington Square Press (paperback)

As you read *Montana 1948,* you quickly forget that it is fiction. In this riveting gem of a book, Watson's narrator, twelve-year-old David Hayden, tells of a harrowing summer in Bentrock, Montana, when his father, the sheriff, takes on the only case of any real proportion he has ever had to face. The sheriff is forced to arrest his own brother, a war hero and doctor accused of molesting numerous Indian women and murdering one of them.

David confides his fears and observations, engaging us bit by bit in a strange story that becomes increasingly complex as it plays out. The tightly woven narrative presents memorable people and dire events that leave you shocked when they are over.

The issues Watson has chosen to spotlight are universal: a young boy's desire to be taken seriously, the untimely death of a loved one, disappointments between husband and wife, the frustrations of dealing with an all-powerful father, the sorrow of finding that family members are far less than the people you'd hoped them to be.

If you enjoy listening to books on tape, this novel is available in unabridged form, with excellent narration by actor Beau Bridges.

Watson, who teaches English at the University of Wisconsin in Stevens Point, is also the author of *Justice,* a collection of short stories that is the prequel to *Montana 1948.* He also wrote the novels *In a Dark Time* and *White Crosses.*

More than anything, MONTANA 1948 *is a meditation on the difficulty of doing what is right. Do you think it was correct for Uncle Frank to be locked in David's basement rather than in the jail?*

The action is told by David forty years after the fact, but expresses the perspective of a child. What aspects of the narrative characterize it as a youngster's view, and how do they add to the sense of mystery?

Watson does a superb job of dramatizing the conflicts beneath the surface in the small town of Bentrock. There is moral ambiguity, simmering anger, and much that is left unsaid. Does the author portray his small-town people with dignity, or is he slamming small-town life?

Divine Secrets of the Ya-Ya Sisterhood, by Rebecca Wells, HarperPerennial (paperback)

This is a book club success story, very probably. Rebecca Wells's poignant novel was around for more than a year when word of mouth among reading groups appeared to push it onto the best-seller list.

At the heart of *The Ya-Ya Sisterhood* is a colorful, satisfying story about four Louisiana girls—their friendship, their travails, their growing old together. Wells has created vibrant characters and has had fun with them, and we are the lucky beneficiaries of her humor and pathos.

The novel focuses in particular on Vivi, the wildest of the four Ya-Yas, and is told from the point of view of her daughter, Sidda. If the book has one major shortcoming, it is that Sidda's story is lackluster compared to that of her mother's. Sidda is a woman of the nineties, a successful playwright planning to marry an apparently perfect man. The fact that her mother is angry at her is not enough to make us care about her; she faces no crucial conflict or dilemma that draws us in. What we do want to know are the heartbreaking secrets of her mother Vivi's past.

Among the most engaging portions of the book are those set in Atlanta during the 1939 world premiere of *Gone With the Wind.* Three of the four teenage Ya-Yas travel to Atlanta with a black chaperone for the opening; Vivi's letters home describing the citywide preparations, the arrival of the film's stars, and author Margaret Mitchell's snubbing of the Atlanta Junior League are fascinating and hilarious.

Rebecca Wells's first novel was *Little Altars Everywhere,* which also includes the Sidda and Vivi characters. Wells is an actor and playwright who tours a one-woman show based on both of her novels.

Wells has a talent for floating the reader up and down on swells of emotion, from rapturous joy to despair. In looking at the mechanics of her writing, can you identify the tools she uses to elicit deep emotion?

There is something about Wells's novel that predisposes women to like it. Are we so anxious to read about rollicking female friendships that it would be hard to write a book about four good friends that wouldn't gain our endorsement?

The Buccaneers, by Edith Wharton (completed by Marion Mainwaring), Penguin USA (paperback)

If you enjoyed *Sense and Sensibility* and *Emma,* you're bound to savor Edith Wharton's work. The author of the renowned *Age of Innocence* and *Ethan Frome,* Wharton set *The Buccaneers* in the polite society of 1870s New York and England. Her novel is a social comedy and romance but is driven by the quest of an ardent young woman who desires more than the superficial pleasures of the elegant life. Among the froth and amusements of her tale, Wharton gives us one honorable heroine in whom to believe.

Wharton died before she could complete *The Buccaneers,* but Wharton scholar Marion Mainwaring has done a fine job of completing the novel, creating approximately the latter 30 percent of the book, following a synopsis that Wharton created.

In Wharton's tale, five young women unable to gain acceptance into New York high society find that the titled aristocrats of England are far more susceptible to their charms, as long as one of those charms is money. With the guidance of a crafty English governess, they win their way into castles and mansions near London, breaking hearts, sometimes their own.

Be warned that the first pages of Wharton's novel center on the thoughts and actions of a minor character in the book, one who is not at all sympathetic. If you had to spend the entire book with her, you might quit after a chapter. However, she is the foolish mother of one of the five adventuresome young ladies, and she quickly slips into the background.

Is it possible to miss Wharton's subtle sarcasm and assume that she takes each of her young men and women seriously?

While Wharton shows us a repressive social structure in both the United States and England, does she give us hope that societal rules might change? Is her ending realistic?

Was it appropriate for Mainwaring to finish Wharton's novel? Is frustration at the incompleteness of a classic writer's work reason enough to accept the participation of a second writer?

Sleeping at the Starlite Motel, and Other Adventures on the Way Back Home, by Bailey White, Vintage Books (paperback)

The best way to enjoy these stories is to be taken by surprise; as you drive down the highway listening to "All Things Considered" on National Public Radio, a soft, southern voice begins to recount a simple tale, and suddenly the road disappears. You're with Aunt Eleanor in her shower as it crashes through to the first floor or with two elementary schoolteachers as they play hooky from a computer class to bet their money at the track.

If you can't tune in to NPR or listen to the tapes, these sketches are also good on the printed page. Read them slowly in some quiet place; they are short and can slip right past you before you know what happened.

In her first book, *Mama Makes Up Her Mind,* White tended to use her Georgia home as the setting, providing a marvelous chronicle of her experiences living with her mother in an odd little house in the country and teaching first grade. In her second book she takes us farther afield to describe the characters and events a quiet, single lady might encounter while crawling through a cave for the first time or observing a wedding at the world's largest and deepest spring.

White is a savvy, amusing observer. Her delight in the eccentricities of others and her amusement at her own foibles is contagious. Her anger at the death of a friend is quietly expressed, but in its spare, careful telling packs a huge puch. By the time you've finished these stories, you've not only seen the world through her eyes, you've had the pleasure of coming to know a very special person.

White is also the author of a novel, *Quite a Year for Plums.*

How is it that some writing is better when read aloud? Is there a certain quality or rhythm of the words that springs forth when they are heard instead of read?

A large part of the charm of Bailey White's stories is her wry, bemused take on incidents and people. Is that the whole of it, or is she an unusual person whose life makes especially good reading?

Fragments: Memories of a Wartime Childhood, by Binjamin Wilkomirski, translated from the German by Carol Brown Janeway, Schocken Books (paperback)

You may have promised yourself not to read another story about the Holocaust because you've learned as much as you can bear. Give it one more chance by reading this unusual book. In a few words clearly expressed, *Fragments* presents the perspective of a preschooler grabbed by the Nazis and imprisoned in their camps. The writing is uncomplicated and, as the title suggests, piecemeal. There is no adult commentary, only the potent images, smells, and feelings of a little boy who barely had language.

Wilkomirski was probably three or so when the Nazis captured him, his mother, and his brothers in Latvia. Years later, emerging from Auschwitz without a family or a home, he was adopted by a Swiss couple and told to forget the nightmare that engulfed his early childhood. There was no conversation, no chance to tell what had happened, until now.

For many of the youngsters who miraculously survived the camps, it was often the same story: They were told to put it behind them; they were children, they would forget. Given the lack of information about their identities, their personal histories were "wiped clean." Writing this book was a way for Wilkomirski to re-create his childhood and to acknowledge memories that never did disappear.

The author makes the story easier for us to stomach by alternating between the horror of his time in the camps and the consolation of his stays at orphanages afterward. Although he was unhappy in the orphanages—and the explanation why is intriguing—he did enjoy ample food, warmth, and human kindness.

This is a short book. You can read it in a day. You'll remember it for a long time.

In February 1999 the TV show 60 MINUTES *did an exposé on Wilkomirski, describing him as a fake. If the author has lied about the authenticity of his story, should his book be totally discounted as a description of the Holocaust? If Wilkomirski had published the book as fiction, would it have been accepted as a piercing, beautiful addition to Holocaust literature?*

***Life on the Color Line: The True Story of a White Boy Who Discovered He Was Black*, by Gregory Howard Williams, Plume (paperback)**

Today Gregory Williams is dean of the Ohio State University College of Law, and if you look at his picture you might never imagine that anyone had defined him as black or that he had to suffer the worst hardships and indignities of minority group status. When he was ten years old in the 1950s and living in Virginia, his parents separated, and Williams and a younger brother were taken by their father to begin a new life as members of the black community in Muncie, Indiana.

The two boys had grown up believing that their dark-skinned, tavern-owner father was of Italian descent; now, separated from their mother and other siblings, they were dumped with unfriendly black relatives into a situation of abject poverty and neglect. Although their new location was just a short distance across town from their maternal relatives, they were cut off from them entirely; the latter refused to acknowledge their existence. In addition to facing the trauma of family breakup, new identity, and rejection by whites, they had to deal with the fact that the black community didn't feel particularly comfortable with them either.

Williams and his brother were saved in large part by a pious woman in the black community who was no relation but who became their second mother.

This is a book you read for the story and not for the writing. While it is adequately told, the narrative at times is awkward. However, *Life on the Color Line* is powerful because of the startling tale it has to tell.

So many questions come to mind: How did Williams have the strength to survive? Could this happen today? Is the "one drop of black blood" school of thought still very much in practice, in which people are defined as black even if their parentage is predominantly other? Is our one hope of abandoning this way of thinking the achingly slow trend toward intermarriage, so that one day it will become impossible to categorize people by one race or another?

Four Letters of Love, by Niall Williams, Warner Books (paperback)

Here's another one of those times when you finish a book and ask, "Who *is* this writer and why haven't I heard of him before?" Irish writer Niall Williams has crafted a tangle of love stories with such beauty and finesse and such accurate observations that he seems an absolute expert in love. His facility with language is bewitching, as repeatedly he presents striking, unexpected word pictures that create characters, feelings, action.

Four Letters of Love is the story of a young man and young woman growing up on opposite sides of Ireland, living apparently unrelated lives, gradually drawing into contact with one another, and thereby sparking serious complications. Along the way, their parents' love affairs and the ties of affection within their families are examined. Williams traces the ebb and flow of emotions, examining how passion can suddenly appear, then disappear, how we can convince ourselves we're in love when we aren't, how parents or spouses can squash, kill, or inspire love without conscious intention.

There's a miraculous aspect of Williams's writing that makes his book seem more authentic rather than less. At first you may feel that certain fantastical events are a matter of interpretation or that the author is exaggerating for effect; as the story proceeds, the author takes greater and greater liberties with reality, until at the end the characters collide in a rush of strange occurrences that are not that surprising, given the groundwork Williams has laid.

Also a playwright, Williams is the author of the novel *As It Is in Heaven.*

Niall Williams believes in miracles and destiny. In FOUR LETTERS OF LOVE *he conjures a story in which fate brings together two soul mates, as weird as the timing might seem. Do you believe that certain people are destined to be lovers?*

Dessa Rose, by Sherley Anne Williams, Quill (paperback)

One of the myths surrounding slavery in the United States was that the enslaved never protested their situation by rebelling. An example of the inaccuracy of this belief is the story of one young pregnant black woman who led a slave revolt in 1829 while she and others were being led to market for sale in Kentucky. Novelist Sherley Anne Williams has taken the liberty of imagining this slave woman, Odessa Rose, meeting up with another apparently heroic figure who lived nearby at the same approximate time, a white woman who took in runaway slaves.

The voices in this book suck you into another reality. Raw, angry, anguished, the voice of Dessa opens up the world of the field slave. Her thoughts are expressed in a rough stream at first, reflecting the tight constrictions on her consciousness. As a field-worker, she has only glimpsed white people at a distance—except for the foreman with his whip. Her waking hours have been split between the fields and the slave cabin. Denied access to education, she has no inkling that the earth is round; as an English-speaker, she is unable to recognize many basic English words. One of the satisfactions of this book is the way in which Dessa gradually gains information and a broader perspective.

Dessa's encounter with Ruth, the unusual white plantation owner, is not what you might expect. There is terrible tension from the start, and part of the suspense of the book arises from the question of whether these two women will ever find a way to understand or talk meaningfully to each other.

Williams is an award-winning author of numerous poetry collections, plays, and short stories. Her book for children, *Working Cotton,* was the winner of a Caldecott Honor.

Did you find it believable that former slaves would risk masquerading as slaves for sale?

Ruth is not enlightened about equal rights or the oppressive conditions of slavery when we first meet her. Did the author do a good job of showing how someone with racist views might be transformed?

Refuge: An Unnatural History of Family and Place, by Terry Tempest Williams, Vintage Books (paperback)

Terry Tempest Williams was a naturalist-in-residence at the Utah Museum of Natural History in Salt Lake City when the Great Salt Lake began to rise to alarming levels in 1983. Her strong connection with the herons, owls, and snowy egrets of the lake's bird sanctuary drew her to the lake repeatedly as water levels grew higher and threatened to obliterate the sanctuary and everything else in proximity.

As she watched this natural calamity, she also had to face a much more personal crisis, the impending death of her mother from breast cancer. In her capable prose, the two disasters become intertwined.

Williams's chronicle of these difficult months is not laden with gloom but rather with an incandescent strength. Her large Mormon family, her gutsy mother, and the dense natural habitat and history of the Salt Lake come to vibrant life. It is the living rather than the dying that occupies Williams's writing.

However, Williams is bitter to discover that when she was a child, she and her family witnessed nuclear bomb tests carried out in the Utah desert by the U.S. government. Although she cannot prove it, she comes to believe that the deaths by cancer of her mother, grandmother, six aunts, and numerous neighbors were caused by nuclear fallout. In handling this awful realization, Williams is once more drawn to seek refuge in the beauty of the wildlife sanctuary at the Great Salt Lake.

Williams is also the author of *Desert Quartet, Pieces of White Shell: A Journey to Navajoland,* and *Coyote's Canyon.*

In establishing a metaphor for her mother's death in the destruction of the bird sanctuary ecosystem, what major insight does Tempest offer about our damaged environment and the loss that occurs in our lives?

Although it is immersed in descriptions of nature, REFUGE *is predominantly a story of human relationships, a description of her family and its heritage. What important gender and cultural issues does the author raise in telling her family's story?*

***The Professor and the Madman: A Tale of Murder, Insanity, and the Making of the Oxford English Dictionary*, by Simon Winchester, HarperPerennial (paperback)**

Here's one more piece of evidence that truth is stranger than fiction. What novelist would dare to write a yarn in which the most significant contributor to the world's preeminent English language dictionary in the late 1800s was a madman confined for most of his adult life to a lunatic asylum?

Simon Winchester describes in edifying detail the odd partnership between James Murray, editor of the *Oxford English Dictionary (OED),* and William Chester Minor, an American doctor institutionalized at Broadmoor, England's harshest insane asylum.

Although Murray and Minor had a twenty-year partnership, and from Minor's hospital cell would come thousands of dictionary entries, it was not until they were well into their vast undertaking that Murray learned about Minor's unusual situation. When he first volunteered to serve as a contributor, Minor wrote to Murray indicating that he was well educated, had access to a considerable library, and had quite a bit of time on his hands.

In addition to describing an extraordinary relationship, Winchester also delivers intriguing historical detail about the development of the dictionary. The *OED,* a huge reference work that can be found in most of the world's English-speaking libraries, took seventy years to compile.

Winchester is the author of twelve other books; among them are *The River at the Center of the World, Pacific Nightmare,* and *Small World.*

Professor James Murray spent forty years working on the OED *and never lived to see it published. Can you imagine someone doing this today? Can you imagine anyone financing publication of a book over a seventy-year period?*

Winchester throws in a generous amount of polysyllabic verbiage. Does this slow his story or give a fitting reminder of the scope of our language?

Medea: A Modern Retelling, by Christa Wolf, Nan A. Talese/ Doubleday (hardcover)

If you were disgusted by the myth of Medea, the sorceress who married Jason of Argonaut fame and then killed their children in a jealous rage, please give this woman another chance. Christa Wolf did, rethinking the whole story, and has come up with a fabulous version of the tale that makes perfect sense—and that shows Medea was given a bum rap and her name tainted through the centuries because she angered the wrong people.

Wolf has reexplained Medea's story using the voices of the major players, with each delivering a different take on the events. The result is a spellbinding tale of palace intrigue in ancient Corinth as well as a study of larger questions such as sexism, prejudice against outsiders, and the corrupting effects of power.

When Medea flees her morally degraded homeland, where she is daughter of the king, she has no idea what she'll find in the kingdom of her rescuers. Having fallen in love with Jason, an heir to the throne of Corinth, she enters a whole new realm of palace politics. Lust, rage, dirty secrets, sorcery, and revenge combine to create intense drama.

Don't skip the introduction by Margaret Atwood; it sets the scene, and, as always, her writing is a pleasure to read.

German author Wolf is one of that country's top literary figures. A prolific writer, she has won numerous awards, including the Vienna State Prize for European Literature. Her works include *The Quest for Christa T.* and *Cassandra.*

In the original version of the Medea myth, Medea's murderous behavior is fueled by her own passions, putting one more log on the fire to support the ancient fear that women are dangerous, sexual beings who must be segregated from men and held in control by religious or social strictures. Did the original story ever ring true to you?

Some have pointed out that Wolf was accused after German reunification of having been an informant for the East German secret police. Do you think she is offering justification for her own actions by revisiting the story of the much-maligned Medea?

This Boy's Life, Tobias Wolff, HarperPerennial (paperback)

Forget the movie, if you happened to see it. There's no way the film could match this book. So much of the charm and impact of *This Boy's Life* is wrapped up in the narrator's voice. Award-winning author Tobias Wolff tells his personal story here, an account of his days set adrift with his mother after her divorce from the ultimate con man. The narrative is amazingly honest, cutting, and funny—and the humor is especially effective because Wolff is ready to laugh at himself as well as the others who populate his gripping autobiography.

This is not a pretty story; at times it is horrifying. From her childhood in Beverly Hills, to her bizarre marriage, to her wanderings through the Pacific Northwest, Wolff's mother seems unable to create a family life that is secure and kind. When at last she settles down, it is with a man of unusual cruelty. Toby's response to all of these difficulties is wild dreaming and bad behavior of his own, and, at last, a crazy act that might save him.

If Wolff's description of his highly unusual father stirs your curiosity, you might want to learn more about him from the point of view of Wolff's brother. When the family split up, one son went with each parent. *The Duke of Deception,* by Geoffrey Wolff, reveals what it was like to depend on a man who got by on outrageous lying and did it in the most engaging way. Also, for the further adventures of Tobias Wolff, check out his account of his days in Vietnam, *In Pharaoh's Army.*

The recipient of numerous honors, Wolff won the PEN/Faulkner Award for his novella *The Barracks Thief.*

Usually it takes a fictional form to allow a writer to portray his or her characters with utter honesty. Wolff's memoir is notable for its grim truthfulness as well as its beautifully wrought prose. Do you think Wolff was unfair to those close to him in revealing an often frightening picture of their lives?

Wolff has consistently been praised for his skills in writing prose. Can you find passages of particular beauty in the book?

Black Boy, by Richard Wright, HarperPerennial (paperback)

Even if you've read widely on the black experience in America, *Black Boy* is an eye-opener. Richard Wright's classic childhood memoir discloses the particulars of life in the South in the early decades of this century, making it clear that daily existence as Wright and other African Americans knew it was almost as degrading as during slavery.

The author, who lived from 1908 to 1960, was the first African American to win prominence in American literary life. He was also the first black novelist to lay bare the rage of African Americans toward the white society that excluded and demeaned them.

Wright's autobiography is thought by many to be his most powerful work. The memories in *Black Boy* are searing; the writing passionate as well as lucid and eloquent.

Wright leads us through his early years, beginning in Natchez, Mississippi, and traveling to other southern cities. His account of repeated, terrible cruelty from white people—and from his own family—would be too much to bear if it were not for the quality of his writing. Reading his well-chosen words, you are reminded that the author survived his hellish childhood to lead a life of talent and creative expression.

Although he attended school only sporadically in his youth, Wright managed to become educated as a teenager, when he discovered the world of books.

Among Wright's many writings are the novel *Native Son,* the collection of novellas *Uncle Tom's Children,* and the nonfiction *Twelve Million Black Voices.* After World War II, the author left the United States to live in Paris.

When first published, Wright's book was seen mainly as an attack on southern white society. Does it read this way now, or is it more accurately a coming-of-age story that draws a complete picture of how one young man developed into a writer?

After reading Wright's story, do you wonder why anyone who had the ability to leave would continue to live in a society that treated him so brutally?

The Ginger Tree, by Oswald Wynd, HarperPerennial (paperback)

The English love this story. They made it a best-seller in their own country and then transformed it into a *Masterpiece Theater* miniseries. Catch it now in its best version, as Oswald Wynd's savory novel.

In *The Ginger Tree,* a young Scottish woman travels to China in the early years of the twentieth century to wed a dashing British military officer. Instead of leading a genteel life among the British in Peking, she scandalizes the European community by falling in love with a Japanese nobleman. We follow Mary MacKenzie through forty years of adventure in the Far East, as she somehow makes her way among two societies that allow little room for women who don't follow the rules.

The author of seventeen novels under his own name and fifteen adventure and suspense books under the pseudonym Gavin Black, Wynd has done more in *The Ginger Tree* than write an engaging saga of one woman's travails and adventures. He has produced a revealing social commentary on early-twentieth-century English and Asian cultures, many of whose mores echo into our own day and age. Wynd has also effectively created two unique characters in Mary and her lover Count Kurihama.

The author spent the first eighteen years of his life in Japan as the son of Scottish missionaries. He served in the British Intelligence Corps for six years and was a Japanese prisoner of war in the 1940s. His writing career began just after World War II with publication of his first novel, the award-winning *Black Fountains.*

Mary seems very much a heroine typical of the latter part of the twentieth century. Did you find it hard to believe that such a fiercely independent woman could have come of age within the confines of a much stricter, earlier Anglo society?

Did you understand the chemistry between Mary and Count Kurihama? Did Wynd lay the groundwork that would make it believable for Mary to sacrifice everything to be with him?

TITLE INDEX

SUBJECT INDEX

FICTION

RECOMMENDED BY . . . 

In addition to the members of my own book club named in the Acknowledgments, each of the individuals listed below offered one or more recommendations based on shared enthusiasm with other book club members, family, and/or friends. Recommendations came from people in northern and southern California, Oregon, Colorado, and New York.

Lynn Allison
American Association of University Women book club, Ukiah
Ron Bean
T. Beller
Rosie Benzonelli
Diane Bertoli
Ann Butler
Kris Cannon
Pam Carroll
Carolina Clare
Nola Colbert, Healdsburg branch, American Association of University Women
Michael Coyle
Cynthia DeMartini
Shane Demir
Patricia Ditzler
Robin Doroshow
Joan Dranginis
Dora Dugars
Wendy Eisler
The fiction committee, Bay Area Book Reviewers Association
Cynthia Florenzen
Kristi Frlekin
Alfred & Dorothy Golden
Ruth Goldhammer
Karen Griffith
Mary Hafner
Lou Hagerty
Vallena Harris
Judy Herman
Cheryl Hulsman
Julie Jackson
Michael Kerry
Carol Lander
Leah Lander
Adele Levin
Jo Loarie
Joyce Manning

Jen Marshall
Michael McMains
Jackie McMillan
Wendy Milner-Calloway
Carol Mork
Laura Mueller
Cindi Newman
Sheila Nitzel, Shakespeare's Twisted Sisters
Philip Nix
Maxine Nunes
Frank Paine
Jacquie Rabinowitz
Gayle Reid
Claudia Rhymes
Tom Richardson
Carol Rinehart
Aaron Rosewater
Penelope Rowland
Marly Rusoff
Judy Schulz
Toni Sciarra
Jim Selman
Lauren Selman
Tina Selman
Gretchen Singer, Ladies' Literary Salon
Bill Street
Jack Street
Danita Tanner
Nakeba Trammel
Greer Upton
Virginia Valentine
Valerie Waidler
Ann Walance
Jim Walter
John Watrous
Ellen Wear